W9-DDK-863

▶ Working with Linguistically and Culturally Different Children

Innovative Clinical and Educational Approaches

Sharon-ann Gopaul-McNicol
Howard University

Tania Thomas-Presswood
Uniondale School District

Allyn and Bacon
Boston • London • Toronto • Sydney • Tokyo • Singapore

To Our Families—
To Ulric, Monique Mandisa, Monica, and Donald
With Love, Gratitude, Tenderness and Respect,
And in Loving Memory of St. Elmo Gopaul

Senior Editor: Carla F. Daves
Series Editorial Assistant: Susan Hutchinson
Manufacturing Buyer: Suzanne Lareau

Copyright © 1998 by Allyn & Bacon
A Viacom Company
Needham Heights, Massachusetts 02194

Internet: www.abacon.com
America Online: keyword: College Online

Library of Congress Cataloging-in-Publication Data
Gopaul-McNicol, Sharon-ann.
    Working with linguistically and culturally different children :
  innovative clinical and educational approaches / Sharon-ann Gopaul-
  McNicol, Tania Thomas-Presswood.
      p.   cm.
    Includes Bibliographical references (p.   ) and index.
    ISBN 0-205-19986-0
    1. Children of minorities—Education—United States.   2. Children
  of minorities—Mental health—United States.   3. Linguistic
  minorities—Education—United States.   4. Educational tests and
  measurements—United States.   5. Educational anthropology—United
  States.   I Thomas-Presswood, Tania   II. Title.
  LC3731.G68   1998
  371.829—DC21   97-23312
                                                                  CIP

Printed in the United States of America

10 9 8 7 6 5 4 3 2   01 00 99 98

Contents

iii

Preface

Given the increased kaleidoscope of culturally and linguistically diverse students entering the United States school system, it is imperative that practitioners and researchers have a framework to more accurately assess and treat these children as they acclimate to American society. Although large inner-city school districts, such as New York City and Washington, D.C. where over 100 languages are spoken, represent a more heterogeneous mix of cultures than are typically found in other parts of the United States, the reality is that the population in the United States has become more diverse in every state.

This book is the culmination of ten years of cross-cultural practice and research with children of various linguistic and cultural backgrounds. As professors in school psychology and as practitioners working in our multicultural agency with approximately 3,200 children in a variety of ways—assessment, treatment, consultation, research, and tutelage, we came to realize that a different approach to assessment, psychotherapy, and tutelage is needed if linguistically and culturally different children are to smoothly acculturate in this society.

This book introduces several models based on the work of the authors who are both bicultural and bilingual, the work of other leading cross-cultural practitioners, and researchers throughout the world.

The principle objectives of these proposed "best practices" are to help mental health professionals more accurately assess, treat, and teach children from various cultural and linguistic backgrounds. The techniques and strategies proposed by these models are indicative of a more comprehensive, eclectic approach to assessment, treatment, teaching, consultation, and research.

An underlying philosophy and perspective runs through all of the chapters in this book: To successfully intervene with a culturally diverse child, the therapist must understand the values and beliefs endemic to that child's cultural upbringing, and must utilize intervention strategies that are culturally sensitive. This book clearly reflects the assumption that all cultural circumstances result in unique responses and unique coping styles based on personal experiences in personal contexts. Although the focus of this book is on linguistic and culturally diverse children, it could be valuable to children of Euro-American heritage. Likewise, although this book is designed to be of use to mental health practitioners and researchers, it may also be useful to educators and speech and language therapists.

The theoretical bases for these models originated from cross-cultural/linguistic psychology, cross-cultural assessment, and treatment with people from culturally and linguistically diverse backgrounds who reside in the three main metropolitan areas—the United States, Canada, and the United Kingdom. As such, these proposed "best practices" suggest that change can be effected both on individual, institutional, and societal levels to people who came from colonized systems around the world. In other words, these models seek to empower the child and his or her family through interactions with multiple systems.

A word is in order regarding the terminology we have used to describe members of the various racial/geographic groups—in part because culturally different children are so diverse, and in part because there is still debate as to how various ethnic groups should define themselves. In general, we have used the term African American or Black to describe people of African ancestry who originated or reside in the United States of America. The term Caribbean was used to describe people who originally came from the English Caribbean countries. Hispanic and Latino were used interchangeably to describe people of Spanish heritage who speak Spanish as a primary or second language. Americans of European descent are referred to as Whites. Members of racial/geographic groups represented in the United States in smaller numbers are called by their specific descriptors (e.g., Chinese). In general, the terms used to describe each of the cultural groups were selected in accordance with the nationally accepted terminology at the time of writing.

Our appreciation goes to the following reviewers for their comments on the manuscript: Ena Vasquez-Nuttall of Northeastern Unversity and Robin Young Porter of Young-Rivers Associates. Finally, thanks to Mylan Jaixen, Carla Daves, Susan Hutchinson, and the rest of the Allyn and Bacon team.

Acknowledgments

To our immediate family, Ulric, Monique Mandisa, and Donald, we extend our most profound gratitude. Your patience and unflagging love throughout this challenging time will be remembered in our hearts forever.

To our parents St. Elmo and Monique Gopaul, Harold and Cecilia Thomas, to whom we owe all who we are and all who we hope to be, we humbly thank you for the vision, the tenacity, and the confidence you instilled in us through your example and eternal love.

To our siblings Gail, Wendy, Kurt, Nigel, Giovana, Liza, Idania, and Kristal; our nieces and nephews Michael, Kja, Michelle, Skyler, Kris, Severio Divier, and Gianni; our dear cousins Doreen, Christopher, and Maria. We thank you for your ongoing support and patience.

To our professional colleagues, all of whom cannot be mentioned, but to whom we extend our gratitude nevertheless, you have fostered in us a clearer understanding of the issues discussed in this book. For all of your guidance, we thank you. In particular we would like to most graciously extend our appreciation to our special friends and colleagues Eleanor Armour-Thomas, Nicola Beckles, Aldrena Mabry, Janet Brice-Baker, Emilia Lopez, Grace Elizalde, Sara Nahari, Giselle Esquivel, Colleen Clay, Miriam Azaunce, Lauraine Casella, Arthur Dozier, Joseph Cesar, George Irish, Delroy Louden, Michael Barnes, James Williams, Frederick Harper, Nancy Boyd-Franklin, A. J. Franklin, Melvon Swanston, Mitchell Schare, Robert Bushell, Jefferson Fish, Rafael Javier, James Curley, Erika Wick, Alina Camacho-Gingerich, Willard Gingerich, Tony Bonaparte, Belenna Lauto, Frank Levenes, Tony Garb, Thomas Capone, Joanne Mckellar, Joyce Schulz, Earl George, Joya Gomez, Charmaine Edwards, Headley Wilson, Susan Lokai, Seretse McHardy, Koreen Seabrun, Sandra Hosein, Jennifer D'Ade, and Joanne Julien.

To the communities and students of Howard University, Uniondale School District, St. John's University, Trinbago Networking Connection,

Ridgewood Bushwick Senior Citizen Council and the California School of Professional Psychology-Los Angeles, we thank you for your support in the nurturing of this project.

We would like to thank all of the publishers who granted us permission to use segments of our own work from our published journal articles, book chapters, and books.

To our deceased loved ones St. Elmo Gopaul, Josephine Fitzgerald, Franklin Ford, and Julia Vane, may God bless you all.

Overview

This book is divided into four parts. Part I examines the major issues and challenges in working with linguistically and culturally different children (Chapter 1). In this chapter the authors introduce the reader to several major ethnic and cultural groups that comprise the United States' population. Each group's history, beliefs, and values are highlighted, with particular emphasis on assessment and treatment issues. These groups were chosen because they represent a significant segment of the immigrant populace as well as the population of the United States as a whole. Part I also reflects the current techniques and their limitations that are still primarily used by mainstream mental health professionals in working with culturally diverse children and their families (Chapter 2).

Part II explores the best practices in assessment and teaching with the linguistically and culturally diverse child. The impact of learning a second language and its resultant effect on assessment is discussed in Chapter 3. Chapter 4 examines issues in intellectual and educational assessment and a model for assessing the intelligence of children—the bio-ecological assessment system is recommended based on the work of the primary author and her colleague Armour-Thomas (1997a & b). Best practices in report writing for the linguistically and culturally different child are explored in Chapter 5. Chapter 6 focuses on how examiners could best assess and ways they could prevent misdiagnosing the emotional/social functioning of culturally different children. By utilizing a culturological approach to assessing personality, examiners are given techniques to which they should be sensitive. Teaching strategies for teachers based on the learning styles and strengths of culturally diverse children are examined in Chapter 7.

Part III offers the best practices in treating and intervening with culturally diverse children (Chapter 8) and a model, the Multicultural/Multimodal/Multisystems (MULTI-CMS) approach, which was developed by the primary author is proposed in Chapter 9. Sample case studies of linguistically and culturally diverse children utilizing this model are presented in Chapter 9 as well.

Part IV offers cross-cultural issues in ethics and law (Chapter 10), culminating with suggestions for the best practices in training mental health professionals to work with linguistically and culturally diverse children. The minimum competencies needed for one to be effective in servicing these children are discussed in Chapter 11. Finally, implications for policy makers and researchers who opt to service these children are proposed in Chapters 12 and 13, respectively.

Sharon-ann Gopaul-McNicol
Tania Thomas-Presswood

▶ 1

The Impact of Culture on the Psychosocial and Educational Needs of Ethnically and Linguistically Diverse Children and Families

The need to develop and advocate a thorough understanding of the impact of culture on the psychological and social functioning of children and families of diverse ethnic backgrounds can be documented in the U.S. Bureau of the Census of 1990. The census reported a total U.S. population of 248,709,873. Contained in that number are 29,986,060 Blacks; 22,354,059 persons of Hispanic origin (of any race); 7,273,662 Asian and Pacific Islanders; and 1,959,234 Native Americans, Eskimos, and Aleuts (U.S. Bureau of the Census, 1990 and 1996). Census data uncovered significant changes in (1) the number and distribution of culturally diverse populations, (2) immigration and migration patterns, and (3) ethnic group population characteristics (O'Hare, 1989; O'Hare & Felt, 1991; O'Hare, Pollard, Mann, & Kent, 1991; Valdivieso & Davis, 1988; Aponte & Crouch, 1995). The U.S. population of Anglo ancestry will constitute no more than 50 percent of the U.S. population by the year 2050 (U.S.

Census, 1990). This growth in ethnic population during the last several decades is due to migration (O'Hare, 1992). World politics leading to unstable economic and social conditions and civil strife (Thorton, 1992) brought about a wave of immigration that was facilitated by changing immigration laws and policies and by minimally protected borders. This increasing diversity of cultural backgrounds will create educational challenges and forge understanding of multicultural issues. Surely, those committed to serving all, rather than selected portions, of a nation's population must demonstrate an awareness of, sensitivity to, and respect for cultural differences (Anderson, 1989).

This chapter will discuss the definition of culture; the influence of culture and multiple social and environmental factors on immigrants, African Americans, Native Americans, and Anglo-European Americans; and the impact of culture in determining the educational needs of children.

DEFINITION OF CULTURE: PROBLEMS AND CONTEMPORARY VIEWS

What is culture? Many anthropologists and other social scientists have been grappling with this question for centuries. Tyler (1871) proposed one of the first definitions of culture. He defined culture as that complex whole that comprises knowledge, belief, art, morals, law, and custom, and includes other capabilities and habits acquired by an individual as a member of society. Frisby (1992) conceptualized culture as the acquired knowledge that people use to interpret experience and to generate social behaviors. These understandings of culture emphasize the accumulated artifacts and experiences of a certain group; however, the problem with these definitions is their failure to specify adequately aspects, factors, or elements of culture so that the term is functional in human experiences (Garcia, 1982).

Krueber and Kluckhahn (1952) surveyed many definitions of culture in the anthropological literature and placed these in six major categories:

1. Descriptive definitions. These enumerate many of the aspects of human life and activity of what is meant by "culture." Culture is viewed as a global entity.
2. Historical definitions. These emphasize the accumulation of tradition over time rather than listing the range of cultural activities.
3. Normative definitions. The focus is on shared, unique experiences and values that govern the activities of a group of people.
4. Psychological definitions. These are concerned with a variety of psychological factors, including adjustment, problem solving, learning, and habits in a group.

5. Structural definitions. These involve the pattern or organization of culture; the central idea is that culture is not a mere composition of customs, but forms an integrated pattern of interrelated features.
6. Genetic definitions. Here the emphasis is on the origin of culture. Culture is viewed as adaptive to the environment of the group, as emerging out of social interaction and out of the creative process that is typical of the human experience.

According to Garcia (1982), culture acts on two levels, explicit and implicit. The explicit level is composed of overt, customary patterns of behaving, thinking, and feeling; the implicit level includes covert, unspoken, and mainly unconscious values and assumptions.

Presently, culture has taken on various shades of meanings throughout social science literature, some of which were discussed by Krueber and Kluckhahn. Frisby (1992) identified six popular connotative meanings that are frequently associated with the word "culture" and "cultural differences":

1. culture as a pattern of living, customs, traditions, values, and attitudes that are associated with broad differences in intercontinental habitation or a society's level of technological sophistication
2. culture as the significant artistic, humanitarian, or scientific achievements of members of the group or one's ancestral homeland
3. culture as "race consciousness"—a common set of attitudes and beliefs that may guide an individual's feelings, interest, or identification with racial or ethnic issues
4. culture as values and norms of the immediate context within which a person is socialized (e.g., culture of the family, streets, etc.)
5. culture as it refers to superficial differences between the macrocultural and microcultural groups (i.e., popular clothing, music, style of religious worship, culinary traditions, and speech and language styles)
6. culture as it refers to outer appearance—persons who are racially different are automatically assumed to be "culturally different"

These shades of meanings used interchangeably in the literature are the source of much confusion. Goodenough (1957) provided a comprehensive conceptualization of culture:

A society's culture consists of whatever it is one has to know or believe in order to operate in a manner acceptable to its members, and do so in any role that they accept for any one of themselves. Culture, being what people have to learn as distinct from their biological heritage, must consist of the end product of learning: knowledge, in a most general, if relative, sense of the term. By this definition, we should note that culture is not a material phenomenon; it does not consist of things, people, behavior, or emotions. It is rather an organization of these things. It is the forms of things that people have in mind, their models for perceiving, relating and otherwise interpreting them. As such, the things people say and do, their social arrangements and events, are products or byproducts of their culture as they apply it to the task of perceiving and dealing with their circumstances (Goodenough, 1957, p. 167).

Such conceptualization of culture reveals how the influence of culturally determined behaviors solidifies a society on a common base of communication and understanding. Acquired cultural knowledge is like a recipe for producing behavior, artifacts, and interpretations of one's reality (Bennett, 1986). The United States is a complex society that brings together people of different nationalities and cultures that coexist with the Anglo-Western European macroculture. The macroculture is the predominate culture that has developed primarily out of Anglo and Western European traditions, and has largely determined the formal institution, official language, social values, and other aspects of life in this society (Bennett, 1986). Moreover, the formal institutions and laws developed by the macroculture determine, through historical contacts, the social position (i.e., socioeconomic status, educational opportunities and resources, social respect, and historical recognition) in the macroculture of a particular microculture. Therefore, it is essential to understand both the macroculture and the microculture that have survived in spite of the influences of different ethnic groups within U.S. society (Bennett, 1986).

INFLUENCE OF CULTURE AND MULTIPLE SOCIAL FACTORS ON CHILDREN AND FAMILIES

Most of who we are is influenced, promoted, and shaped by our cultural heritage. For many, cultural, language, and ethnic origins continue to be a major part of their overt identity (Lynch, 1992). Nevertheless, culture, language, and ethnicity are not the only determinants of our values, beliefs, and behaviors (Lynch, 1992). Anderson (1989) noted that in working within the concept of culture, one must remember that cultures are not static entities, and that cultural tendencies are in no way fixed or rigidly adhered to by any individual or family. Culture is viewed as an ongoing process in which individuals steadily rework new ideas and behaviors within their cultural framework (Anderson, 1989). Anderson (1989) further states that it is equally important to recognize that general cultural attributes are tendencies, not absolutes, and to ascribe to cultural tendencies a more deterministic role results in potential stereotyping of ethnic and racial minorities or majorities. Situational specific factors also play a pivotal role in shaping the lives of children and families. Situational specific factors refer to socioeconomic status, occupational skills, educational background, immigration status, and so forth, that may limit or enhance the choices and possibilities of a family within the broader sociocultural context (Anderson, 1989). Moreover, as noted earlier, the macroculture decides, through its belief, history, and practices, the social position and treatment of microcultures that are part of its society. All of these forces have a unique impact on the microcultures that exist in the macroculture. This impact is predicated on a number of factors: voluntary/involuntary immigration status, socioeconomic level, acculturation, language, educational/employment status, social support and network, ecological living conditions (urban/suburban/rural), biological stressors (health issues), and cultural history in the native land and in the United States. These factors operate together and exert forces that shape the experiences of individuals and families. In the United States, numerous microcultures or ethnic populations, for educational purposes, can be classified into three major groups: immigrant children and families, African Americans, and Native Americans. These will be examined next, along with macro or mainstream cultures (i.e. Anglo-Western European) traditions and experiences.

IMMIGRANT CHILDREN AND FAMILIES

Most ethnic groups in the United States have been immigrants, with the exception of Native Americans. However, the vast diversification of ethnic groups makes it difficult to unerringly generalize about the immigrants living in the United States. They bring to the macroculture their unique histories and political relationships with the host nation that dictate their status within the new society. They live in various parts of the country, exhibit different birth and mortality rates, form different family structures and living arrangements, achieve different levels of income and educational status (Aponte & Crouch, 1995), and earn different levels of acceptance into the mainstream culture. Multiethnicity is also salient within racial groups.

Valdivieso and Davis (1988) observed that Hispanics of Mexican ancestry account for 62 percent of Hispanic Americans, followed by Puerto Ricans (13 percent), Central and South Americans (12 percent), and Cubans (5 percent). Hispanic groups have settled in various geographical regions of the United States based on their ability to find work and safe havens, point of entry, and historical relationship with the United States (Aponte & Crouch, 1995). Mexican Americans tend to concentrate in the Southwest (California and

Texas) and Midwest (O'Hare, 1992; U.S. Bureau of Census, 1991; Valdivieso & Davis, 1988); Puerto Ricans and Dominicans settle mostly in the Northeast (New York metropolitan areas); and Cubans are concentrated primarily in southern Florida (Aponte & Crouch, 1995). Racially speaking, Hispanics are even more diverse; this ethnic group has been influenced by Spanish and African cultures as well as by the indigenous people of the Americas.

The Asian-American community is equally diverse in terms of language, education, generations in the United States, countries of origin and cultural traditions, religion, and sociopolitical relationships with the United States. Although some groups are more recent immigrants to the U.S., such as Vietnamese, Cambodians, and Laotians, the U.S. Census data reveal that most Asian Americans are Chinese (22 percent), followed by Filipinos (21 percent), Japanese (19 percent), Koreans (10 percent), and East Indians (10 percent) (Aponte & Crouch, 1995). West Indians (i.e., immigrants from the English, French, and Dutch-speaking Caribbean Islands) constitute a small percentage of the U.S. population, but in states such as New York, Florida, and California, their presence is being felt and recognized. In New York City alone, from 1983 through 1987, 95,783 West Indian immigrants were documented (New York City Department of Planning, 1985; Gopaul-McNicol, 1993). West Indians are an heterogeneous group of people whose customs have been influenced by African, Spanish, British, Dutch, Asian, and American cultures (Gopaul-McNicol, 1993). Although large-scale immigration to the United States by people from the Middle East dates back to the late nineteenth and early twentieth centuries, most recently the beginning of the Iranian Revolution, the occupation of Afghanistan by the Soviet Union, the Iran-Iraq war, and the occupation of Kuwait by Iraq led to the migrations of large numbers of Middle Easterners to the United States (McGoldrick, Pearce, & Giordano, 1988).

Despite these differences, immigrant experiences and challenges are similar across ethnic groups. There are factors common to the immigrant experience that educators, clinicians, and mental health workers must understand. These factors uncover the cultural specificity that makes each group unique and that would allow professionals to service these communities more effectively. Factors surrounding the broader dynamics of immigrants and immigration are: acculturation processes, socioeconomic level, social support and network, educational and employment background, language proficiency, immigration status, and social and political standing in the mainstream culture. These are important variables that immigrants must adjust to in a new culture or society.

Acculturation Processes

An individual arrives into a new society with an understanding of how the world works. This understanding, or worldview, shapes cultural tradition and customs. Worldview is defined as the way an individual perceives his or her relationship to the world (e.g., nature, other people, animals, institutions, objects, the universe, God, etc.) (Sue, 1981). Brown and Landrum-Brown (1995) noted that the concept of worldview is often used to illustrate how diverse individuals and cultural groups tend to experience the world in different ways. Moreover, worldviews are learned ways of perceiving one's environment; therefore, they can become relevant factors in shaping the way that an individual perceives and responds to individuals and events in the environment (Brown & Landrum-Brown, 1995). In order to effectively work with ethnic children and families, educators and clinicians need to understand the unique worldview and life experiences of the cultural group they serve and to develop culturally appropriate interventions (Lee, 1989).

When researchers speak of acculturation, they refer to the process whereby the worldview or behaviors of persons from one culture are modified as a result of contact with a different culture (Moyerman & Forman, 1992). This process of mutual cultural exchange results from contact between cultures, during which each culture influences the other (Rick & Forward, 1992). However, the macroculture contributes more to the flow of cultural elements (Berry, 1980; Nicassio, 1985; Rick & Forward, 1992; Teske & Nelson, 1974) toward smaller groups such as immigrants (Yinger, 1981). Some scholars describe this process as a unidirectional process of assimilation by which an individual relinquishes his or her ethnic values, beliefs, customs, and behaviors for those of the mainstream culture (Aponte & Barnes, 1995; Garcia & Lega, 1979). Others view acculturation as a bidirectional process in which the ethnic individual is assimilated by the mainstream culture, yet retains his or her ethnic culture identity (Aponte & Barnes, 1995; Berry, 1980; LeVine & Padilla, 1980; Mendoza & Martinez, 1981).

Berry (1980) and Berry and Kim (1988) identified five phases in the process of acculturation:

1. Precontact phase, in which each independent ethnic and cultural group brings its own system of beliefs or worldview
2. Contact phase, in which groups begin to interact with each other
3. Conflict phase, when pressure is exerted on the microculture to change in order to fit with the macroculture
4. Crisis phase, in which the conflict comes to a head
5. Adaptation phase, during which relations between the two groups (micro and macrocultures) are stabilized into one of several modes of acculturation

As an individual travels through these phases, stress is produced, which affects psychological functioning. The amount of stress experienced varies according to the acculturation phase (Aponte & Barnes, 1995; Berry & Kim, 1988;

Berry, Kim, Minde, & Mok, 1987). The immigrant person's experiences during the acculturation phase influence the mode of acculturation (Aponte & Barnes, 1995). Based on their work over the past decade, Berry et al. (1987) proposed a model that consists of five modes of acculturation:

1. Assimilation, in which the individual surrenders his or her cultural identity and assumes the beliefs, values, attitudes, and behaviors of the majority group (Aponte & Barnes, 1995; Berry, 1986; Berry & Kim, 1988).
2. Integration, the maintenance of cultural integrity, as well as the movement to become an integral part of a larger societal framework (Berry, 1986; Thomas, 1995).
3. Separation, which entails self-imposed withdrawal from the mainstream society (Aponte & Barnes, 1995).
4. Segregation, which occurs when this withdrawal or separation is imposed by the mainstream society (Berry, 1986).
5. Marginalization, which develops when the ethnic individual can identify with neither his or her traditional culture nor with the mainstream culture (Aponte & Barnes, 1995). Berry also refers to this mode as deculturation and notes that it is characterized by feelings of alienation, loss of identity, and stress (Berry, 1986; Thomas, 1995).

Acculturation is a fluid process, and an individual can drift back and forth from one phase and mode to another. Moreover, individual members of a family may acculturate at different rates based on their exposure to and type of interaction with the mainstream culture. Length of time residing in the United States is a significant factor as well. Burnam, Hough, Karno, Escobar, and Telles (1987) observed that the selectivity of the migration stream from Mexico to California tends to create a psychologically robust first-generation immigrant population that feels less deprived, because migration has increased his or her standard of living; in contrast, the Mexican American born in the United States feels more deprivation because of much higher but unrealized aspirations. The process of acculturation is influenced by factors such as socioeconomic status, educational level, immigration status, social support, time residing in the United States (Garcia & Lega, 1979; Thomas, 1995).

Experiences confronted by an ethnic person as part of the acculturation process can produce anxiety, depression, guilt, anger, and other psychological disturbances suggestive of adjustment problems. Many studies have explored the relationship between migration and mental health, numerous ones pursuing the idea that stress experienced during the acculturation process places immigrant individuals and families at risk for various psychological disorders, social maladjustments, and physical ailments (Cleary, 1987; Faris & Dunham, 1960; Golding & Burnham, 1990; Lynch, 1992; Van Deusen, 1982;

Westermeyer, 1989). However, the acculturation process should not be viewed as a direct path to psychological distress and psychiatric disorder.

Oberg (1960) introduced the concept of "culture shock" and suggested that it is precipitated by the anxiety that results from losing all familiar signs and symbols of social intercourse (Furnham & Bochner, 1986). Culture shock is the result of a series of disorienting encounters that occur when an individual's basic values, beliefs, and patterns of behavior are challenged by a different set of values, beliefs, and behaviors (Lynch, 1992). Westermeyer (1989) referred to this concept as "migration readjustment experiences." This type of stress, considered a natural and inherent aspect of the immigrant experience, is often referred to as acculturative stress (Thomas, 1995). Acculturative stress includes those behaviors and experiences generated during acculturation that can be mildly pathological and disruptive to the immigrant and his or her family (e.g., depression, feelings of marginality, substance abuse, anxiety, psychosomatic symptomatology, adjustment disorders, etc.) (Berry, 1986). Children may exhibit behavioral problems in school, appear withdrawn, or have difficulty achieving and socializing.

Because each person brings different needs and resources to the situation and finds ways to cope that slow or hasten the journey through the stages of acculturation, the time it takes to pass through the stages is not predictable (Lynch, 1992). In some instances, as a function of limited language proficiency, low socioeconomic status, limited education, and poor social support, an immigrant person may spend many years feeling disillusioned, alienated, and unaccepted by the mainstream culture. Acculturative stress is a normal reaction that is part of the routine process of adaptation to cultural stress and the manifestation of a longing for a more predictable, stable, and understandable environment (Furnham & Bochner, 1986). The greater the dissimilarity with the host culture, the greater the acculturative stress in the immigrant; conversely, the lesser the dissimilarity with the host culture, the lesser the degree of acculturative stress experienced by the immigrant and his or her family (Berry, 1986). Thus, a Japanese person in Fiji, a Native American person in New Delhi, or an Italian person in Beijing is more likely to experience acculturative stress or culture shock than the Bostonian in southern California, the Texan in New York, or the West Virginian in Las Vegas (Lynch, 1992). Even age presents itself as a relevant factor. Individuals who migrate after the age of 14 experience higher levels of stress that those who migrate prior to age 14 (Aponte, Rivers, & Wahl, 1995). Among late immigrants (after age 14), the combination of self-imposed pressure to succeed in the new country and lack of communication and other skills provide a high-risk situation for the development of psychosocial conflicts (Salgado de Snyder, 1987).

Changes on all levels are necessary in immigrant family life to facilitate acculturation (Thomas, 1995). Berry et al. (1987) identified changes in a number of areas:

1. Physical changes. The person must cope with living in a new place, including such elements as increased population density, pollution, and a different climate.
2. Biological changes. The individual encounters dietary differences and propensity to diseases (e.g., hay fever, allergies, etc.) (Thomas, 1995; Westermeyer, 1989).
3. Cultural changes. Political, economic, technical, linguistic, vocational or educational, religious beliefs, and social institutions become altered, or are interchanged for new ones.
4. Social changes. The immigrant family must function within new social networks, both in-group and out-group.
5. Psychological and behavioral changes. Alteration in mental health status resulting from cultural readjustment experiences almost always occurs as individuals attempt to learn the ways of the new environment.

The more similar the worldview and customs of the ethnic person to that of the mainstream culture, the fewer the changes that are experienced. For example, the values and experiences of Russian refugee groups are more congruent with European Americans than the values and experiences of Mexicans who migrate from rural areas (Delgado-Gaitan, 1994). This allows the Russians to participate more fully in their U.S. communities and allows the Russians to belong without losing their cultural identity (Delgado-Gaitan, 1994), and hence facilitates the acculturation process. Moreover, the cultural distance between Russians and Americans is reduced due to the educational and literacy traditions that the Russians obtained in their former homeland (Delgado-Gaitan, 1994). Often, in school settings teachers compare the adjustment and achievement of children from different cultural traditions, without considering the different worldviews and experiences that each ethnic child brings to the educational setting.

Marlin (1994) pointed out that the central conflict in immigration rests in the following: How can one mourn all that is lost and yet not lose connection to one's past? How can one live in a new culture and sustain one's longing to return to one's native land? How can one go forward in one's return to the past? Which values, beliefs, and practices should be kept and which should change? By achieving a balance this conflict can be resolved, and the acculturation process is an attempt to reach that balance. The process of acculturation is continuous, dynamic, and open-ended; it is rarely complete, especially for adult immigrants.

Understanding the acculturation process helps educators, psychologists, social workers, and other mental health workers serve the immigrant community more effectively. It provides a framework that enables these people to recognize the immigrant's feelings, analyze the cause of these feelings, and alter problem-solving approaches to better manage the immigrant's emotions and experiences in order to regain emotional equilibrium (Lynch, 1992). Furthermore, Aponte and Barnes (1995) noted that the determination or knowledge of an ethnic individual's degree of acculturation is important for several reasons:

1. It leads to a deeper understanding of the person by providing a picture of the individual's view of him/herself, view of others of the same or different ethnic groups, and view of the mainstream culture.
2. Lack of it can lead to stress and to the development of psychopathology in the person (Berry & Kim, 1988; Berry et al., 1987).
3. It influences how immigrant individuals present their problems (Dinges & Cherry, 1995).
4. It is related to the utilization of mental health services.
5. It is of crucial importance in guiding the treatment of ethnic or immigrant persons, in determining the success of therapeutic interventions, and in understanding performance on psychological and psychiatric assessments.

Acculturation involves changes at an internal and external level that must be resolved in order to have a successful adaptation. All this work needs to be accomplished in a new environment, and at a time when survival depends on securing basic needs and acquiring new skills and attitudes (Richards, 1994).

Socioeconomic Level, Education, and Occupation

Socioeconomic status (SES) serves as a moderating factor in the process of acculturation (Aponte & Barnes, 1995). Its influence starts even before an immigrant family arrives in the United States and the process of acculturation begins. For example, an immigrant family from Colombia of upper socioeconomic status may have been exposed to American ways and customs more than a family of minimal income who lives in the most rural regions of the same country. In general, if a family with greater income migrates to the United States, that family would acculturate more rapidly and smoothly than its lower income counterpart. The United States Immigration and Naturalization Services reported that the majority of those who migrate are from lower socioeconomic levels and are usually unskilled workers (U.S. INS Statistical Yearbook, 1982–1987). Based on a review of studies concerning the poor, Hoppe and Heller (1975) indicated that lower SES populations across nations possess a number of similar characteristics, including distrust of the world outside family and friends, perception of the world in general as chaotic and catastrophic, heavy involvement in familial and peer relationships, and lack of community participation (Briones, Heller, Chalfant, Roberts, Aguirre-Hauchbaum, & Farr, 1990). These characteristics have a negative influence on an immigrant individual or family by limiting access to resources (medical and mental health), slowing acculturation processes, reducing political power, and limiting exposure to growth producing academic experiences and instruction. Level of income and education were identified as significant predictors of one's capacity to cope with stress (Mosley & Lex, 1990).

The impact of SES on a number of factors, such as mental and physical health, utilization of services, quality of education, living conditions, and so forth has been studied for decades. Nevertheless, most studies involving immigrants have concentrated on the effect of migration on mental health. Specifically, there has been much interest in how the stress involved in migration places immigrant families at risk for various psychiatric disorders and social maladjustment (Faris & Dunham, 1960; Golding & Burnham, 1990; Van Deusen, 1982; Westermeyer, 1989). Research findings suggest that individuals from low SES backgrounds exhibit more psychopathology, utilize mental health services less, and have fewer successful treatment outcomes than do middle-class and upper-class individuals (Malgady, Rogler, & Constantino, 1987; Briones et al., 1990; Aponte & Barnes, 1995). According to Dohrenwend and Dohrenwend (1981) and Lorion and Filner (1986), being from a low SES background can increase an individual's exposure to more stressors than that found in middle- and upper-SES experiences. Moreover, individuals from low SES can experience more victimization (stressful life experiences stemming from prejudice and racism), are more vulnerable (have fewer personal resources because of limited education and job skills and less social support), experience more additive burdens (combined effects of stressful events, have limited personal resources, and limited social support), and are subjected to more chronic burdens (long-term personal and situational stressors) than are persons from higher social classes (Aponte & Barnes, 1995). Thus, high SES mitigates many of the effects of minority status by placing persons in a prestigious and affluent network of relationships and memberships that protect them (Aponte & Barnes, 1995). However, research also suggests that having a meaningful support network constitutes a pivotal link between ethnicity and socioeconomic status and the presence of psychopathology; the alienating effects of minority status and lower SES membership are buffered by having a meaningful support network (Aponte & Barnes, 1995). Social support and network can consist of social interactions or relationships that provide aid to a person and embed that person within a social system that offers love, care, and a sense of attachment or belonging (Aponte & Barnes, 1995), as well as provide an atmosphere in which similar language, tradition, and cultural customs are shared.

Although many immigrants who enter the United States are of low socioeconomic status, for most ethnic groups this has improved over the last several decades (O'Hare, Pollard, Mann, & Kent, 1991). Nevertheless, the gap between these groups and Whites remains a significant one. Most other ethnic groups have a higher poverty rate than Whites (Aponte & Crouch, 1995; U.S. Bureau of Census, 1990). For total populations, Hispanics had a poverty rate of 28.2 and Asian or Pacific Islanders, 14.1. Whites had a poverty rate of 9.8, and the United States as a whole had a poverty rate of 13.1 (Aponte & Crouch, 1995).

Adler, Boyce, Chesney, Cohen, Falkman, Kahn, and Syme (1994) noted that several factors can be viewed as constituting socioeconomic status: occupation status, income, and education. There is great diversity in socioeconomic status across and within immigrant groups. For example, although the distribution of occupations for Asian Americans and Pacific Islanders is more likely to be in managerial or professional positions or manufacturing and trade jobs, and their mean household income is higher than Whites, the relative economic good standing of Asian/Pacific Islanders taken as a group does not reflect the subgroup differences within this broad ethnic group (Aponte & Crouch, 1995). More recent immigrants from China, Vietnam, Laos, Thailand, and Cambodia would tend to earn much lower incomes than those Asian Americans who were born in the United States (Aponte & Crouch, 1995). For Hispanics, research and census data indicate that 13.1 percent of Hispanics can be found in managerial and professional occupations (U.S. Bureau of Census, 1990), and that a relatively high concentration of Hispanics are in the farming, fishing, and forestry categories because of the large number of Hispanic migrant farm workers (Aponte & Crouch, 1995). Several reasons account for these findings: limited English proficiency and economic opportunities, as well as poor educational background and occupational skills (Aponte & Crouch, 1995; Thomas, 1992).

Socioeconomic status and educational background at the time of entry into the United States can facilitate or slow down the acculturation process and the immigrant family's overall adjustment to the new culture. Educational and occupational skills open the door to income and economic opportunities in this country. Nonliteracy impairs the ability to function in the host culture. Limited financial resources curtail the ability of ethnic families to live in neighborhoods where their children can receive adequate school instruction and exposure to good English language models. Poor occupational skills lead to unemployment or minimum wage jobs that are barely capable of meeting immigrant families' basic need for food, clothing, and shelter. It is frequently necessary for immigrant parents to obtain several jobs or work long hours to support the family, which in turn negatively affect the quality of family life and the parent's availability to their children. This combination of factors often can send an immigrant family on a downward spiral, preventing family members from obtaining the skills necessary to escape poverty. Middle to high SES, good educational preparation, and occupational skills can improve an immigrant's standing in the new culture by providing experiences that are valued in the mainstream culture and access to services that safeguard the immigrant person against psychological distress.

Ecological and Biological Stressors

Ecological and biological changes create stressors that the immigrant family must overcome. Ecological stressors include increased population density, a high crime rate, expensive housing, pollution, and climatic differences; biological stressors consist of dietary and nutritional changes, propensity to diseases, and so forth. Many immigrants migrate to urban areas because employment opportunities are more readily available. However, a large number of immigrants are migrant workers who live in rural areas. Urban life presents a number of potentially stress-evoking events. The immigrant family of limited financial resources that lacks occupational skills must often settle for low-paying jobs that offer no health care plan or job security. It is not uncommon to hear of employers who exploit immigrant workers (e.g., sweat shops, seasonal farm workers, etc.). The immigrant parent guided by financial constraints may choose to live in dilapidated public housing in a poor, crime-ridden urban neighborhood because rent is cheaper. The parent is also motivated to live in the city because schools are closer to home, even though the schools might be overcrowded and unprepared to deal with the needs of immigrant children. Victimization because of crime becomes a real possibility as many immigrants are victims of scams because they are often reluctant to go to the police. Urban children of low socioeconomic status have been found to experience more stressful events than suburban children of higher socioeconomic status (Aponte & Barnes, 1995). Middle-class immigrant families may settle in suburban areas where housing is more adequate, neighborhoods are safer, and schools are more effective.

Pollution and climatic changes may activate health conditions that may not have existed previously, such as asthma, allergies, sinusitis, hay fever, upper respiratory problems, and so on. Living in a new ecological environment can expose immigrants to disease agents not encountered in their native country. Dietary changes occur because one might not be able to find the ingredients used in preparing ethnic dishes. In some cases, the ingredients used to prepare ethnic foods are available but might be too expensive to purchase on a regular basis (e.g., a mango that is 35 cents in one's country might cost $1.25 in the United States). Climatic changes have an impact on the immigrant family's life. If the climate of the country of origin is similar to that of the new country, then the adjustment is minimal; however, if a family from the Caribbean settles in New York, for example, the adjustment would be greater given the difference in climate.

Migrant workers experience stress and disruption that are inherent in the lifestyle typical of farming. Housing for farm workers is frequently substandard or nonexistent; consequently, many farm workers may camp in the open or sleep in their vehicles (Aponte et al., 1995). The urgency to accomplish tasks according to nature's timetable forces farm workers to labor in the fields in all seasons and weather, to relocate or move to other farms seeking work, to be exposed to unsanitary working and housing conditions that make workers vulnerable to diseases no longer a threat to the general public, to come in contact with pesticides and chemical fertilizers that can be toxic to humans, and to frequently disrupt their children's education, which in turn impacts negatively on school achievement (Aponte et al., 1995).

Intercultural experiences and high to middle socioeconomic status can help mitigate or exacerbate these stressors. Prior intercultural experiences, such as having lived in an urban setting, play an important role. West Indians who migrate first to the United Kingdom and then to the United States tend to adjust better because of their previous experience of living elsewhere (Gopaul-McNicol, 1993).

Language Proficiency

Language is the primary means of accessing services, and understanding and communicating with the host culture (Lynch, 1992). A lack of language skills has often emerged as a major stressor for an immigrant individual and family. An inability to communicate creates a dependency on relatives and alienates the individual from the society he or she wishes to join.

Language learning involves acquiring the phonetic system (the sounds of the language), the morphologic system (how words are formed in the language), the syntactic system (the structure and grammatical system of the language), and the semantic characteristics of the language (the actual meaning of the utterances spoken and heard) (Walker, 1985). Linguistic proficiency refers to an individual's level of mastery over these aspects (Walker, 1985). To achieve proficiency in a second language, it is necessary to be exposed to the second language in a variety of settings and contexts. Learning appropriate patterns of discourse means learning a verbal repertoire for each social context in which speech is used (Walker, 1985). The attainment of proficiency in the second language is a slow process. A language barrier can be a difficult obstacle to overcome for adult immigrants for several reasons: immigrant adults who have little education tend to be intimidated by formal methods of learning English, and those with limited economic resources must work (Homel, Palif, & Aaronson, 1987). Basic English skills are learned on the job, helping the adult communicate with coworkers and get around in the community. Acquisition of a limited number of everyday expressions and the ability to shop and travel can take months (Westermeyer, 1989). The need to know English for employment is crucial, and the relationship between English fluency and successful resettlement and employment is strong (Walker, 1985). Greater English language proficiency brings increased opportunities, economic enhancement, and associated feelings about one's ability to function in society (Padilla et al., 1988).

Research focusing on second-language acquisition has identified a number of individual characteristics such as cognitive factors (learning style, intellectual potential, etc.), attitudinal factors (attitude about learning English), motivational factors, personality factors, native-language proficiency (literacy and educational background) (Hamayan & Damico, 1991) that are instrumental in facilitating or debilitating the acquisition of a second language. Age of the immigrant is also an important factor. Middle-aged immigrants may never reach social fluency, but can usually attain adequate language for work and ordinary social interactions; moreover, elderly immigrants often do not reach a level adequate even for self-sufficiency (Westermeyer, 1989). Gender, too, is a factor; men seek more English language training and develop more proficiency in English than women (Reder, Cohn, Arter, & Nelson, 1984). Immigrant women who do not work are frequently isolated at home, and the absence of child-care facilities denies them exposure to English-speaking models (i.e., friends, neighbors, English language classes, etc.) (Walker, 1985). Inability to communicate is frequently one of the reasons many immigrants choose to live in ethnic neighborhoods or enclaves. Children generally master English more rapidly than their parents because they receive more exposure to English in addition to formal instruction in school. It is not uncommon for children to become translators for parents. However, children do experience difficulties in school associated with second-language acquisition (see Chapter 3). Language usage and fluency can be viewed as both a component and an outcome of the acculturation process (Aponte & Barnes, 1995). To integrate into the new culture, the family must be able to communicate in the language of the macroculture.

Another important aspect of language are the cultural messages and beliefs that are transmitted in the way words are used, their connotations and denotations, as well as in the interpretation of information received. Language is an expression of culture (Jones & Thorne, 1987). Attention to language can be useful in discerning attitudes and beliefs in addition to facilitating communication (Anderson, 1989).

Immigrant and Legal Status

Numerous reasons motivate people to migrate to the United States. Some migrate seeking economic opportunities; they leave their native country pursuing freedom from poverty. Others flee oppressive regimes, and religious and political persecution; a small percentage of people leave their native land to better their education and professional experiences, and then return home. Understanding a family's reason for migrating to a new country is important and provides insight into stressors affecting the family. Immigration and legal status (i.e., voluntary or involuntary, documented or undocumented) are instrumental in molding the immigrant family's experience in this country.

   Voluntary immigrants are those who intentionally migrate seeking better social and economic conditions; migration for these families is planned and carefully orchestrated. Involuntary immigrants are forced to leave their native land due to political instability, civil unrest, or ideological and religious persecution. Refugees are considered involuntary immigrants, and African Americans are also an example of involuntary immigrants, because their presence in the United States was not voluntary.

   The way in which a society assists in resettlement and absorbs new people depends both on the adaptive characteristics of the newcomers as well as the nature of the society to which they come (Walker, 1985). Although Cubans make up the largest group of political refugees that has ever come to the United States (Grosjean, 1982), a large number of refugees also has come from Southeast Asia, namely Vietnam, Laos, and Cambodia. Most recently, the United States has accepted refugees from Haiti and Cuba (the third and most recent wave of Cubans was in 1994). Due to the nature of their immigration, refugees have had experiences that place them at a higher risk for psychological disorders. They may have been victims of torture or witnessed acts of terror; they may have lost family members either through death or relocation; they may no longer have community and social support; they may not be able to practice their religion in the same manner; they may have had to withstand great material loss as well as loss of status; and they may have lived in asylum camps in another country under austere conditions before finally resettling in the United States. Urban living is a new venture for refugees of rural backgrounds, many of whom have lost the skills, status, and roles that were theirs in their homeland (Walker, 1985). Underemployment and unemployment status are high among the refugee population, and as a result of insufficient job skills and training, many refugees cannot find work (Walker, 1985). A large number of refugees rely on public assistance to support their family; unfortunately, the cycle of welfare dependence is part of the new culture of resettlement (Walker, 1985). Even when families have been reunited and have settled in ethnic communities in which similar cultural values, language, and tradition are shared, the insulation of ethnic enclaves has failed to stem widespread culture shock (Walker, 1985). High rates of anxiety, depression, and adjustment problems have been found among refugees (Aponte & Barnes, 1995; Westermeyer, 1993; Mollica & Lavelle, 1988). Meredith and Cramer (1982) interviewed a refugee community (a Lao ethnic group called Hmong) in four states and found that 92 percent of those interviewed reported stress-related illness. Refugee families must also respond to the severe disintegration of traditional family structures, role hierarchies, and social support systems as well as persistent cultural conflicts and challenges to long-held beliefs, values, and socialization practices (Chan, 1992, p. 210).

   The experience of some refugee groups has been mitigated by their socioeconomic status, education, exposure to American culture, and language skills. For example, many Cubans that migrated in 1960, after the 1959 revolution headed by Fidel Castro, were businesspersons, lawyers, teachers, nurses, and skilled workers who set up their own businesses (Grosjean, 1982, p. 99). However, for many Cuban immigrants in the first wave, the belief that they would be able to return eventually to a free Cuba constrained some of their acculturation achievements (Zuniga, 1992, p. 153).

The legal status of an immigrant family that is undocumented (without legal immigration papers to live or work in the United States) or documented (with legal permission to live, work, or study in the United States) significantly affects their quality of life. Without proper documentation, many immigrants fear deportation (Congress, 1994). Living in the United States under constant fear of discovery and deportation has a detrimental effect on the functioning of immigrant families (Congress, 1994). Some undocumented immigrants (i.e., illegal aliens) are smuggled into the United States under less than humane conditions in trucks or cars; some just run across the border; others come hidden in the cargo of ships; others come on aircraft as tourists or students and never return once their visas expire. They seek employment as domestics, factory workers, gardeners, and farm workers, willing to do any type of task that allows them to make a living without a "green card." This undocumented status makes these immigrants susceptible to exploitation from employers who pay them less than minimum wage, provide no health care, and demand long working hours, knowing that they are afraid of losing their income or of being deported. Undocumented immigrants also avoid interacting with institutions such as schools, hospitals, police, and so forth. Parents do not attend conferences at school, do not inform police when they have been victims of crime, and only seek health care in cases of emergency. Although plagued by difficult circumstances, many undocumented immigrants remain in the United States because, despite their hardship, they hope to provide a better life for their children.

Social Support and Network/Family Life

Migration success is not only based on learning new sociocultural norms and behaviors, but also relies on social support from relatives, co-nationals, and the social acceptance of the host group (Zuniga, 1992, p. 159; Boekestijn, 1984). Immigrant families often depend on one another for emotional, psychological, and financial support; this support can alleviate stress and contribute to the immigrant's adaptation, which is paramount because it is often the only source of support during times of crisis (Zuniga, 1992). Research in this area has consistently yielded similar results that identify social support as an important factor in buffering individuals against psychological distress (e.g., depression, anxiety, adjustment disorders, etc.) (Briones et al., 1990). Social support comes in many forms: family and relatives, compatriots, ethnic communities, churches or religious congregations, and the like. Many immigrant groups have traditionally depended strongly on their immediate and extended families for social support. The social network of the immigrant can also help secure contacts important to obtaining employment (Thomas, 1995). Employment is frequently secured through contacts that an immigrant was able to make through a family acquaintance in the United States (Thomas, 1995). Immigrants with little or no social support are more susceptible to psychological distress and feelings of alienation. Living in an ethnic neighborhood can have a positive effect on the immigrant family's adjustment, influencing the impact of the family's cultural heritage on their lives (McGoldrick et al., 1982). Lee (1989) noted that for the Chinese living in Chinatown, the Chinese community support system provided a temporary cushion against the stresses of migration that usually surface in the next generation; in contrast, those living in areas with a small Chinese population generally had more trouble adjusting and felt pressured to assimilate more rapidly. However, although living in an ethnic neighborhood can provide social support because individuals share cultural traditions, beliefs, and language, it can attenuate the acculturation process because interaction with the mainstream culture might lessen the adjustment process.

Family life is irrevocably changed by migration. Interaction between children and parents, children and grandparents, husbands and wives, relatives, and siblings are altered by the exposure to the values, beliefs, and traditions of the mainstream culture. When the values of the mainstream culture come in contact with those of the immigrant family, results can include intergenerational conflicts; marital difficulties; in-law conflicts; sibling rivalry; hostile, albeit dependent relationship with sponsors; communication problems; and crises in parenting strategies (Lee, 1989). The family can grow from these challenges or can become dysfunctional. It is crucial to understand both the effect of acculturation on the family and the level of acculturation of each family member.

Lee (1989) identified four specific cultural orientations of immigrant families based on their position in the acculturation process: traditional families, transitional families, bicultural families, and "Americanized" families. Traditional families usually consist of all family members who were born and raised in the country of origin. These families tend to be recent arrivals with limited contact with the Western culture. They are older at the time of immigration, speak the native language exclusively, practice and strongly hold on to cultural values, sex roles, and traditions. They tend to function as extended families. Transitional families consist of parents and grandparents with strong traditional beliefs living with the younger generation who are Westernized. These families immigrated a decade ago, or are families with American-born children (Lee, 1989). They also tend to function more as extended families. Bicultural families consist of parents who are professional, English-speaking, and quite "Westernized" like their children. Their family background tends to be of middle to upper SES, and they have had early intercultural exposure (Lee, 1989). They are bilingual and bicultural, and can move between each culture with ease and comfort, allowing them to take advantage of what both cultures offer. They are very similar to a "typical American family" and can function as a nuclear family. "Americanized" families consist of parents and children who are born in the United States and have been in this country for several generations (Lee, 1989). They communicate in English only, and are not as committed to transmitting cultural traditions. Moreover, they have never visited relatives in the country of birth of their predecessors or practiced rituals rooted in ethnic traditions. They tend to function as a nuclear family and embrace American values and beliefs. While these categories were originally proposed for Chinese families in the United States, they are applicable to many immigrant families because they provide a framework that helps to explain how different families interact as a result of acculturation and exposure to the mainstream culture.

Because family members acculturate at a different rate as a function of age, gender, length of time in the United States, exposure to the mainstream culture, language proficiency, and educational background, differences in acculturation can create conflicts between family members. In traditional families, the younger members of the family usually develop better proficiency in English while older members (parents or grandparents) continue to speak exclusively their first language. This mismatch of language skills brings about communication difficulties between parents and children. Besides, it is not atypical for children to serve as translators for their parents; this role frequently diminishes the parent feelings of independence and control over the children, because the immigrant parent may now be dependent on the child to communicate with the mainstream society.

Intergenerational conflicts emerge when children acculturate at a faster pace than their parents. Children are exposed to American values and behaviors in school and on television. A need to fit in and to like and be liked by their American peers motivates them to embrace trendy fashions and behaviors. Moreover, not fitting in at school can open an immigrant child to constant teasing and ridiculing from American peers who may not be sensitive to cultural differences. Traditional and transitional parents are often urged to keep their cultural traditions as a means of preserving their identity, pride, respect, and ties to their homeland. When children begin to adopt the behaviors, manner of speech, clothing styles, and so forth, of the majority culture, parents fear their children are rejecting and losing their cultural tradition and language. Some immigrant parents may limit their children's experiences with the mainstream culture by keeping them at home or closely supervising their friendships and interactions with their American counterparts (Aponte et al., 1995). This further alienates the child and increases the chasm between parent and child. Immigrant children usually find themselves confronted with the difficult task of trying to develop values in two conflicting social and cultural situations, each demanding a different content (Thomas, 1992; Esquivel & Keitel, 1990; Brown, 1969). The more dissimilar the cultural values between both cultures, the greater the struggle to accommodate both groups, and the propensity for intergenerational conflicts increases.

Similarly, transitional families may experience difficulties resolving parent–child conflicts, gender role differences, and marital disharmony (Lee, 1989, 1982). Gender-role related problems can develop between spouses because of the changes required to survive in the new society. In the United States, a two-income household is essential for social mobility and survival. In cultures where women ascribe a more passive and submissive role than males, the gender expectation of a more egalitarian society places stress on a couple's relationship. Women, whose role was traditionally in the home and in childcare, now change to working outside the home, perhaps making a salary equal to or higher than her spouse. The male may begin to feel that he has lost status and respect in the family because sex role delineations are suddenly blurred. In many instances, women obtain employment more rapidly than their husbands, further wounding their egos and place of hierarchy in the family. Employment outside the home for women may give them a feeling of independence and autonomy that comes into direct conflict with their husband's role in the family. Communication problems between spouses are not uncommon, because demands (domestic, financial, and parenting) on the family may require more direct communication (Agbagani-Siewert, 1994). Bicultural families tend to be more adaptable, and members of "Americanized" families may face issues of cultural identity (Lee, 1989).

Many immigrants upon entering the United States first live with a relative or sponsor. By living with a relative, they are able to save money to eventually have their families join them. They are then able to support family members left behind in their native country, or to pay off debts to friends or relatives who pool their money to make the trip possible. However, many times the relationship with the sponsor deteriorates as the immigrant becomes more dependent or feels that the sponsor (who is more acculturated) has become too "Americanized," and no longer rigidly adheres to cultural practices and rituals. Another relevant issue is the type of child–parent conflict that results from parents having to leave their children behind to live with relatives or close friends for several years before being able to financially bring them to the United States. These parents may have missed their child's important developmental milestones, and may now be a stranger to that child (Thomas, 1992). The child may feel rejected and may rebel at every attempt the parent makes at disciplining, correcting, or advising. Parenting strategies must change because discipline practices of the homeland may not be considered appropriate in the new society. For example, corporal punishment is still the preferred method of correcting children in many cultures, but in the United States, there are laws against such practices. Smith-Hefner (1993) reports in a study of Khmer parents and generational conflicts that those who come from poor rural backgrounds cannot understand why police and the courts protect a misbehaving child rather than support a parent who is trying to correct his or her child.

The experience of migration forges changes in the immigrant families' ability to operate as they did in their homeland. While these changes initially produce a state of disequilibrium, many families successfully negotiate these obstacles to reach a balance that allows them to function in the mainstream culture.

Prejudice and Racism

Race has played a critical role in the economic, social, and political structure of American society from its precolonial beginnings to the present (Carter, 1995). Racism, prejudice, and discrimination are moderator variables emanating from the larger society or majority group that have a direct impact on the acculturation process (Aponte & Barnes, 1995). Racism can be external to the family and experienced as discrimination, or internalized in a sense of shame about oneself (Boyd-Franklin, 1989). Racism can be expressed in two ways, attitudinal and structural. Bem (1974) defined attitudes as a positive or negative evaluation of people, objects, ideas, or events. Attitudinal racism can mean that the mainstream or majority culture behaves toward ethnic groups by teasing, labeling, scapegoating, neglecting, and denying equal opportunity and equal rights (Aponte & Barnes, 1995; Adams, 1990). Institutional racism involves a pattern of rules, regulations, and behaviors that are exclusionary and exploitive, and are part of an organization or social system (Aponte & Barnes, 1995). Prejudice refers to a negative attitude toward or evaluation of a person due solely to his or her membership in a group, while stereotype refers to a set of beliefs about the characteristics of people in a particular group that is generalized to almost all group members (Crider, Goethals, Kavanaugh, & Solomon, 1989). For example, despite any evidence, many American citizens, including high-level government officials, initially assumed that Middle Easterners were responsible for the Oklahoma bombing in 1995.

Racism contributes immensely to how a culture evolves in the mainstream society. Racism affects the immigrant's work, self-esteem, and interpersonal relationships. In a study reported by Martinez (1993), respondents indicated that part of the stress faced by Latino immigrants was due to discrimination; for example, many indicated that U.S. citizens treated them unfairly and had negative stereotypes of them. Mexican Americans have experienced job discrimination, immigration restrictions, school segregation, and electoral disenfranchisement (Martinez, 1993; Montejano, 1987). The history of Asian Americans in the United States offers other examples of race's influence, specifically the Exclusion Act of 1882 against Chinese immigration and the forced internment of Japanese American citizens during World War II (Carter, 1995). Race also plays an important role. Light-skinned immigrants usually encountered a more favorable reception in the United States than dark-skinned immigrants (Montejano, 1987). In fact, the more similar the immigrant is in race or phenotypic traits to the majority culture, the better he or she would be accepted in that society. It becomes very clear to the non-Anglo immigrant that it is a disadvantage to be non-White, and this impacts on self-identity as well as self-esteem. Gopaul-McNicol (1993) indicated that racial self-perception plays an important role in the overall adjustment of immigrants of color from the West Indies. Those who perceived themselves as Blacks before they migrated tend to adjust more easily with respect to the European or American definition of "Black." Those who perceive themselves as White (people of mixed descent: European and African, and East Indians) usually go through a period of denial when they are termed "Black" by the European or U.S. societies (Gopaul-McNicol, 1993). Most immigrant groups who are linguistically diverse have experienced discrimination and prejudice as it applies to the opposition to bilingual education programs in this country (Aponte & Barnes, 1995), despite research and scientific support to its effectiveness in developing English proficiency.

Racism, prejudice, and discrimination can have a pervasive effect on the ethnic immigrant's quality of life and experiences in this society. They contribute to feelings of alienation, substance abuse, domestic violence, child abuse, and suicide (Lopez-Bushnell, Tyne, & Futness, 1992; Ho, 1990). Therefore, the experience of racism and discrimination are stressors that interfere with the adjustment, psychological functioning, and social adaptation of ethnic groups in the mainstream society (Aponte & Barnes, 1995).

AFRICAN-AMERICAN CHILDREN AND FAMILIES

Many African Americans arrived on the American continent as slaves, and it is within this historical context that the African-American experiences have evolved. African Americans and the richness of their culture have been a part of the United States since its founding (Willis, 1992), and this is evident in their achievement in literature, science, politics, art, and sports. Their contribution to trade, industry, and agriculture was significant and immeasurable; African Americans distinguished themselves in major wars, and were an integral part of the building of pre- and post-Revolutionary America (Willis, 1992). Yet, despite their contribution to this nation, racism and prejudice have shaped the lives of African Americans in the United States. During slavery, the African-American family was separated; mothers and fathers were brutally beaten; wives, sisters, or daughters were raped; children were sold; and families were intentionally kept illiterate. During nearly 300 years of slavery, individual slave owners exerted complete authority over the slave family (Fohlen, 1965). Even after the Emancipation Proclamation in 1863, the Reconstruction (1865–1877), and Black Codes or "Jim Crow" Laws (1865–1866), African Americans continued to be victims of terrorist acts such as physical violence, lynching, and property damage (Aponte & Barnes, 1995). By 1901, Black Codes had become the fabric of how the races would relate to one another (Willis, 1992). Considerable time and energy by many states were expended in the implementation of laws separating the races in schools, housing, jobs, public facilities, and services; due to the stranglehold of Black Codes, African Americans could not partake of the vast resources and opportunities of that period (Willis, 1992) and future decades to come. The denial of access to education, employment, and adequate housing created economic conditions that kept many African Americans poverty stricken with little to no option for social mobility. In the 1890s, an exodus of African Americans began and continued through World War II. They migrated from the South to the North due to economic hardship. During this period, an influx of European immigrants was also settling in the North and East, creating considerable crowding (Leigh & Green, 1982) and competition for limited resources (e.g., jobs, housing, etc.). While charity organizations staffed by wealthy volunteers provided services to newly arrived European immigrants, African Americans were viewed as physically present in American society but culturally distinctive because of appearance, African origins, and the experience with slavery (Leigh & Green, 1982). Willis (1992) noted that as a result of the prejudice encountered in the North, poor urban living conditions developed and became the homes for many African Americans, poor immigrants, and disenfranchised groups. Because very little was done to assist African Americans in obtaining education, housing, and employment, the circumstances that engendered these social conditions persist to this day.

The Civil Rights Movement of the 1960s was born out of African-American frustration with pervasive and destructive racist practices and beliefs. The Civil Rights Act, the Economic Opportunity Act of 1964, and the Voting Rights Act of 1965, and other landmark legislation succeeded in changing racist practices; however, racist attitudes and beliefs had become such an inherent part of the Anglo-American psyche that practices that were once overt and legal are now covert in nature. Consequently, the complexity of ideas and attitude toward African Americans have been transformed into a set of insidious and surreptitious policies and rules and informal networks that operate in major institutions (politics, economics, and education) to keep African Americans "in their place" (Vontress, 1995; Majors & Billson, 1992).

To this day, housing and employment discrimination continue, and at least one-third of African Americans live under conditions of extreme racial segregation (Massey & Denton, 1993). Therefore, although the U.S. Congress enacted many laws to provide African Americans and other ethnic groups with educational and employment opportunities, only a small percentage of the African-American population has been able to take advantage of these opportunities given the decades of exclusion. Nevertheless, those who effectively utilize the system to move forward (e.g., educated African Americans) often experience a societal projection process in which they are made to feel inferior by the implication that they have attained their status solely as a consequence of affirmative action concession (Boyd-Franklin, 1989).

Clearly, the African-American family has been affected directly by racism; this is reflected in the long years of slavery, lynchings, legal segregation, and the continued struggle to enjoy rights and opportunities other Americans take for granted (Vontress, 1995). Against this backdrop the African-American community has been forced to grow resilient and develop socially. The impact of these circumstances is present today when one looks at the African-American social, economic, and educational conditions. The effects of racism continue to be experienced on a psychological level even as African-American families move into a more middle-class socioeconomic level (Boyd-Franklin, 1989). African Americans still have reason to be suspicious of the police; they are frequent victims of bias crimes; they are often unable to obtain bank loans to buy a home or to open a business, and so on. A "healthy cultural paranoia" engendered in African Americans as a consequence of experience with racism and prejudice has been identified, and involves a general distrust and suspicion of the majority institution (Aponte & Barnes, 1995; Di-Angi, 1976; Jones, 1990).

Frisby (1992) described African-American children and families as extremely diverse, and he illustrated this point in the following statement:

African Americans reside in all types of environments (inner-city, suburban, rural) and can be found along the entire range of the economic spectrum (poverty to upper middle-class). African-American family structure is diverse (two-parent, single-parent, extended families, step-families), and black parents can be found to hold a range of occupations (skilled, semiskilled, professional, blue collar, white collar, etc.). African-American children attend a variety of schools (public, private, alternative), and manifest the entire range of academic achievement levels (i.e., from gifted achiever to unmotivated dropout). Black children are the product of various degrees of interracial mating and as a result have skin shades that range from white to yellow to brown to blue-black. African-American children manifest a variety of personality traits, temperaments, attitudes, and values (p. 535).

Yet despite this diversity, one cannot escape the reality that although African Americans constitute 12.3 percent of the U.S. population, they have a poverty rate of 29.5 percent (U.S. Bureau of Census, 1990). In addition, 16.5 percent of African Americans are in managerial and professional positions and 22.9 percent are in semiskilled labor positions (U.S. Bureau of Census, 1990). African Americans make up the majority of the population in major inner-city areas of the United States, where crime, poor housing, unemployment, and lack of access to services are prevalent (Willis, 1992). A consequence of living under these conditions where problems of poverty, overcrowding, violent crime, illegal drug trafficking, and lack of services are widespread is that children and families have a higher risk of infant mortality, poor health, and psychological problems (Willis, 1992; Allen & Majidi-Ahi, 1989; Randall-David, 1989). These ecological conditions have taken their toll on families and children. The African-Americans mortality rate is high compared to Whites. There are multiple reasons: a high infant mortality rate (17.6 infant deaths per 1,000 live births/8.5 infant deaths per 1,000 for Whites); higher death rates from illnesses—African Americans are 3.4 times more likely than Whites to die of AIDS, 2.8 times more likely to die of kidney disease, and 2.4 times more likely to die of diabetes; and a high homicide rate—African-American males are 7.6 times more likely to die by homicide than White males (Aponte & Crouch, 1995; O'Hare et al., 1991). However, one strength that is steadily demonstrated by African-American families is the ability to survive and handle difficult economic and social adversity (Boyd-Franklin, 1990).

According to Boyd-Franklin (1990), research has delineated five key areas of strength in the African-American community: (1) the bond of the extended family, (2) the adaptability of family roles, (3) strong religious orientation, (4) an integral belief in the value of education and the work ethic, and (5) the ability to develop and utilize effective coping skills in the face of socioeconomic hardships. The formation of the extended family is facilitated by a constant interplay of complex historical, socioeconomic, and marital factors (Wilson, 1989). African Americans have a heritage of shared loyalty and strong kinship ties that predate to historical origins in Africa, and in today's society, reliance on a kinship network, not necessarily limited to linear genealogical patterns or "blood lines," remains a chief mode of "familial interactions" (Boyd-Franklin, 1990). The value of group effort for the common interest is taught as a more enduring strategy for the survival of the African-American community, as opposed to individual effort for private gain (Billingsley, 1974). Willis (1992) notes that a significant aspect of the message about survival infused within the context of the family is the value of independence—the ability to stand on one's own feet, to have one's "own thing." Socialization is an important function of the extended family. The main socialization task of the African-American family is instilling in its members a sense of who they are and of their heritage (Billingsley, 1974).

Role flexibility developed as an answer to economic necessities (Boyd-Franklin, 1989). To address the needs of the family, a high percentage of women and adolescents have had to work to support the family, and this has led to versatility of family members in assuming and fulfilling family roles (Boyd-Franklin, 1989; Hill, 1972). For example, older children substitute as parents and caretakers; mothers assume the role of both parents or switch traditional roles with fathers (Boyd-Franklin, 1989). Moreover, Boyd-Franklin points out that if the roles in a family are flexible, then that family is better able to adapt to ever-changing social, political, and economic changes in society. Religion has traditionally been the source of spiritual fortitude in the African-American family (Randall-David, 1989; Willis, 1992), and it has been used as a survival mechanism for generations (Boyd-Franklin, 1989). From its beginnings, the African-American church has been the place where community members learned the values and responsibilities of leadership and organizational skills, and where role models for young members are available, because in the past these experiences have not been available to African Americans in the larger society (Willis, 1992).

African-American families place great emphasis on the value of education. These parents often expect their children to surpass them in achieving a better status and quality of life (Boyd-Franklin, 1990). The promise of education has always been a guide for many African-American families, and individuals who have accomplish high educational goals come not just from the middle-class families, but from families with a variety of status levels and fortunes (Willis, 1992). However, opportunity is often what differentiates between those who attain their educational goals and those who do not (Billingsley, 1974). The African-American family's ability to survive and cope when confronted with economic and social adversity have always been an area of strength (Boyd-Franklin, 1990). Boyd-Franklin (1990) encapsulates this idea when she notes that the flexibility of familial roles, and the ties of the extended family that offer a viable support network when faced with adversity, are two of the coping strategies African-American families effectively use to perpetuate and maintain a familial structure.

Despite historical constraints placed on African-American families, many have been successful within the societal milieu that they value and select; yet there are those who are not making it, in part because major societal institutions, still driven by underlying racist ideology, have failed to address their complex needs (Willis, 1992).

NATIVE-AMERICAN CHILDREN AND FAMILIES

Native Americans are highly diversified people who should not be approached stereotypically (Everett, Proctor, & Cantwell, 1983). While there are vast intertribal and interclan differences in customs, practices, family structure and roles, beliefs, and attitudes (Everett et al., 1983), they share common experiences of oppression (Aponte & Barnes, 1995) and discrimination.

A quest for fortune and land was responsible for the European presence on the American continents. The European conquest, which took almost 400 years, devastated Native-American tribes politically, economically, and socially throughout the American continents and the Caribbean (Joe & Malach, 1992). Before the arrival of the European conquerors, Native-American cultures had a well-established and rich history of great accomplishments. The cultural and historical roots for Native Americans date back thousands of years to generations of ancestors whose footprints in history left evidence of their advanced societies in religious rites, mounds, and burial sites that have revealed pottery, clothing, basketry, ornaments, weapons, tools, and use of metals such as copper and gold (Joe & Malach, 1992). Moreover, the Mayan and Aztec civilizations created great cities, and had achievements in the arts and sciences that equaled or exceeded those of the Europeans (Joe & Malach, 1992).

Even though the American continents were inhabited by indigenous peoples, the arrival of the Europeans rapidly depopulated the land through wars and the introduction of communicable diseases that unleashed great epidemics (Joe & Malach, 1992; Washburn, 1975). The European perception of the indigenous people and the European reason for arriving in North America defined the relationship and interaction that would exist between Native Americans and European Americans for centuries to come (Joe & Malach, 1992). European immigrants changed forever the culture and world of the Native Americans, and most of these changes were negative (Joe & Malach, 1992) and destructive to the Native-American way of life. Historically, the nature of intervention experienced by Native Americans had been plagued with attempts by various groups to change their traditions, practices, and beliefs (Everett, Proctor, Cantwell, 1983); these interventions attempted to dehumanize and "deculturize" Native Americans.

The federal government, under the policy of the Manifest Destiny, intervened repeatedly with unfavorable consequences for Native Americans (Everett et al., 1983). Native Americans have experienced the impact of a majority culture that imposed European values, beliefs, and practices on them and removed them from their ancestral lands in the early history of the United States (LaFromboise, 1988). Whole nations of people were uprooted from their homes and lands and transported to places that were so different in geography and ecology as to be almost incapable of supporting life as the tribes knew it (Everett et al., 1983), and destined them to a life of poverty (Joe & Malach, 1992). The European-American obsession with the acculturation or "Europeanization" of Native Americans led to numerous practices that were discriminatory and oppressive to Native Americans. Many Native-American children were placed in boarding schools or put up for adoption far from their tribes, where tribal language and cultural practices were discouraged in an overt attempt to weaken oral tradition and connectedness with tribal culture (Joe & Malach, 1992; Trennent, 1988).

Today, although the passage of the Indian Child Welfare Act of 1978 assured Native Americans that a serious effort would be made to keep their children in traditional settings, 25 to 35 percent of Native-American children are still placed in non-Native-American homes where exposure to their cultural heritage is limited (Choney et al., 1995; Kessel & Robbins, 1984). Consistent with the federal policy of assimilation, traditional Native-American spiritual/religious activities were outlawed in the late 1800s. This encouraged missionaries to set out on a goal to Christianize or convert Native Americans, and created division within tribes. It remained illegal to practice "native religions" until the federal government passed the American Indian Religious Freedom Act of 1978 (Choney et al., 1995). According to Dana (1993) and Trimble (1987), the discriminatory and oppressive experiences of Native Americans can be described as that of a conquered people who have been displaced from their land, had children removed from their families, had the roles of males in their family and community undermined, and had their language eliminated (Aponte & Barnes, 1992). Effects of these oppressive acts have carved the conditions that now plague Native-American societies today. The impact has been visible on social, cultural, economic, and psychological fronts.

According to the U.S. Census Bureau (1991), there were approximately 2 million people identified as Native American/Alaskan Native in 1990. Within these 2 million people, 542 tribes are represented and over 150 Native-American languages are spoken. The median ages range from 18.8 to 26.3 years on reservation lands, with those Native Americans living within tribal jurisdictional areas having slightly higher median ages (22.7 to 27.2 years) and those in Alaskan Native villages slightly lower (16.8 to 25.0 years) (Choney et al., 1995, p. 74). Twenty-three percent of the Native-American population continues to live on over 300 existing reservation and trust lands, with approximately 15 percent living within tribal jurisdiction, Alaskan Native villages, or tribal designated areas (Choney et al., 1995). Choney et al. (1995) indicated that 62.3 percent of Native Americans are divided between rural and urban areas. Joe and Malach (1992) purported that the profile of many reservation communities today parallels that of developing countries: high birth rates and mortality rates. Social indicators suggest that Native Americans and Alaskan Natives confront higher poverty levels and lower educational accomplishments than do other groups (U.S. Bureau of the Census, 1991). An endemic cycle of poverty contributes extensively to the poor health and well-being of many Native-American families (Joe & Malach, 1992).

The four leading causes of Native American deaths are alcohol related (i.e., accidents, cirrhosis, homicides, and suicides) (French, 1989). Fetal alcohol syndrome and alcoholism are major health problems among Native Americans (French, 1989), and are becoming a significant threat to the survival and functioning of future generations of Native Americans. Regarding Native-American adolescents, the Senate Select Committee on Indian Affairs in 1990 listed in its report problems such as developmental disabilities, depression, suicide, anxiety, alcohol and substance abuse, low self-esteem and alienation, running away, and dropping out of school as high priority areas (Choney et al., 1995). The forced acculturation, racism, and discrimination continually experienced by tribal people in the United States was a threat to personal integrity; moreover, the encounter of two conflicting cultures can produce a unique sort of stress—acculturative stress—that is accompanied by physiological distress (Berry, Kim, Minde, & Mok, 1987; Choney et al., 1995). A number of studies have suggested that culture and acculturation influence drinking patterns and habits (French & Hornbuckle, 1980; Hughes & Dodder, 1984; Weisner, Weibel-Orlando, & Long, 1984). Nevertheless, Native Americans have experienced a great many social and psychological problems that can be traced to their earlier experiences with White European cultures, and this is responsible for their present status in this country (LaFromboise, 1988).

French (1989) placed the Native-American cultural continuum in three categories: traditional Native Americans, middle-class Native Americans, and marginal Native Americans. However, Choney et al., (1995) proposed a more comprehensive model that viewed the acculturation of Native Americans from a cognitive, behavioral, affective/spiritual, and social/environmental perspective. The model consists of five levels of acculturation: traditional, transitional, bicultural, assimilated, and marginal. Traditional Native Americans' psychological perspective represents most the aboriginal tradition, beliefs, and practices (e.g., harmony with nature, present-time orientation, cooperation, sharing wealth, work for present needs, anonymity, submissiveness) (French, 1989). They speak little English (or may refuse to speak English) and are fluent in their respective tribal language. Transitional Native Americans are very proficient in their tribal language. They understand some Anglo-European customs, but fully embrace their tribal traditions. Although they participate in some mainstream society activities and socialize with some non-Native Americans, they remain closer to their tribal way of life and ethos. Bicultural Native Americans speak English and the tribal language well. They understand both tribal and Anglo-European customs and participate and socialize in both cultures. The bicultural Native American can move with ease in both cultures while maintaining his or her "Indianness." Assimilated Native Americans are considered the most affluent (wealth, status, education) by the standards of the mainstream society. However, they are not respected by other Native Americans because they subscribe fully to the norms of the mainstream society, and are rewarded by the majority culture for their "assimilation" (French, 1989). They do not speak the tribal language. They socialize and live mainly with non-Native Americans. Marginal Native Americans are caught between their traditional cultural heritage and the expectations of the mainstream society. They want to embrace their "Indianness," but do not have the social mechanisms to do so. Those who live on reservations have greater access to knowledge about their heritage; however, those who live in urban and rural areas have less interaction with other Native Americans and less exposure to their heritage (French, 1989). They are more vulnerable to feelings of alienation and depression as well as alcoholism; furthermore, those who live in urban areas are also prone to the perils of typical urban life (i.e., crime, poor housing conditions, etc.) (French, 1989; French & Hornbuckle, 1980).

Traditionally, most Native-American families include extended family members as well as the immediate family (Joe & Malach, 1992). Members of the extended family have responsibilities to and for one another; the extended family is a resource network for many Native Americans (Everett et al., 1983)—the base of support and stability. All knowledge about tribal heritage, pride, and spirituality is transmitted through the tribal elders and extended family. Great emphasis is placed on anonymity, humility, and submission of the self to the welfare of the tribe, all of which are important values in the Native American culture (Foster, 1988). Family members are interdependent, and needs are met in a variety of ways (Everett et al., 1983) because everyone has a responsibility to one another.

Native Americans remain committed to advancing tribal identity, and to seeking the right to self-government, equal access to quality health care and education, and an appreciation and encouragement for fostering their tribal language and culture (Joe & Malach, 1992) despite racist and oppressive sociopolitical underpinnings.

ANGLO-EUROPEAN CHILDREN AND FAMILIES

The anticipation of a new land rich in resources such as gold and spices, coupled with the post-medieval interest in explorations and conquest, provided the impetus that brought the first European explorers to the American continent (Hanson, 1992). Land was the lure; to Europeans, the possession of land meant economic independence and more desirable social status (Critoph, 1979). They could now practice the ideal of the free individual, and they did not have to accept a predetermined life as they would have in Europe

(Critoph, 1979). The land was sparsely populated by Native Americans who did not change the land and who were spread across the vast land based on their practices and lifestyles (Hanson, 1992). As the presence of early European settlers increased in North America and as they began to acquire land, Native Americans were systematically displaced and segregated because they stood in the way of social, economic, and cultural expansion. Native Americans fought for their rights as previous inhabitants of the land; yet, centuries of conflicts, hostilities, and distrust still define the relationship between Anglo Europeans and Native Americans to this day. Many Africans were brought to America to help build the new nation, but they came as slaves and were denied access to the riches of the new land (Hanson, 1992).

Increased migration and the birth of new citizens augmented the presence of Europeans who began establishing a nation by forming a government and trading with other nations. The new colonists brought the accumulated cultures of Western Europe; agrarian traditions; the traditions and literature of the classical world; and the institutions, theologies, religions, and philosophies of Europe. Moreover, they were free to practice their own religion, to acquire land, and to pursue their own political philosophies (Hanson, 1992). The Anglo-Saxon origins of this country established English as the primary language, and in these Anglo-European roots the mainstream culture of the United States finds its beliefs, values, and practices (Hanson, 1992). Additionally, because the majority of migrating Europeans gained their livelihood from the soil during the first three hundred years of American history, agrarian principles formed the foundation of American traditions (Critoph, 1979).

Given the expansion of the population, the Anglo-American model has endured, with most subsequent immigrants adapting to its canons (Hacker, 1992). Other European immigrants not only learned English, but also adjusted their lives to the economy and technology associated with that prototype (Hacker, 1992). For example, following 1848, Germans arrived in the United States in large numbers; they rapidly learned English and studied the customs of their new land (Hacker, 1992). Because many were merchants or farmers, familiar with the rules of a market economy, they quickly found a niche; through intermarriage, moves to mixed neighborhoods, and service in the Union Army during the Civil War, the process of assimilation was accelerated (Hacker, 1992). After generations, very few neighborhoods retained true vestiges of a German influence. However, acceptance was not readily granted to every early European immigrant group. For example, Irish immigrants struggled to be accepted because, even though they arrived speaking English, their rural-folk ways slowed their adjustment to an urban nation (Hacker, 1992). Moreover, at the time of their entry into the United States, Catholics were not regarded as "Whites" (Hacker, 1992). At the turn of the century, many Jews arrived on U.S. shores, and were first kept at the margin of "White" America because they were not Christians (Hacker, 1992). Yet through education they gained acceptance. Nevertheless, European ancestry has never presented an insurmountable barrier to achievement (Alba, 1990).

The staggered arrival of European immigrants and their varied economic backgrounds and initial success led to a perceptible ethnic hierarchy: Protestant groups from the British Isles occupied the top; groups from northern and western Europe were in the middle; and groups from eastern and southern Europe were at the bottom (Alba, 1990). In spite of some conflicts between European immigrants and the mixture of other European nationalities through immigration or intermarriage, the Protestant British remained secure in their language and customs, government and laws, and religious institutions (Alba, 1990).

According to Hacker (1992), World War II accelerated the process of assimilation, and its aftermath brought about the acceptance of people from every corner of Europe as "White," and the consciousness of ethnicity gradually disappeared among Europeans (Alba, 1990). However, the further the immigrant ancestor's cultural identities differed from the White Anglo-Saxon Protestant image of the "real" American, the greater the pressure to assimilate (Howard, 1993). A number of factors contribute to European immigrants developing an "American identity" and shedding their ethnic differentiation: generational progression among individuals and families, equalization of educational and labor-market opportunities of ethnic groups, inability to speak the mother tongue, and interethnic marriage (Alba, 1990). The erosion of ethnic identity facilitates assimilation, yet the transformation of ethnicity among Whites does not imply the elimination of ethnicity but instead the formation of a new ethnic group, one based on ancestry from anywhere on the European continent (Alba, 1990).

The cultural backgrounds and practices of immigrants from the British Isles and Western Europe, along with the conditions and opportunities encountered in the new land, shaped the major cultural values and practices of the American people (Hanson, 1992). Althens (1981) identifies cultural values and customs embedded in the American culture:

- Individualism and privacy: the belief that each person is a distinct entity
- Egalitarianism: the belief that all human beings are equal
- Action orientation: doing is better than being
- Definition of persons in terms of their work and achievement
- The belief that competition is the best way to motivate people
- The belief that hard work leads to success
- The idea that there is generally a best way of doing something
- Unnecessary qualification: the tendency to quantify parts of experience
- Emphasis on the present and not the past
- Placing a higher value on utilitarian parts of experience than on aesthetic ones

- Impatience: the tendency to be annoyed by the pace of activities, if it is slow by one's standard
- The tendency to make comparative judgments
- The belief in self-help
- The willingness to offer one's services for the benefit of the "common good"
- Directness and assertiveness

These values and customs have translated into belief systems that reflect the culture's philosophies regarding childrearing, medical or health care practices, the causation and treatment of disabilities (Hanson, 1992), and education and social policies and practices.

The American family structure has gradually changed since the early agrarian family unit (i.e., a nuclear family). The contemporary American family structure is becoming quite diverse and includes nuclear families and single-parent families. In the Anglo-European American tradition, a family consists of a mother, a father, and children. Grandparents and other family members do not participate in decision making and day-to-day functioning of the family. The male is typically considered the head of the household, but today, in more contemporary households, there seems to be a move toward a more balanced distribution of power in the family, with females participating in the decision-making process as well as contributing financially to the family's subsistence. The family is "child centered," and children participate actively in day-to-day family activities. Children are encouraged to be independent and self-sufficient, and parents begin early to provide the children with the skills they need to be independent. Education is important to self-development, social mobility, self-respect, and independence. Parents are expected to be involved actively in the education of the children as well as in school policies. Most Anglo-European Americans ascribe to a Judeo-Christian belief system, and Christianity constitutes the religion practiced by the majority of people (Hanson, 1992).

Despite many cultural commonalities, Anglo-European Americans are a diverse people; they differ broadly across extremely different cultures of origin and continue to be diverse in religion, politics, economic status, and lifestyles (Alba, 1990; Howard, 1993). Many White Americans have maintained direct and strong ties with their European roots, and they continue to call themselves Irish Americans, Italian Americans, Croatian Americans, or Russian Americans—terminology that recognizes the two sides of their identity (Howard, 1993). In attempting to understand the history and culture of European Americans, it is important to recognize the pain, suffering, and loss that were frequently associated with their immigrant experience (Howard, 1993). For example, Jews, Catholics, Eastern Europeans, Southern Europeans, and members of minority religious sects receive a strong message: Forget your home language, make sure your children do not learn to speak it, change your last name to sound more American (Howard, 1993), and do not divulge your religious affiliation if it is different from that practiced in the main-stream culture. Because many aspects of culture are transmitted through lan-guage, many ethnic Europeans who did not pass on their mother tongue to subsequent generations lost contact with their ethnic roots (Alba, 1990). The pressure to assimilate forced many ethnic Europeans to lose contact with their ethnic identity and adopt an "American Identity."

In 1990, Anglo-European Americans constituted 75 percent of the popu-lation of the United States (U.S. Bureau of Census, 1992), but the recent wave of immigrants with non-Anglo cultural affiliation from Central and South America, Caribbean, and Asia are increasing the ethnic and racial diversity of the U.S. population. This has become a challenge for the Anglo-European American mainstream culture, who must learn to evaluate new social philoso-phies about educating and treating new citizens from ethnically and linguis-tically diverse backgrounds.

THE IMPACT OF CULTURAL, LINGUISTIC, AND IMMIGRATION FACTORS ON THE EDUCATION OF CHILDREN

The United States has traditionally struggled with the dilemma of the assimi-lationist and pluralist perspective of its social structure (London, 1990). The as-similationist position espouses establishing a dynamic American identity (Kallen, 1924; London, 1990; Sowell, 1981; Thomas, 1981); in contrast, the plu-ralist position advocates a view of self-respect and the maintenance of ethnic identity (Bennett, 1981; London, 1990; Longstreet, 1978). Today, this dilemma has become more pronounced because it has been shoved to the forefront as a consequence of the continuing diversification of the U.S. population. Resis-tance to bilingual and multicultural education, affirmative action, and other educational services to improve the school performance of culturally and lin-guistically diverse children, and the undying effort to establish "English Only" laws bear witness to this dilemma. There seems to be an underlying fear that by condoning biculturalism and bilingualism, the United States will lose its "American identity," and that this threatens the fabric of American society. Educational institutions have long been the vehicle of acculturation; indirectly and directly, they inculcate the values, beliefs, and practices that are thought to embody the "American identity" and exclude all elements of "foreignness" from the curricula of schools (Banks & Banks, 1989). Middle-class White val-ues and ethics are generally espoused to all pupils. London (1990) impressed that as a larger and visible social institution, schools reflect in their operation, organization, and structure the stresses of the society.

The increasing cultural diversification of the U.S. population has been met with ambivalence at best. On the one hand, cultural diversity is a desirable feature of life; exposure to diversity brings us in contact with different people and customs (Aponte et al., 1995). After all, many Americans travel abroad each year. On the other hand, when cultural and linguistic differences are great, when they become part of the fabric of our society, and when they occur in the context of formal schooling, significant problems emerge (Dana, 1993). While cultural diversity itself is not a problem, our sociopolitical insularity and consequent inability to accept and accommodate diversity is the source of conflict and controversy.

Cultural conflict is one of the main problems faced by culturally and linguistically diverse children in U.S. schools (London, 1990). The major discrepancy is between the culture of various ethnic groups and the Anglo-European culture upon which the public school system is based and implemented throughout the United States (Aponte et al., 1995) fueled by an ambivalence to embrace a multicultural framework and context. Unfortunately, membership in a racial or ethnic group is often correlated with lack of school achievement (National Assessment of Educational Program, 1985). Specifically, the schools have not been successful in educating these children, as evidenced by high drop-out rates, low academic achievement, and high rates of referral to special education (Ortiz, Garcia, Holtzman, Poyzoi, Snell, Wilkinson, & Willig, 1985). This is even more significant considering that by the year 2,000, it is estimated that approximately one-third of public school children will be from culturally and linguistically diverse backgrounds, with Hispanics being the largest ethnic group (U.S. Department of Education, 1994). Therefore, educators, school psychologists, and social workers must be prepared to efficiently teach, assess, and counsel children who are from racially or ethnically diverse groups, who speak a different language, and who are less secure financially and physically (Yates & Ortiz, 1991, 1995).

The ever present concerns and priorities for educators are to provide educational programs and experiences that are most appropriate and most effective for various student populations (Baca & Bransford, 1981). School and clinical practitioners often attempt to fit culturally diverse children into a system that is frequently at odds with the way they are, the way they think, and the way they behave (Dana, 1993). To effectively address the educational needs of culturally and linguistically diverse students, it is paramount to first examine and understand the positive and negative elements that these children bring to the educational system and how these impact upon their academic preparation. The elements are numerous; however, research data identify several important factors: cultural variables, language proficiency, ecological and social conditions, educational background, and family characteristics. Moreover, the school system also brings other elements, namely, preparation of school staff, academic expectations, educational services available, and attitudes toward culturally and linguistically diverse students and families. Student and school elements intertwine and determine whether these children would be successful in U.S. society.

STUDENT ELEMENTS THAT IMPACT ON EDUCATIONAL NEEDS

Cultural Variables

Learning to learn is a dimension of the cultural information that is passed from adult to child in a family network (Walker, 1985). Understanding how to learn is culturally determined and transmitted by the family and society. The ways in which people learn are a reflection of their culture's framework for teaching and learning, which is in turn manifested in the values that society wants transmitted to its children (Walker, 1985). For example, Asian cultures generally have been depicted as encouraging rote, passive learning (Walker, 1985), while African Americans are said to be more active and cooperative learners. In the American mainstream classrooms, competition is encouraged; doing better than others is often proof of mastery (Goldman & McDermott, 1987). This attitude is pervasive in society, including the classroom (Chamberlain & Medinos-Landurand, 1991). In contrast, for children raised in cooperative societies, competition is generally not understood or valued; for these children, working together is a mutual goal (Chamberlain & Medinos-Landurand, 1991). Children who are raised in a cultural value system that does not ascribe to the notion of competition are at a disadvantage in U.S. schools. Social-emotional issues arise when behaviors that are appropriate in one environment are inappropriate in another (Smith, 1992). According to Cloud (1991), another variable related to achievement is the value placed on education by the family and by the larger ethnic community. This value is culturally determined. The degree of focus placed on education is influenced by factors such as economic conditions, educational level of the parents, gender of the child, the degree to which the family believes that education will guarantee their child's advancement in society, and the degree to which the family believes their child is being provided with a quality education (Cloud, 1991). For example, Smith (1992) found that although Khmer parents recognize the value of education for their children, other traditional ideals concerning the proper role of young women continue to dictate parental attitudes toward their daughters' education. These same role expectations are the basis for intergenerational conflicts concerning the education of Khmer girls in the United States and strongly influence the direction and duration of these girls in school (Smith, 1992). Ogbu (1981) presents a similar view when he affirms that many minority students are aware that the system works to their disadvantage; therefore, they do not adopt the behaviors necessary for school success because they reject the White American societal values that those behaviors embody (Hayes, 1992).

Other cultural variables include level of acculturation, the notion of time, kinetic orientation (active/passive), proximity (social space between individuals), touching, eye contact, gender, locus of control, and cognitive and perceptual styles. The mismatch between a child's native culture and that of the schools may have profound impact upon this child's communication, motivation, and performance (Chamberlain & Medinos-Landurand, 1991). The impact of cultural variables in learning is discussed fully in Chapter 7.

Ecological and Social Conditions

Understanding the social and environmental conditions under which students live is critical to establishing an educational atmosphere that would address their academic needs. A history of poor health or poor nutrition may result in missed opportunities to acquire various skills and abilities (Zeichner, 1993). Emotional and educational deprivations surrounding the lack of stimulation in infancy negatively influence the neurological wiring that facilitates learning at critical periods in a child's development. Children who live in poverty confront a number of interactive variables, including (a) higher rate of poor prenatal care and complications during and after birth, (b) continuing problems related to health and cognitive development, including malnutrition, lead poisoning, and poor parental care, (c) a lack of stimulation and exposure to growth producing educational experiences (Dana, 1993), and (d) possible drug use by parents, as well as HIV infection or AIDS. Poor health care for immigrant and ethnic families and children is likely to continue throughout the child's development or school years due to many barriers to health care access, from both the consumer's and the provider's perspective (Lequerica, 1993). These barriers include lack of familiarity with the language and culture of consumers, limited access to bilingual staff or interpreters, and urban institutions (hospital, schools, and mental health facilities) that are large, overcrowded, and understaffed, thus offering impersonal, limited, and fragmented services (Lequerica, 1993). Other issues include limited English proficiency, and unfamiliarity with the health delivery system and the cultural assumptions in which this system is embedded (Lequerica, 1993).

Some culturally and linguistically diverse children experience great mobility in their lives (Smith, 1992). Many children, as a result of socioeconomic factors, are homeless and live in unstable situations (e.g., migrant workers, political refugees); others move whenever the landlord increases the rent. These children may experience disruption and dislocation in their education that often adversely affects both physical and mental abilities as well as school performance (Smith, 1992). It is imperative to understand a child's circumstances and how they facilitate or interfere with learning and school performance.

Children who migrated to the United States due to wars or civil strife in their homeland may bring to the school system a variety of emotional and health problems that may interfere with learning. The political turmoil in today's world has precipitated wars or civil strife in countries like Iraq, Kuwait, Guatemala, Nicaragua, El Salvador, Haiti, Cambodia, Azer Baijan, Armenia, North Ireland, South Africa, and Lebanon; children in these regions had to suffer the effects of war hostility, unpredictable turbulence, and basic dislocation (Elbedour, Bensel, & Bastrieu, 1993). Moreover, the chaos and violence in many inner cities have created such dangerous conditions, filled with sudden, violent deaths, that many children growing up in the cities have equally been traumatized (Elbedour et al., 1993) and exhibit similar patterns of behaviors. A child's war-time experience, fueled by the trauma war can create, may find expression in a host of psychological symptoms, including anxiety, excessive fearfulness and feelings of helplessness, feelings of shame, blame of self or others, social isolation, and a general lack of hope and purpose; many show signs of mourning and grief, depression, suicidal ideation, somatic illness, difficulty focusing attention, acting out behaviors (rage, anger, and aggression), susceptibility to traumatic dreams that at times results in an inability to sleep (Elbedour et al., 1993). Some may exhibit signs of traumatization that is short-term, some may show a delayed response (typical of post-traumatic stress disorder), and others may not show signs of trauma (Elbedour et al., 1993).

Language Proficiency

Language is probably one of the most visible and major obstacles that some ethnic children face in school. Children who are culturally and linguistically diverse have language and communication differences that raise educational issues (Smith, 1992). According to Walker (1985), linguistic differences between the first language and English, combined with cultural characteristics of the learners, are significant predictors of success in learning English. Limited English proficiency (LEP) refers to a pupil who comes from a home in which a language other than English is primarily used for communication and who has sufficient difficulty in understanding, speaking, reading, or writing the English language. This denies him or her the opportunity to learn successfully in classrooms in which the language of instruction is English (Baca & Bransford, 1981). Non-English proficient youngsters (NEP) are those who do not speak English and whose dominant language for communication in all settings and context is a language other than English. The level of proficiency that children have attained in their native language at the time they begin to learn the second language directly affects how easily and efficiently they will attain proficiency in the second language (Hamayan & Damico, 1991). Children who have limited command of their first language may experience more difficulty learning a second language than children who are proficient in their native language. Moreover, many of the school problems encountered by children who are learning a second language are similar to those commonly used to identify children who are learning or language impaired. Many educators and diagnosticians are not fully informed as to the processes involved in second-language acquisition and how they affect learning; consequently, many limited English proficient as well as non-English speakers are overrepresented in special education in some categories while underrepresented in others (U.S. Department of Education, 1995). The processes inherent in second-language acquisition and its effect on learning and assessment are discussed in Chapter 3.

Educational Background

Some linguistically and culturally diverse students were born in the United States, whereas others resettled in the United States as immigrants, refugees, or as the children of migrant workers (Cloud, 1991). Their educational experiences are varied: Some have been involved in a continuous educational process; others have interrupted and fragmented schooling background; some attained proficiency in their native language and experienced academic success in their native land; and others did not attain a strong foundation in the native or first language prior to beginning schooling experiences in English (Cloud, 1991; Hayes, 1992). These experiences have profound effects on the achievement and academic performance of these children.

A great obstacle to academic progress in many immigrant children is lack of an educational foundation on which to build new knowledge. Political instability and economic devastation in many countries provides the impetus for migration and also results in inadequate educational preparation in a number of children and adults who immigrate to the United States. In the case of refugee children, many finally settle in the United States after living in several countries where they may or may not have attended school. Often, they may have attended several schools in which they were exposed to various language and instructional strategies. Many immigrant children enter the U.S. public school systems with no formal schooling. Others move back and forth between the parents' place of birth and a resettlement community of relatives and friends in the United States (Cloud, 1991). For example, a number of Puerto Rican youngsters move between urban northeastern United States and Puerto Rico. Other groups show similar patterns of frequent migration, such as Mexicans in the west and southwest United States, and Dominican and Haitian students in the Northeast (Cloud, 1991). This instability and disruption in schooling fractures the type of continuity necessary in a learning environment for educational growth and achievement.

Family Characteristics

There is very little doubt that family characteristics do influence school achievement (Feuerstein, 1980). The family's attitudes and practices related to education and its ability to provide for a child's social and emotional development are critical factors in shaping the child's educational experience (Giles, 1990). Parents' attitudes about education and learning a second language, literacy level, involvement in school, and English language proficiency are factors that impact on children's achievement.

The adjustments an immigrant family must make to build a solid economic foundation in the United States often create problems. Economic reasons tend to force both parents to be employed and to have long working hours. Quite often parents hold more than one job to meet the family's basic needs. Consequently, parents have very little time to spend helping their children with homework, attending parent–teacher conferences or school functions, or providing their children with the type of support they need to facilitate acculturation. Parents' nonparticipation in their children's education also occurs when parents have limited English proficiency, their immigration status is undocumented, and their cultural expectations surrounding school involvement are different. For example, Giles (1990) indicated that a number of factors contribute to the low level of contact Haitian parents have with their children's schools in the United States: limited English skills, shame at their own lack of education, time constraints created by their heavy work schedules, and fear of being reported to Immigration and Naturalization Services by school staff if they are illegal. Moreover, while Haitian parents have a sacred belief in the value of education, when in the United States they often play a low-key role in their children's education because in Haiti, the school takes a comparatively greater responsibility for children's education (Giles, 1990; Joseph, 1984). A similar pattern of belief about parent–school participation has been observed with some Latino parents. Latino parents deliver their children to school trusting the wisdom of teachers who assume the role of "parent" in the school. Latino parents respect the advice and decisions of school staff and are often willing to accommodate these decisions, despite doubts, on behalf of their children. However, educational practitioners tend to interpret this culturally determined role as "passivity" or "disinterest." In a study of Filipino-American families and culture, Agbagani-Siewert (1994) noted that Filipino community leaders and social service workers in Los Angeles and Seattle reported increasing adolescent gang problems; the lack of supervision and support from extended family in the United states, economic issues, and the stress stemming from the acculturation process impel some parents to seek the help of extended family members in the Philippines by sending problematic children back to the homeland.

Parents' level of literacy is another relevant variable. The level of literacy in the home and community may influence the pupil's achievement in school (Hamayan & Damico, 1991). Children whose parents read a lot at home in the presence of their children and who read to their children expose them to enriching educational experiences and promote an atmosphere that encourages academic achievement. Weinstein (1984) notes that literacy level greatly affects second-language learning facility, such that pupils who come from a literate home have a significant advantage over those who do not. Moreover, parents whose language skills are deficient or who are limited in English proficiency can only provide limited proficiency to their children, because exposure to appropriate language models are inadequate. A general orientation toward literacy does not simply constitute a set of mechanical coding and decoding skills, rather, it represents a way of processing information (Hamayan & Damico, 1991) and understanding the culture and world they are now part of. According to Weinstein (1984), the skills come out of specific socialization patterns acquired in the home environment that prepare a child for the cognitive and social expectations placed on them in a classroom setting.

ISSUES AND CONTROVERSIES

The growing diversification of the U.S. population has engendered a need to understand how best to create social and educational policies to prepare all American citizens to participate fully and equally in our society. To address the educational and social needs of all sectors of American society, it is critical to not only acknowledge but understand the impact of factors such as socioeconomic status, cultural and historical backgrounds, language, acculturation, ecological and biological influences, and immigration experiences on psychological and educational functioning. Understanding must lead to interventions with strategies that truly address their needs. Our inability to understand the impact of these factors on educational and social systems has led to practices and philosophies that have failed to help prepare children and families of socially, linguistically, and culturally diverse backgrounds to take advantage of the opportunities afforded to middle- and upper-class White Americans.

Our failure to incorporate the needs of socially, culturally and linguistically diverse children and families into our operating frameworks can be documented in the following realities:

- The over or underrepresentation of children from diverse social, linguistical, and cultural backgrounds in special and remedial programs in the educational system
- The low expectation of teachers and minimal involvement of these parents in schools
- The ineffective instructional strategies used in many schools with these children
- The high drop-out rate of these children from schools
- The social and economic marginalization of these families and children
- The underutilization of health and mental health services of these families
- The lack of understanding of culturally determined attitudes and beliefs about psychological issues on the part of educators and clinicians
- The lack of assessment and clinical strategies and interventions that are culturally appropriate
- Minimal competency of educators and clinicians to work with multiethnic/multilingual groups

To decrease the educational, social, and economic inequalities in our society, serious efforts must be made to incorporate ethnically diverse groups into all aspects of American society.

▶ 2

Issues in Working with Culturally and Linguistically Diverse Children and Families

Traditional practices in the psychological assessment and treatment of children and families from diverse cultural and linguistic backgrounds have been under close scrutiny by mental health and educational practitioners due to limited success in addressing the needs of this population. Despite almost two decades of research devoted to the investigation of adequacy of the psychotherapeutic services and treatment practices for ethnic-minority populations, mental health practitioners and psycho-educational diagnosticians continue to be perplexed by the problem of how to increase the effectiveness of mental health and educational services to culturally and linguistically diverse children and families (Sue & Zane, 1987). In this chapter, current practices in the delivery of psychotherapeutic services and psycho-diagnostic assessment as well as the effectiveness and shortcomings in working with culturally and linguistically diverse children and families will be examined.

Cultural beliefs, values, and practices, and linguistic issues have a definite impact on delivery of services to populations dissimilar to that of the mainstream culture. Although there is a proliferation of studies suggesting that culture may influence psychopathology and assessment results (Lambert, Weisz, Knight, Desrosiers, Overly, & Thesiger, 1992), most professional practices in treatment and assessment are being guided by research on the Anglo-Eurocentric population in the United States. In this Eurocentric context, most disorders are assumed to exist within the person, caused by genetic predisposition, brain chemistry, and/or early learning rather than being produced by societal or environmental factors influencing life experiences (Dana, 1993, p. 91). Assessment and psychotherapeutic procedures based on this worldview ignore relevant factors that have demonstrated impact on psychological adjustment in school, at home, and in the community. An individual's cultural understanding of psychological distress and mental illness, the role of mental health professionals and the family in the therapeutic process, and sociocultural, language, and socioeconomic issues (e.g., acculturation, educational background, English language proficiency) can make traditional approaches to treatment and assessment less effective with culturally and linguistically diverse children and families. For decades, the field of psychology and social work have operated under an assumption that culturally and linguistically diverse individuals are deficient. This "deficit hypothesis" (Katz, 1974) purports that culturally and linguistically diverse communities have historically experienced isolation and continued economic and cultural deprivation, and that impoverishment, powerlessness, and disorganization brought about psychological deficits in such areas as intellectual performance (Jones & Thorne, 1987; Guthrie, 1976) and emotional adjustment. Many contemporary social scientists (Allen & Boykin, 1992; Boyd-Franklin, 1989; Bradley & Bradley, 1977) reject the "deficit" model and embrace a model that emphasizes the notion of cultural difference. However, most still ascribe to the "deficit hypothesis." Baruth and Manning (1992) warn psychologists, psychiatrists, social workers, and other mental health practitioners against using cultural and ethnic backgrounds as a basis for determining propensity toward experiencing problems. Professionals who conduct psychological assessments and therapy should look at individual children and their families as well as their problems, socioeconomic class, gender, and family life situation to guard against labeling and stereotyping.

HOW CULTURE AND LANGUAGE INFLUENCE PSYCHOLOGICAL ASSESSMENT AND TREATMENT

Psychological Assessment

Assessment is the process of collecting data for the purpose of (a) specifying and verifying problems and (b) making decisions about a person. Other scholars have defined psychological assessment as one person's attempt to know, understand, or size up another (McReynolds, 1975); as a process of developing images, making decisions, and checking hypotheses about another person's behavior in interacting with the environment; and as a process of solving problems (Maloney & Ward, 1976) and helping people cope with problems. Psychological tests, behavioral observation, and current and historical information are used as vehicles to collect meaningful information about the person and his/her environment.

The assessment process embraces a number of assumptions about the examiner's qualifications, instruments and methods of assessment, goals of assessment, and behaviors in testing. These assumptions state that:

1. The person administering the tests has adequate training and competence in the administration, scoring, and interpretation of cognitive, achievement, and personality tests as well as an understanding of the pitfalls and limitation of the instrument of choice. The examiner should be licensed and certified to practice in the area in which he or she is assessing. In addition, it is assumed that the examiner is capable of establishing rapport, understanding nonverbal language and the cultural beliefs, values, and practices of the individual to be assessed (Dana, 1993). Moreover, the examiner should speak the language of the individual to be assessed or reasonable accommodation should be made (e.g., use of a trained interpreter).

2. The instruments chosen for assessment are expected to have appropriate norms that represent the population group of the individual being assessed. The instruments should have appropriate validity and reliability.

3. The type of language used on the instrument of assessment or the words used hold similar meaning to different people and the experiential background of the individuals being tested is about equal. The assumption is that individuals exhibit similar level of acculturation and worldviews and that they understand what is expected in a testing situation.

4. Standardized tests are the ideal and preferred way of assessing the individual's cognitive abilities and unassisted performance is the best format for assessment. The scores obtained on these standardized tests are compared to the norms and a determination is made on the individual's standing compared to his or her peers. This actual level of functioning reveals more or less accurately the individual's inner abilities and the primary purpose of testing is to predict future functioning and to classify the individual according to his or her level of functioning (Kozulin & Falik, 1995).

5. The behavior sampled is adequate in number and representative of the individual's abilities that are the target of assessment. Based on this information, the assessor can make reasonable decisions about the individual being assessed.

These assumptions guide the psychological assessment process in the area of cognitive, personality, and personnel testing. When evaluating individuals with non-Eurocentric cultural influences, many of these assumptions are violated, and they compromise, if not invalidate, the findings and the decision-making process.

Many practitioners are not trained to assess children from culturally and linguistically diverse backgrounds. Often they do not understand how cultural incompatibilities bring about practices that suppress the performance of an individual from a culturally and linguistically diverse population. The lack of testing procedures that guide administration of psychological tests and interpretation of results adds to the inability to properly assess this population. The instruments often chosen to assess culturally and linguistically diverse children tend to be inadequate and unable to yield results that reflect the true potential of this population. The standardization norms of these tests frequently do not represent the group of the individual being assessed when he or she is from a non-Western-European culturally influenced background. Hence, decisions about education and treatment are often grounded in inaccurate data.

A number of landmark litigation cases were influential in the field of assessment of limited English proficiency and bilingual children by mandating more appropriate testing procedures. In California, the case of Diana v. State Board of Education (1970) prohibited the use of English intelligence tests because they unfairly classified some children of average intelligence as disabled. Other cases such as Guadalupe Organization Inc. v. Tempe Elementary School District (1972), United States v. Texas (1971), and Aspira of New York Inc. v. New York Board of Education (1972) have increased the demands on school districts to test bilingual children in their primary language. Prior to these litigations and their court decisions, it was common practice to test bilingual or non-English speakers in English. Their performance, which reflected their inability to speak and understand English, was often interpreted as a cognitive deficiency. Today, the failure to establish the bilingual student's level of proficiency in both languages and to consider the process of second-language acquisition leads to misassessment and misplacement.

To accommodate the limited English proficiency or the bilingual students, many assessors who do not speak the language of the individual use interpreters. Interpreters facilitate the work of psycho-diagnosticians who do not speak the language of the individual to be assessed or interviewed. Their involvement in the assessment process allows monolingual assessors to obtain information, to conduct an evaluation or interview, and to be more aware of cultural factors. However, the research on the reliance on interpreters has revealed a number of pitfalls. Interpreters must be trained and must meet certain minimal competencies. According to Toliver-Weddington and Meyerson (1983), poorly trained interpreters may provide results that could be more invalid than those resulting from not using an interpreter. Inadequately trained interpreters may err in their translations, in their role definition, in analysis and interpretation activities, and in building rapport and transmitting information to a youngster's parent or to the individual assessed (Chamberlain & Medinos-Landurand, 1991; Langdon, 1988; Juarez, 1983; Marcos, 1979). The interpreter is expected to speak both target languages proficiently, to develop vocabulary and comprehension skills to interpret information effectively, to understand the idiosyncrasies of both languages (e.g., idioms, the social meanings, and indigenous folklore), and to have good facility in the vocabulary of both languages to interpret simultaneously. An interpreter should also be able to understand dialectical variations in the language. For example, the Spanish spoken by Puerto Ricans in New York varies (due to idiomatic expressions, anglicism, lifestyle, and influences particular to that region) from that spoken by Mexicans in Texas, and the Spanish spoken by Puerto Ricans on the island of Puerto Rico varies from that spoken by Puerto Ricans born and raised in New York City.

Because interpreting requires specific abilities and skills, the interpreter must also be able to paraphrase effectively, have a working knowledge of technical educational terminology, and have an understanding of child development, cross-cultural issues, and educational procedures (Chamberlain & Medinos-Landurand, 1991, p. 137). Moreover, the interpreter should be bound by ethical constraints similar to those of the assessor. For example, the interpreter must maintain confidentiality and impartiality, respect the feelings and beliefs of the individual, as well as respect the role of other professionals (Chamberlain & Medinos-Landurand, 1991).

Another strategy used to evaluate non-English speakers is to translate assessment instruments made for the English-speaking American population. The translation of American psychoeducational assessment instruments into other languages has been a common practice in spite of problems associated with translating and validating tests used in another culture (Bracken & Fouad, 1987). The problems with translation are significant. The body of research in the area of cross-cultural psychology has revealed that (a) translations are rarely equivalent across languages (Brislin, 1980), (b) individuals' expectations about tests (procedures and directions) and test-taking behaviors may differ from one culture to another (Butcher & Pancheri, 1976), (c) psychological constructs are not constant or universal across languages or cultures (Van de Vijuer & Poortiga, 1982), and (d) content validity is not assured across cultures (Fouad & Bracken, 1985). Furthermore, given the varied linguistic experiences of most bilingual American children, norms that reflect local and regional linguistic influence are most appropriate for the assessment of individual children's performances (Carrow-Woolfolk, 1978). Consequently, there might not be any one best set of norms for bilingual (e.g., Spanish) children nationwide (Wilcox & Dasby, 1988). Additionally, as Jones and Thorne (1987) argue, the creation of new norms, while it acknowledges the pluralistic nature of our society, reflects a static view of society and rests on the assumption that linguistically and culturally diverse communities maintain their culture in a stable, enduring fashion. Difficulties are also encountered on personality tests that require extensive verbalization. Due to their limited

English proficiency, children and adults may have difficulty articulating their thoughts and ideas. Simplistic vocabulary and paucity of projective material might be the result, and they may reflect the individual's poor command of the language and not necessarily a psychiatric condition.

Other professionals involved in the assessment of children, including school and clinical psychologists and educational evaluators, have incorporated additional modifications such as providing culturally and linguistically diverse individuals with modifications in the procedures of standardized tests. For example, the assessor may not time the individual during timed tasks and may simplify the directions or provide demonstrations. One major factor in testing individuals from other cultures with instruments developed for Americans is the level of acculturation of the individual. If the individual was not exposed to the tasks used by the instrument to assess various cognitive skills, a low score may be an indication of the level of acculturation or inexperience rather than a deficit. For example, a child that has very little experience with blocks or puzzles may not perform as well as would be expected from an American child. Differences in familiarity with test materials can generate marked differences in test performance and results (Neisser, Boodoo, Bouchard, Boykin, Brody, Ceci, Halpern, Loehlin, Perloff, Sternberg, and Urbina, 1996, p. 80). Moreover, the medium used by the instrument to assess a particular skill also has an impact on the individual's performance. For example, Neisser et al. (1996) reported that Zambian and English children reproduce patterns in three different media—wire models, pencil and paper, or clay. The Zambian children excelled in the wire medium with which they were more experienced, while the English children were best with pencil and paper. The English and Zambian children worked equally well with clay.

An individual's learning styles are also culturally influenced. A difference between the learning style or problem-solving strategy of the individual and the instrument's reference group can produce results that are artificially low. Conversely, in some cases in which members of cultures that have cognitive functioning styles congruent with that expected of the reference group on which an instrument was standardized would meet with more success not only on the tests but also in school (Tharp, 1991). Therefore, the learning strategy that an individual employs, the individual's adaptive strategies when faced with failure, the individual's reaction to the examiner and testing situations, and even the overt acceptance of testing are moderated by cultural practices and beliefs (Chamberlain & Medinos-Landurand, 1991). Parents play a pivotal role in transmitting to their children the culturally prescribed behavior for success in school. For example, Okagaki and Sternberg (1993, p. 37) suggest that most parents acting in accordance with culturally defined notions of intelligence will socialize their children in ways that they believe will maximize the intelligence of their children in their home/community context rather than in the school context.

Cultural factors bring to the assessment process subtle and pervasive confounding variables, particularly in the interpretation of behavioral profiles (Tollman & Msengana, 1990). Children and families internalize the social norms, the communicatory cues, the mannerisms, the aspirations, and even the thinking modes of their particular culture (Tollman & Msengana, 1990). Therefore, accurate and valid interpretation of behavioral composites can only be carried out by individuals familiar with the culture of the individual under assessment (Tollman & Msengana, 1990). Tollman and Msengana (1990) studied the problems in evaluating the higher mental functioning of Zulu-speaking people using traditional Western techniques. They reported a behavioral profile that appears to suggest pathology because it is characterized by "impoverished speech, paucity of content, and emotional bluntedness, which according to Westernized criteria may be considered deficits. However, when evaluated in the context of the Zulu tradition, their behaviors may very well be culturally generated and not an indication of pathology or emotional disturbance.

Chamberlain and Medinos-Landurand (1991) highlighted a number of test-taking behaviors (social and cognitive skills) required of children from diverse cultures to be at par with their Anglo-American peers on standardized tests: (a) monochronic orientation—the ability to focus on one activity at a time, (b) a passive style in physical interaction—referring to bodily movement (restrictive range of motions as opposed to expansiveness), (c) close proximity—physical closeness instead of space between people, (d) minimal physical touching, (e) frequent and sustained eye contact, (f) flexibility in gender role expectation—the ability to perform equally well for a female or male assessor, (g) individual orientation—being able to be motivated by the assessment process and to do well for oneself, (h) understanding of verbal and nonverbal communication of the majority culture; (i) internal locus of control—taking personal responsibility for one's success or failure, (j) field independent perceptual style—the ability to perceive details apart from the whole, and (k) a reflective, methodological, and analytical cognitive style. All these characteristics are directly related to the level of acculturation of the individual being assessed and his or her family. When assessing the cognitive potential of a youngster of a culturally diverse background, the examiner must be knowledgeable of how these factors may adversely influence the testing process and control their impact by making appropriate modifications (Thomas-Presswood, 1997).

Treatment

In the area of treatment and counseling, culture and language also bring to the forefront issues of interpretation of behavior and treatment strategies appropriate to accommodating cultural differences. Moreover, the mental health worker must be able to, when necessary, identify those issues in the therapeutic setting that are the result of the acculturation process, cultural practices and beliefs, or psychopathology. Researchers have identified problems in the delivery of mental health services to individuals of diverse linguistic and cultural background. These problems include underutilization of services on the part of ethnic groups, high premature termination rates, and ineffectiveness of traditional mental health services for culturally and linguistically diverse clients (Cheung & Snowden, 1990).

The source of these problems are multiple: (a) failure of psychology training programs to provide training experiences relevant to culturally and linguistically diverse communities (Bernal & Padilla, 1982; Carney & Kahn, 1984; Casas, Ponterotto, & Gutierrez, 1986; Corvin & Wiggins, 1989) and to deal with racial and cultural matters in counseling or treatment (Carter, 1995); (b) differential or discriminatory forms of treatment (e.g., unequal access to good treatment facilities) (Yamamoto, James, & Palley, 1968), (c) therapist preferences for clients' characteristics that place ethnic and linguistic minorities at a disadvantage; (d) lack of bilingual therapists, and (e) stereotypes therapists harbor about ethnic and linguistically diverse clients (Sue & Zane, 1987). Research on the delivery of mental health services to linguistically and culturally diverse communities has been consistent in focusing attention to inadequacies in the provision of services (Sue & Zane, 1987). When one surveys the literature, seven factors emerge as relevant to the therapeutic process when working with linguistically and culturally diverse children and their families: race, belief about mental illness or psychological distress, expression of symptoms, communication styles, language, acculturation, and religion.

1. Race in Treatment and Counseling

The lack of understanding of cultural and racial issues in the therapeutic process is a significant factor in the effectiveness of the delivery of mental health services. Most therapists were trained in methods and strategies based primarily on White-Anglo-American beliefs, values, and lifestyles. Additionally, most are unable to provide or devise culturally responsive forms of treatment (Sue & Zane, 1987). Carter (1995), in discussing his Racially Inclusive Model, draws attention to the fact that race has been ignored in personality and human development despite the fact that theory building comes from knowledge of, and interactions with, people who have distinct racial legacies (p. 23). Although most mental health practitioners or psychotherapists embrace one of a number of unique treatment approaches, or a combination thereof, for working with clients, these strategies for understanding human behavior and motivation are all grounded in a Euro-American worldview (Carter, 1995).

These treatment approaches are developed within a cultural value system that emphasizes an individual's intrapsychic or interpersonal life to the exclusion of other factors (e.g., race, culture, and language) that also shapes the individual's psychological perspective (Carter, 1995). Because race in the United States historically has been an integral aspect of sociopolitical life and can influence one's life choices (e.g., where one lives, learns, finds job opportunities) (Carter, 1995), being able to recognize and understand the role of sociopolitical and historical factors in the therapeutic relationship is essential to success in treatment. When these factors are not recognized in the therapeutic process, it can be difficult to assess the client, to conceptualize the problem, and to form a therapeutic relationship (Carter, 1995). For example, Sue and Sue (1990) reported in a study addressing community mental health services for ethnic minorities than although many African Americans use the system, they tend to exhibit relatively little positive change, terminate quickly, and average fewer sessions than other culturally and linguistically diverse groups. The failure of mental health practitioners to address the issue of race impacts on the success of the therapeutic process.

2. Belief about Mental Illness in Treatment and Counseling
Whether an individual seeks therapy or remains in therapy is influenced in part by the individual's belief about mental illness, psychological distress, or disability. These beliefs are shaped by the individual's culture. Research in the field of illness and culture documents that cultural beliefs constrain the perceptual, explanatory, and behavioral options (e.g., help-seeking behavior) that individuals have at their disposal for understanding and responding to illness (Angel & Thoits, 1987; Kleinman, 1980, 1982). For example, Sue and Sue (1990) reported that although mental illness generates a negative reaction in the mainstream American culture, the degree of stigma and shame associated with emotional difficulties is most likely greater in the Asian-American community.

In the Asian-American value and belief system, mental illness in a family member is considered a failure of the family system itself, and the weakness of a member of the family is viewed as a disgrace to the family unit (Sue & Sue, 1987). Sue and Sue (1990) point out that an individual's or family's view of mental illness can influence whether or not psychotherapy is sought. Because Asian Americans were more inclined to conceptualize mental illness as associated with organic or somatic variables and to believe that mental health involves the avoidance of morbid thoughts, many Asian Americans seek medical treatment instead of psychotherapy (Sue & Sue, 1990). Western-type treatment approaches often emphasize disclosure and examination of intrapersonal, emotional, and intrapsychic conflicts that are believed to underlie all mental illness or distress. Introspection also plays a very important role in the process. However, this type of approach has been ineffective in addressing the needs of the Asian-American community as well as other ethnic groups given their cultural beliefs about mental illness and a worldview that focuses on the community and family and not on the individual.

Morrow (1987) discussed several beliefs that Southeast Asians (including Vietnamese, Cambodians, and Loatians) hold about disabilities. Disabling conditions such as mental retardation, emotional disturbance, and physical or sensory disabilities carry a great stigma because they are viewed as the consequence or punishment for sins or moral transgression committed by the individual's parents or his ancestors (Morrow, 1987). Another belief is that a disabling condition results from the demonic or evil spirit possession of the disabled individual or child, or from an imbalance in the mind–body relationships (Morrow, 1987). Psychologists, psychiatrists, social workers, other mental health professionals, and educators who work with children and families from different cultures must be aware of the cultural significance or meaning that a disabling condition may carry in a particular cultural group.

3. Expression of Symptoms of Psychopathology

A major issue and common point of contention in the area of cross-cultural diagnostics and treatment is the generalizability of Western concepts of mental illness and psychiatric diagnosis to other cultures (Williams, 1986). Cross-cultural research in the area of psychopathology clearly documents that the expression of symptoms of psychological distress or mental illness differs from culture to culture (Lopez & Nuñez, 1987; Westermeyer, 1993; Kleinman & Good, 1985; Cuellar & Roberts, 1984; Al-Issa, 1982; Marsella & White, 1982; Adebimpe, 1981; Draguns, 1980). Tseng and McDermott (1981) noted that behaviors that are called pathological in one culture may be viewed as normal or appropriate in another. Consequently, both mental health practitioners and the client who comes from a diverse cultural background may have dissimilar perceptions of normalcy and pathology, and may not understand the norms of each other (Williams, 1986). Thomas and Schare (in press) reported, in a cross-cultural study of alcoholism that compared American and Panamanian alcoholics using the Minnesota Multiphasic Personality Inventory and the Alcohol Use Inventory, that despite similar amounts of alcohol intake, participants endorsed different test items and experienced different symptoms that appeared related to cultural beliefs about alcohol use, acceptance of alcoholism as a disease, family values, religion, and fulfillment of gender-role responsibilities as culturally prescribed. Another cross-cultural study of depression conducted by Tanaka-Matsumi and Marsella (1976) comparing three groups (Japanese nationals, Japanese Americans, and Americans) found that subjective meaning and experience of depression differs across the three cultural groups.

Culture specific symptomatology has been observed. Malgady, Rogler, and Constantino (1987) discussed a cultural phenomenon called "ataque nervioso," or nervous attack, that has been observed in Hispanic individuals. The nervous attack is characterized by screaming, falling, fainting, lack of communication, and agitated motor activity. Malgady et al. (1987) indicated that this condition is believed to be a culturally patterned, acute hysterical re-action to an extremely stressful situation, and that if this is not viewed in cul-tural context, it could be misdiagnosed as a major pathological disorder (e.g., schizophrenia). Arriving at an accurate psychiatric diagnosis when working with individuals from diverse cultural backgrounds can be very complicated, not only because clients from different cultures may have different meanings for terms (e.g., depression, anxiety, etc.) and can present with different symp-toms, but also because the cultural experience of the mental health practi-tioner can influence how he or she interprets the symptoms or behaviors observed or reported (Williams, 1986).

4. Communication Styles in Treatment and Counseling
Therapy is a process of interpersonal interaction and communication (Sue & Sue, 1990). There is an interchange of verbal and nonverbal information be-tween the therapist and the client. It is paramount to the therapeutic process that in this interchange both parties interpret the information transmitted ac-curately in order to establish a working and helping relationship. The term communication styles refers to those behaviors that are nonverbal yet are an integral part of the communication process. These behaviors are highly influ-enced by culture. Sue and Sue (1990) elaborates on five behaviors: proxemics, kinesics, paralanguage, high-low context communication, and kinesthetic.

Proxemics has to do with the use of personal and interpersonal space. Ap-propriate distance in social interaction is established by culture. Different cultures ascribe to different distances between individuals. For example, Hispanic-American children tend to stand close, touch, and avoid eye contact, whereas Anglo Americans ascribe to greater physical distance between indi-viduals, avoid touching, and maintain eye contact (Baruth & Manning, 1992).

Kinesics has to do with bodily movement such as facial expression, ges-tures, posture, and eye contact. There is great variation cross-culturally and cross-linguistically in the specific interpretation of gestures (Brown, 1987). All human beings move their heads, blink their eyes, and move their arms and hands (Brown, 1987, p. 210), but different cultures have designated different meanings to these bodily movements or expressions.

Paralanguage refers to other vocal cues that are used to communicate, such as volume and intensity of speech, and turn taking. These aspects of lan-guage are culturally prescribed. For example, Sue and Sue (1990) advised therapists not to be premature in interpreting the function of speech volume, because speaking loudly may not indicate anger, hostility, poor self-control, or over-emotionality; conversely, speaking in a soft voice may not be a sign of weakness, lack of self-confidence, shyness, or depression.

High-low context communication should also be taken into account when considering communication style. Individuals who are high-context communicators rely on nonverbal cues and behaviors that are shared by other members of the group. Low-context communicators rely on the verbal part of the interaction or the spoken word.

Kinesthetic refers to touching, another important aspect of nonverbal communication. Touching in some cultures indicates a very personal and intimate gesture, while for other cultures extensive touching is commonplace (Brown, 1987). Touching can be easily misunderstood, and it is an aspect of communication that the therapist should understand when working with an individual from a different cultural background.

In a therapeutic relationship, many misunderstandings due to misinterpretation of behavior can result from the therapist's inability to read the cultural script that the client brings to the process. The therapist must be able to identify his or her own cultural script or communication style in order to work with individuals from culturally and linguistically diverse groups.

5. Language in Treatment and Counseling

Language differences in the therapeutic process also present another obstacle to treatment success. English language proficiency of the client impacts the therapist–client relationship when the therapist is not bilingual or exhibits limited proficiency in the primary language of the client. Misinterpretation of symptoms by the mental health professional may invalidate diagnosis and treatment. Some researchers have argued that in an interview the limited English proficient client may spend so much time trying to say the words correctly in order to be understood that he or she may displace affect in what is being said (Marcos, 1976). Consequently, one of the primary implications for psychotherapy with bilinguals is that a lack of integration between affect and experience is not necessarily an indication of a psychiatric disorder (Ponterotto & Casas, 1991). The mental health professional should have achieved a level of proficiency in the language of the client so that he or she can correctly interpret the idiosyncrasies, subtle nuances of the words, and idiomatic expressions. The ability to speak the language of the client can also enhance the client–therapist relationship by increasing therapist credibility and the level of trust the client may place in the therapist.

6. Acculturation in Treatment and Counseling

The acculturation process entails changes and accommodations in the individual's life and environment, which impinges in new ways upon his or her psychological well-being (Roger, Cortes, & Malgady, 1991). Recent immigrants who have been uprooted from a familiar and supportive environment may experience great anxiety as they learn new customs, language, and job skills. The stress is experienced by all family members, including children who may act out in school or become withdrawn. On the other hand, during the phases of acculturation, a client may become more acculturated than other members of the family, giving rise to generational conflicts. Anxiety, depression, and other psychological and somatic symptoms might be experienced as the individual becomes more and more acculturated. In a treatment situation, the mental health professional must be able to assess and diagnose difficulties that result from the acculturation process in order to devise effective treatment strategies.

7. Religion in Treatment and Counseling

The role of religion has been largely ignored in the literature on psychotherapy. How religion plays itself out in the therapeutic process is a question rarely discussed in psychological literature even though the majority of patients who seek relief through psychotherapy consider themselves spiritual in one form or another (Gopaul-McNicol, 1997). Boyd-Franklin (1989) emphasized that in examining the strengths and coping skills of African-American families, family therapists must be sensitive to the role that religion and spirituality play in the daily lives of many African-American people (p. 78). In the African-American community, churches are multifunctional, serving the varied needs of individuals who are disenfranchised or who are victims of racism by providing an escape from painful experiences caused by social and emotional problems (Gopaul-McNicol, 1997; Boyd-Franklin, 1989). Peck (1993) briefly described four stages of spiritual development:

1. Chaotic/antisocial, or lawlessness and absence of spirituality
2. Formal/institutional, or rigorous adherence to the letter of the law and attachment to the forms of religion
3. Skeptical/individual, or a stage of principled behavior characterized by religious doubt or disinterest, but albeit accompanied by inquisitiveness about other areas of life
4. Mystical/communal, or the state of adherence to the spirit of the law as opposed to one of the letter of the law

Lack of understanding of the stages of spiritual development has clear implications for the diagnostic process and treatment strategy. Errors can be made in diagnosis, which may then misguide the therapeutic process. Another issue that becomes prominent in the diagnostic and treatment process is the religious beliefs of clients. These beliefs may guide the client's understanding of mental illness or psychological distress. These beliefs are embedded in indigenous healing practices, such as herbalism, sorcery, exorcism, spiritualism, and personal sacrifices (e.g., celibacy, wearing clothes of one color for a year, donating great sums of money to charity, walking an inordinate amount of miles on one's knees, etc.) to receive a particular blessing, healing, or to give thanks. These non-Western healing practices often employ spiritual forces to help address a variety of physical and emotional issues (Lee, 1989). Many cultures believe that special people in the community are "anointed" with special healing powers and spiritual gifts that can provide them with insight into medical and emotional difficulties. This "spiritually anointed" individual has different names in different cultures. In the English-speaking Caribbean, this individual is called Obeah Healer; in Haiti, Voodooist; in Korea, Mansin; in the Hispanic communities, Santero or Curandero; in the Native-American tradition, Shaman or Medicine man. Frequently, a parent may take a child who is exhibiting behavioral problems in school to the healer to remove "evil spirits" while allowing the child to be treated in a Western setting using traditional Western-type strategies. Because indigenous models of helping continue to exist throughout the non-Western world in spite of the growing influence of Eurocentric medical and psychological practices (Lee, 1989), mental health practitioners must understand the role of indigenous healing practices if they are to establish a trusting and effective therapeutic relationship and effective treatment strategies.

SUMMARY

Psychological assessment practices and therapeutic strategies are currently being guided by research and instruments developed for individuals of an Anglo-European cultural tradition. These methods have been ineffective when working with individuals from linguistically and culturally diverse backgrounds. Research has documented high attrition rates in therapy, low success rates in treatment, misdiagnoses, inadequate training for working with culturally and linguistically diverse communities, poor quality of services, instruments and tools insensitive to cultural issues, and a lack of policies at the university or training level regarding the importance of preparing future practitioners (of all racial, ethnic, and language backgrounds) to understand and work with culturally and linguistically diverse populations. Although surveys of the literature in cross-cultural psychology have identified the previously discussed seven factors as having an impact on the therapeutic process when working with individuals from different cultures and language backgrounds, the impact of these factors on treatment and diagnostic processes has not been incorporated into a comprehensive treatment approach to effectively work with such individuals.

▶ 3

Learning a Second Language and Its Impact on Assessment

The number of limited English-proficient (LEP) children in U.S. schools is rapidly increasing. The U.S. Department of Education (1994) estimated that for the period of 1992 to 1993, over two million LEP children were enrolled in schools throughout the United States. In New York City (NYC) alone, 157,839 children were identified as LEP for the 1994–1995 school year (Office of Bilingual Education, 1995). The top five languages spoken by the students in NYC's five boroughs were Spanish (110,971), Chinese (13,455), Russian (8,194), Haitian Creole (7,375), and Korean (3,128). Other low-incident languages spoken by NYC school children included Italian, Serbo-Croatian, Hindi, Pilipino, and Albanian. This influx of school-age children who have very few communication skills in the English language brings linguistic and instructional needs to educational settings. Although many children who speak English as a second language (ESL) do not experience any problems in school, others enter the classroom setting exhibiting a variety of academic and learning difficulties that are due to learning a second language (Lopez & Gopaul-McNicol, 1997), and only a small number can be identified as being truly learning or language disabled. Very few teachers in the public school system nationwide understand how learning a second language impacts on achievement. This misunderstanding leads to referrals to school psychologists and other educational diagnosticians to determine the need for special education intervention. Many students with limited English proficiency have been misdiagnosed as having learning or language disabilities because of their poor performance on standardized tests (Cardoza & Rueda, 1986; J. R.

Mercer, 1983). Many psychologists and educational diagnosticians frequently do not comprehend the processes involved in learning a second language and their effects on the assessment tools used to determine the need for special education services. Furthermore, educational practitioners are unable to distinguish between a true disability (e.g., learning disability) and problems in achievement that are the result of limited English proficiency, educational deprivation, or low literacy levels. The ability to distinguish between a learning disability and behaviors resulting from normal responses that occur when a student is placed in an English-dominant environment is the essential factor in successfully limiting bias during assessment of bilingual and LEP students (Kretschmer, 1991).

This chapter examines the process of learning a second language and discusses how this process impacts on instruments used during a traditional psychological assessment model when determining the presence of a learning disability or a language impairment. The goal of the authors is to present information that would allow non-bilingual and bilingual educational and clinical diagnosticians to minimize misassessment and inadequate school placements of linguistically diverse children.

SECOND-LANGUAGE ACQUISITION PROCESS

A number of issues—such as how a second language is acquired or learned, the effects of bilingualism on achievement, the appropriate age to begin teaching a second language, and the consequences of different patterns of bilingual language use in the homes of LEP students on achievement—have been heatedly debated in the literature for several decades. Over the past 17 years, research findings have begun to provide a clearer picture as to how children acquire proficiency in a second language and how the process of second-language learning affects achievement, learning, and assessment. However, within the past ten years research findings in this area have begun to trickle down to educational practitioners and diagnosticians. Still, the process of learning a second language is not fully understood by most mainstream teachers who work with linguistically diverse children. Although most school districts with a large LEP student population have implemented programs such as English as a Second Language (ESL) and bilingual education, educational practices aimed at preventing referrals for special education services have not always been seriously considered. The crux of the problem is that many behaviors used to identify monolingual children who are learning disabled are the same behaviors (limited vocabulary, difficulty following directions and discriminating and producing many sounds) that occur as a normal product of the process of learning a second language. Moreover, some achievement difficulties are the result of other sociocultural issues, such as poor educational background in the country of origin or cultural incompatibility between the culture of the school and that of the student, and not necessarily the result of an intrinsic learning problem. Consequently, many children have been identified and labeled learning disabled or language impaired because well-meaning psychological and educational diagnosticians used a data interpretation model that did not recognize the special issues relevant to administration and interpretation when assessing or evaluating linguistically diverse children.

Learning a second language is a long and arduous process. Not every individual who is learning a second language achieves native-like proficiency; this level of proficiency is the exception and not the rule (Hamayan & Damico, 1991). Two aspects of language proficiency have been identified: theoretical and practical. Theoretical language proficiency emphasizes the underlying capacity to learn and process language structures regardless of the language spoken. Practical language proficiency refers to the degree of control or command an individual has over a particular language (Hamayan & Damico, 1991). The practical aspect of language proficiency also involves language abilities such as listening, speaking, reading, and writing. These factors operate together as well as independently, so that an individual might be able to speak a language well, but not be able to write or read it and vice versa. In the same way, being able to speak a language facilitates being able to read and write it (Hamayan & Damico, 1991). Command of a language does not only involve having mastery of the sounds, vocabulary, and grammar discourse rule (McNamara, 1967) but also has social aspects that are essential to communication in that language. Sociolinguistic skills that refer to the ability to make requests, suggestions, and complaints are integral to the communication process (Canale & Swain, 1980).

When a child is beginning to learn a second language, he or she makes errors in the production and comprehension of the second language and also faces some difficulty processing information presented in the second language (Hamayan & Damico, 1991). Most second-language learners acquire most of their second language skills via social interaction with peers, parents, teachers, and siblings (Krashen, 1982). Krashen (1982) postulated that children learning a second language progress through several stages:

Preproduction. In this stage, also called the comprehension stage, the learner is developing comprehension skills even though expressive skills in the second language are minimal. Listening is essential because the learner is beginning to associate sounds and meaning. The second-language learner is able to obtain a main idea from key words in a sentence and to understand basic direction (involving physical activities and movement) and conversation. Some researchers have observed that second-language learners experience a silent period where the learner does not communicate orally (Homel, Palif, & Aaronson, 1987). This silent period can last from a couple of weeks to several months.

Early production. During this stage the learner's comprehension and word usage are developing and progressing. One or two word utterances or even short phrases are beginning to emerge. The learner may mispronounce words, and may begin using telegraphic speech (i.e., short phrases with missing articles) (Lopez & Gopaul-McNicol, 1997).

Speech emergence. In this stage, the second-language learner is now beginning to use longer and more complex sentences or phrases. The learner even begins to generate his or her own sentences and is able to retell stories in English or the second language. Errors in grammar are common and are related to the transference of rules from the first language to the second language (Lopez & Gopaul-McNicol, 1997).

Intermediate fluency. This stage is characterized by the production of connected narratives. The second-language learner engages in conversations and interacts more with native speakers of the second language. While the learner's receptive language skills are adequate and he or she makes fewer errors in the second language, information processing is slower in the second language than in the first language. This is because the second-language learner is still translating information in order to facilitate understanding of the content of communication in the second language (Dornic, 1979).

Advanced fluency. During this stage, the second-language learner exhibits better developed receptive and expressive skills in the second language. However, the learner continues to process information at a slower rate in the second language in areas such as retrieval, memorization, and encoding (Lopez & Gopaul-McNicol, 1997). Dornic (1979) noted that this slower rate of processing may persist even after many years of using the second language because the process of decoding in a new language demands time and practice. Moreover, information encoded in the first language might be more easily retrieved in the first language, initially forcing the learner to translate information (e.g., if the adult student first learned to read and write in Spanish, when faced with a task such as filing in the second language, he or she may first recall the alphabet in Spanish) (Thomas & Damino, 1985).

The implication for mainstream teachers who work with limited English-proficient students is clear. Even after developing what appears to be adequate expressive and receptive language skills, the second-language learner may continue to process academic information at a slower rate. Frequently, teachers refer LEP children for special education intervention when, after two years in an ESL program, the student continues to process language mediated information in the second language in a concrete or superficial manner. What these teachers are recognizing is not necessarily the sign of an intrinsic learning or language impairment; it is a natural and normal progression in the process of learning a second language. The research in second-language acquisition and bilingualism has identified different facets of language proficiency. Cummins (1984, 1989) conceptualized two different aspects of language proficiency: Basic Interpersonal Communicative Skills (BICS) and Cognitive Academic Language Proficiency (CALP). According to Cummins (1984), BICS can be defined as the manifestation of language skills in everyday communicative contexts. It refers to those language skills that are needed for everyday personal and social situations. Basic Interpersonal Communicative Skills refers to a type of surface fluency that the second-language student learns when he or she interacts with peers and teachers; it is basically social language. Basic Interpersonal Communicative Skills may take two to three years to develop in the second language, and it is a universal aspect of language proficiency that is typically acquired by all native speakers of any language (Cummins, 1981).

Cognitive Academic Language Proficiency refers to aspects of language such as vocabulary–concept knowledge, metalinguistic insights, and knowing how to process decontextualized academic language (Cummins, 1989). Cognitive Academic Language Proficiency refers to those language skills that are essential to transcend ordinary social language. It is a significant factor for reasoning, problem solving, or other cognitive processes required for academic achievement in subject matter, and it is associated with literacy and cognitive development (Cummins, 1981). Moreover, strong literacy skills in the first language facilitates development of CALP in the second language. Children need between five and seven years, on the average, to approach cognitive proficiency level to support grade-level performance on academic tasks. This is significantly more time than it takes children to acquire conversational fluency in English (Cummins, 1984). In Cummins' (1984) work, he further posited the major points embodied in the BICS/CALP distinctions: Some neglected aspects of language proficiency are notably more important for children's cognitive and academic progress than are the superficial manifestation of proficiency frequently emphasized by educators. Furthermore, educators' failure to recognize these differences can have unfortunate consequences for linguistically diverse pupils (p. 138).

PATTERNS OF LANGUAGE USE IN SECOND-LANGUAGE SPEAKERS

Second-language learning involves a developmental progression through various patterns of language usage. By a gradual process of trial and error and hypothesis testing, second-language learners slowly succeed in establishing successive approximations to the system used by native speakers of the second language (Brown, 1987). This normal process brings about several patterns of language use: interlanguage, fossilization, interference, code switching, and language loss.

Interlanguage

Interlanguage refers to a separate language system that has a structurally intermediate status between the native and second or target language. It is an internal language system that encompasses a combination of English rules, the student's native language rules, and ad hoc rules adapted from both languages (McLaughlin, 1977). The resulting language form is neither the system of the native language nor the system of the target language, but instead falls between the two (Brown, 1987). The development of this interlanguage is a normal and systematic state of acquiring a second language and not a case of poor or impaired English language learning (Hamayan & Damico, 1991, p. 61). Additionally, it is not static; it is constantly changing as the speaker becomes more proficient in the target language. It approximates more and more the second language as the learner is exposed to new vocabulary and linguistically rich experiences. However, if the learner is removed from an enriching second-language environment, his or her interlanguage may revert to an earlier form, because the student may forget what he or she previously mastered.

Fossilization

Once the second language has been learned, the student has a language system that resembles or closely approximates that of the native speakers (i.e., a true bilingual); however, in many instances the student stops learning after achieving a certain level of fluency, and as a result the interlanguage becomes fossilized (Grosjean, 1982). What becomes fossilized are those items, rules, and subsystems that second-language speakers tend to keep in their interlanguage while learning a second language; that is, these aspects of the interlanguage become permanent and will never be eliminated for most second-language learners, regardless of extensive explanation and instruction (Omaggio, 1986) and what is otherwise a fluent command of the language (Brown, 1987). This permanent incorporation of incorrect linguistic forms into a person's second-language competence and this tendency to maintain a less-than-perfect interlanguage form is called fossilization (Brown, 1987), and is believed to be a normal aspect of second-language acquisition. Research studies (Gardner & Lambert, 1972; Richard, 1972; Selinker, 1972) have identified several factors that are responsible for some people not reaching total fluency in the second language. The factors are mostly social in nature. One factor identified involves the level of fluency needed for everyday communication. When a second-language speaker realizes that he or she has sufficient competence in a language to function in the mainstream culture, then that individual stops learning. Richards (1972) elaborates on several other factors that can lead to fossilization in immigrant groups: area and pattern of settlement, the group's numerical strength, educational level, and cultural cohesiveness.

Interference

In interference, errors that can be attributed to interference from the native language (or language transfer) can be found at the level of pronunciation, morphology, syntax, vocabulary, or meaning (Omaggio, 1986). For example, in Spanish the word for bookstore is *libreria* while the Spanish word for library is *biblioteca*. Note that *libreria* and library are similar in spelling but different in meaning. A native Spanish speaker who is learning English may confuse these two words. He or she may say, "I am going to the library to buy a book" when he/she really means to say "I am going to the bookstore to buy a book." Transfer errors in vocabulary and the encoding of meaning can occur when learners use strategies such as literal translation or language switch to communicate (Omaggio, 1986).

Code Switching

Code switching is a type of verbal interaction in bilinguals in which they shift from the grammatical system of one language to another (Hamayan & Damico, 1991). For example, the bilingual student may begin a sentence in one language and complete it in another, such as "I am going to the store para comprar comida." Code switching is not the sign of impoverished vocabulary or inadequate language skills. Research has provided insight into this phenomenon and has suggested that it is a complex, rule-governed occurrence that has meaningful social and psychological implications that require a high level of proficiency (Aver, 1984; McClure, 1981). Bilingual students code switch in specific situations and contexts, and with particular individuals. A person may code switch with family members and close friends as a way of expressing close ties and cultural solidarity. Code switching is also used to convey subtle meanings that would be difficult to do in the target language.

Language Loss

Language loss refers to the process of losing proficiency in the native language. It can occur when a young second-language learner receives inadequate linguistic exposure, experiences, and training in the first language in order for the native language to continue to develop. Consequently, the first language begins to erode, and proficiency is lost. The child may even begin to exhibit limited proficiency in both languages and show behaviors that are similar to a monolingual learning-disabled or a language-impaired student.

TYPES OF BILINGUALISM

Because language proficiency is a complex, multileveled, multifaceted, and variable process, and because most second-language learners do not achieve equal proficiency in both languages, use of the term bilingualism usually refers to different levels of proficiency in the two languages (Hamayan & Damico, 1991). Two levels of bilingualism have been examined: balanced versus non-balanced and additive versus subtractive.

Balanced versus Nonbalanced Bilingualism

Balanced bilingualism refers to equal proficiency and high command of all aspects of communication in both languages regardless of setting or context. The speaker is comfortable speaking in one language or the other. Balanced bilingualism is very rare. Dornic (1979) noted that a nonbalanced bilingual is more typical than a balanced one. A nonbalanced bilingual is one who has developed higher proficiency or dominance (i.e., listening, speaking, writing, and reading) in one language and operates better in that dominant language in a variety of situations and contexts. Hamayan and Damico (1991) pointed out that it is possible for a bilingual individual to have mixed dominance in the two languages (e.g., be dominant in one language in speaking skills and have equal proficiency in listening skills in both languages) (p. 42). They further note that this type of mixed dominance is quite typical in bilinguals born in the United States where the native language is spoken in the home and English is used in the school (Hamayan & Damico, 1991). The implication for psycho-educational assessment is great, because a student's dominant language might not be readily evident; consequently, language proficiency must be thoroughly assessed and analyzed in different settings and contexts.

Additive versus Subtractive Bilingualism

Various factors may influence the type or level of language skills that a second-language learner may attain. Additive bilingualism occurs when an individual who has achieved an expected level of proficiency in the primary language adds on a second language to his or her already-established language system. The individual continues to grow in his native or primary language while learning the second language; the first language is not negatively affected by the incorporation of a second language because it is strongly developed. Additive bilingualism is said to have a positive cognitive effect. In contrast, in subtractive bilingualism, the addition of a new language inhibits the development of competence in the first or primary language. The incorporation of a second language has a detrimental effect on the primary language and can even slow down or arrest the progressive growth of the first language because the second-language learner may lose his or her first language. In subtractive bilingualism, the first or native language is not strongly developed. The individual does not attain a level of linguistic competence in the first language to support the addition of a second language. Cummins (1984) maintained that subtractive bilingualism can result in inadequate proficiency in both languages. Premature exposure to a second language coupled with insufficient training and exposure to situations that would facilitate the development of linguistic competence in both languages brings about subtractive bilingualism. These findings also led Cummins (1984) to submit that a threshold level of linguistic competence may have to be reached by bilingual students to benefit from learning a second language.

What conditions are conducive to the development of additive or subtractive bilingualism? These conditions are more social than cognitive. Children who exhibit subtractive bilingualism present a certain profile that includes: (a) home environments that do not promote a variety of individual enriching linguistic experiences in either languages and where objects are not labeled in either language (Nelson, 1985), (b) low literacy level of parents or poor educational backgrounds of parents (Hamayan & Damico, 1991), and (c) being a member of a society that does not value the cultural background and language of the child. Individual characteristics (e.g., personality factors, attitude toward target language, and cognitive abilities) also play a role. However, research findings in this aspect of subtractive bilingualism are limited.

Subtractive bilingualism has a significant impact on children's emotional, academic, linguistic, and cognitive development (Homel, Palif, & Aaronson, 1987). These children tend to experience difficulties in school due to their poor language skills. They become frustrated by their inability to succeed in school or to be on par with their peers. These behaviors may foster feelings of inadequacy and low self-esteem.

FACTORS THAT INFLUENCE SECOND-LANGUAGE COMPETENCE

Children do not acquire a second language in a vacuum. The factors that facilitate or hinder the development of proficiency in a second language have their origins in three global areas: cognitive, affective, and social. They exert an influence on the individual and societal levels. Research has unveiled a number of situations and conditions that are conducive to success in second-language acquisition. These conditions include language proficiency in the first language, literacy level in the first language, cognitive and learning style in the classroom, individual characteristics of the learner, motivation and attitude toward the second language, literacy level of parents in the home, and level of acculturation in the family.

Language Proficiency in the First Language

As noted earlier in this chapter, highly proficient skills in the first language facilitate learning a second language. A five- or six-year-old student who has a rich linguistic experience in Spanish at home would be able to learn English in school with relative ease (Cummins, 1984). He or she would most likely undergo an additive bilingual experience in which the first language would continue to develop. A good linguistic foundation and mastery of the first language is essential to building skills in a second language.

Literacy Level in the First Language

The ability to read and write in one's first language improves one's ability to learn a second language. Research suggests that students with good social and academic language skills in the primary language develop high levels of language abilities in the second language (Cummins, 1984), because the common underlying proficiency between the two languages permits children to transfer their skills from the first language to the second language (Lopez & Gopaul-McNicol, 1997). Being literate and proficient in one's native language provides a kind of framework for understanding and processing academic information in the second language. Children who are not literate in their first language experience great obstacles in learning a second language and in managing and processing academic information. Their academic and learning difficulties often resemble that of learning disabled children, yet the root of their problem in learning is very different.

Cognitive Learning Style

Intellectual abilities have an impact on second-language learning only when the second-language learner has a deficit in cognitive abilities that is significant enough to affect all aspects of learning. Learning style has a greater influence on second-language acquisition. According to Hamayan and Damico (1991), learning styles affect second-language learning to the degree that there are compatibilities between the child's learning style and the style in which the second language is being instructed. Learning style can be defined as the manner in which an individual processes information from the environment, or as the way in which an individual learns. Several types of cognitive processing and functioning styles have been discussed in the literature: field dependence versus field independence and verbal/analytic versus visual/

holistic. Field-dependent learners are those who are able to see details only in relation to the whole (Chamberlain & Medinos-Landurand, 1991). For example, when assembling a puzzle, a child may need to understand that the puzzle makes an elephant in order to solve the puzzle. Field-independent learners are those who can draw out specific details from a complex pattern regardless of the whole. For example, in assembling a puzzle, a child can look at the disparate pieces and draw a relationship between the pieces in order to solve the puzzle. The child does not need to know what the puzzle is in order to solve it. If a field-dependent learner is being taught a second language in a manner that requires the student to remember specific rules of grammar independent from a context in which he or she may draw some meaning, this type of learner may experience some difficulty because he or she tends to learn better if the information is presented within a context. In verbal/analytic processing style, the whole is revealed through the unfolding of the sections (Tharp, 1989). The visual/holistic cognitive functioning system states that the pieces derive their meaning from the pattern of the whole (Tharp, 1989). This model includes observing first and gaining competence before performance, and learning by doing rather than through verbal instruction (Tharp, 1989). Children who are verbal/analytic learners are similar to field-independent learners and would flourish in a second-language learning environment in which they are provided with step-by-step orally mediated information.

Individual Characteristics of the Learner

The way a child feels about him or herself and how motivated that child is to learn a second language contributes to the process of learning a second language. Personality factors play a role in second-language acquisition. If a student is outgoing or extroverted, he or she is more likely to engage in social situations that would increase exposure to the second language. An outgoing student would learn to express him or herself in a second language faster than a child who is introverted and afraid of taking risks (Tucker, Hamayan, & Genesee, 1976). To learn in any type of context, the learner must feel comfortable and experience very little anxiety. A high anxiety level interferes with learning a second language because it not only impairs memory but it also decreases the learner's willingness to take risks and practice the new language. Therefore, the optimum learning characteristics of a second-language learner would be someone who is eager to learn the second language, who is confident and willing to take risks, who is outgoing and not anxious, and who lives in a home and community where learning a second language is stressed while still showing appreciation for the first language.

Motivation and Attitude Toward the Second Language

Language is not only an instrument of communication, it is also a symbol of social or group identity—a badge of group membership and solidarity (Grosjean, 1982). As an instrument of communication and as a symbol of group identity, language is accompanied by attitudes and values held by its users and also by the mainstream culture or society at large (Grosjean, 1982). The willingness to learn a language to identify with a particular social group can be a motivating factor to acquire a second language; however, a strong motivation to belong to a social group that does not participate in the mainstream culture can become an obstacle to gaining second-language proficiency (Lopez & Gopaul-McNicol, 1997). Hence, if a child lives in a society that rejects his native language or looks at it in disfavor, this attitude can have profound effects on the psychology of the child and on the child's use of the language (Grosjean, 1982). The listener's negative attitude exhibited by school staff toward non-native English speakers' speech patterns presents an obstacle to both LEP and culturally and linguistically diverse children because it tends to lead to inappropriate referral and lowered expectations (Cummins, 1984; Rodriguez, Prieto, & Rueda, 1984; Eisenstein, 1983; Taylor, 1973). In a series of studies focusing on the relationship between attitudes and language success, Oller, Hudson, and Liu (1977), Chihara and Oller (1978), and Oller, Baca, and Vigil (1978) were able to identify several clusters of attitudinal variables that correlated positively with attained proficiency. These studies found that positive attitudes toward self, the native-language group, and the target-language group enhanced proficiency (Brown, 1987). The negative attitudes of the mainstream culture or dominant group (usually the politically, economically, and educationally stronger group) toward the linguistically diverse group are often adopted in part by this minority group, and are amplified to such a degree that members of the minority group also downgrade themselves (Grosjean, 1982). The family and community should not only value learning the second language, but should respect and appreciate the native language. If the second-language learner lives in an enclave where he or she is able to function without speaking the second language, then he or she may not be very motivated to master the second language. In the same way, if the student's family does not show interest in the student learning a second language, this lack of interest may impact on the child's motivation to learn the second language.

Literacy Level of Parents or the Home

Educational background of the parents not only influences a student's academic performance in school but also second-language acquisition. Weinstein (1984) observed that the level of literacy in the home greatly affects second-language learning facility in such a way that children who come from a literate home have a significant advantage over those who do not. Children who are exposed to a home environment where reading and writing are strongly emphasized, regardless of whether they are in the native or second language, benefit because prereading skills are transferable from one language to another (Hamayan & Damico, 1991; Cummins, 1989). Hamayan and Damico (1991) further stated that parents who are LEP can only offer their children limited exposure to English.

Acculturation

Brown (1987) stressed that second-language learning in many ways involves the acquisition of a second identity. Aponte and Barnes (1995) submitted that acculturation is a fluid, ongoing process that comprises learning facts about the new culture (e.g., tradition, practices, and history); incorporates behaviors representative of individuals within the host culture (e.g., the language, social courtesies); and adopts values, norms, and worldviews representative of the mainstream culture. Acculturation brings about adjustment to changes and incorporation of new beliefs and values into one's cultural schema. An individual's worldview, self-identity, and modes of thinking, behaving, and communicating can be disrupted by a change from one culture to another (Brown, 1987). Language is the most visible expression of culture (Brown, 1987). Being unable to communicate with the mainstream culture limits the economic and social opportunities of the second-language learner; by the same token, embracing the new language may distance the second-language learner from his cultural group. Consequently, learning a second language can create feelings of alienation from members of one's culture, the mainstream culture, and from oneself.

COMPONENTS OF ORAL LANGUAGE

Oral language is comprised of several basic elements that a child must master in order to communicate competently in a language. When determining the presence of a language disorder, the speech and language pathologist assesses the development of these components because they are the foundation of any language. These basic elements are phonology, syntax, semantics, pragmatics, and prosody.

Phonology

Phonology refers to the study of speech sounds that form words and that constitute spoken language. A unit of sound is called a phoneme (e.g., the letters *d* and *v* make different sounds). Children are expected to learn how to discriminate and produce orally these sounds in order to articulate words. Although being able to master all sounds of a language is developmental (e.g., a 24-month-old child might not be able to produce the sound for *w*), a native speaker should have mastered most sounds of that language within the first five years of life.

Syntax

Syntax refers to how words are formed and organized to produce meaningful phrases and sentences with grammatical structures. Children are expected to understand how words are organized in the English language to produce grammatically correct and meaningful sentences.

Semantics

Semantics refers to the meaning of words and sentences. Speakers of a language are expected to gain competency in word knowledge and multiple meanings. Based on the understanding of words, speakers should be able to make inferences and understand figurative language.

Pragmatics

Pragmatics refers to the ability to use and manipulate language in social communication or in a given context (e.g., physical distance between speakers, gestures, eye contact, turn-taking). Pragmatics includes nonverbal language, and is highly influenced by culture (e.g., while Americans interpret direct eye contact in a conversation as an indication of honesty and confidence, in other cultures, such as Asian, avoidance of direct eye contact is a sign of respect). Children are expected to know how to manipulate language to communicate meaning and get their thoughts across.

Prosody

Prosody refers to an understanding and correct use of the rhythm and intonation patterns of a language (Berry, 1980). Children are expected to develop an understanding of the rhythm and intonation patterns of a language and be able to use them to convey information.

While these basic elements of language form the foundation of every language, they are different across languages. For example, the sound system, syntactic rules, and semantic structures of the Russian language are different from those of the English language (Myers & Hammill, 1990). Moreover, even within a language, variations may occur as a result of ethnic influences and the second-language acquisition process.

Ethnic Language Variations

Ethnic language variation refers to different speech patterns that might be regional or cultural (e.g., Black English/Ebonics, English Creole/Jamaican English). Students who speak Black English may follow different rules in phonology, syntax, and semantics. As discussed earlier in this chapter, variations of the English language can also be observed in second-language learners due to the process of acquiring a second language. These variations in English are not considered "substandard language," but they are considered significantly different from those expected and needed for success in mainstream American schools (C. D. Mercer, 1987) and society. More importantly, when these variations are not acknowledged in a language-assessment situation, they could be construed as symptoms of a learning disability or language disorder (see Table 3–1). Diagnosticians must also be aware that even when translated tests are used (e.g., English-language tests translated to Spanish and standardized on a Spanish-speaking population), ethnic variation in that language may produce invalid or biased results. For example, the Spanish spoken by Puerto Ricans in New York might be different in terms of semantic or prosody than Spanish spoken by Mexicans in California. Moreover, the Spanish spoken by these two groups might be different from that spoken by Mexicans in Mexico or Puerto Ricans in Puerto Rico.

IMPACT OF SECOND-LANGUAGE LEARNING ON ACHIEVEMENT

How does second-language acquisition influence school achievement? Cummins' (1981, 1984, 1989) work, along with that of other researchers (Kagan, 1986; Ortiz, 1984; Wong Fillmore, 1982) over the past twenty years has tried to provide insight into how language proficiency affects achievement or academic performance in school. Today, it is understood that competencies in expressive and receptive languages are essential for successful performance of almost every aspect of academic tasks, including reading, writing, and participation in classroom activities (Worlfalk, 1995). Academic performance is facilitated by language proficiency in either language (native or English). Teachers make serious errors when they assume that communicatively competent students should have no difficulty in understanding concepts presented in standard English (Garaway, 1994). Additionally, the fact that ESL and bilingual programs exit children after two or three years of instruction and assume that because they have acquired sufficient language skills to converse

TABLE 3–1 Similarities Between Ethnic Language Variations and Learning Disability Symptoms

Components of Oral Language	Definition	Standard American English (SAE)*	English as a Second Language (ESL)	Black English (Ebonics)
Pragmatics	Refers to the ability to use and manipulate language in social communication or in a given context (e.g., turn-taking, pauses, eye contact). This includes nonverbal language (e.g., gestures, nodding one's head, etc.).	Children are expected to know how language works and how to mold it and change it to their advantage.	Children from different languages are influenced by their cultural milieu, so that an Asian or Hispanic child may not look an elder in the eye.	African-American children demonstrate differences in understanding as a result of cultural patterns developed simultaneously with linguistic patterns (C. Mercer, 1987).	LD children may demonstrate difficulty in understanding the social rules in communicative exchanges (e.g., turn-taking). They may have trouble reading social cues. At times viewed as poor social skills.
Prosody	Refers to an understanding and correct use of rhythm, intonation, and stress pattern of the language (Berry, 1980).	Children are expected to have developed the ability to understand and use different intonation to convey information.	Different languages have different intonation and rhythmic patterns that may influence a child's second-language speech.	In Black English, stress might be placed on different syllables than in SAE (e.g., *po´lice/po lice´*) (Fasold & Wolfram, 1975).	Prosodic deficiencies have been evident in the speech of some neurologically disabled and language-impaired children (C. Mercer, 1987).
Phonology	Refers to the study of speech sounds that constitute spoken language, and to the organization of these sound units and pronunciation rules. A phoneme is a unit of sounds.	Children are expected to comprehend acceptably and to produce and sequence individual phonemes necessary to normal speech and language development.	ESL children often have difficulty discriminating and producing many sounds in SAE (C. Mercer, 1987) and, on occasion, in their native language due to dialectical differences.	Children who use Black English do not discriminate and produce many sounds in SAE (e.g., the /r/ and /l/ sounds are pronounced as "*uh*" like in "*sistuh*" instead of "*sister*") (Fasold & Wolfram, 1975).	LD children may have difficulty discriminating and pronouncing many sounds of the language. These are categorized as articulation problems (Kochnower, Richardson, & DiBenedetto, 1983; Wiig & Semel, 1976).

Continued

TABLE 3–1 *Continued*

Components of Oral Language	Definition	Standard American English (SAE)*	English as a Second Language (ESL)	Black English (Ebonics)
Syntax	Refers to how words are formed and organized to produce meaningful phrases and sentences with grammatical structure.	Children are expected to acquire an understanding of the appropriate order of words in a sentence to communicate a specific meaning (e.g., word order in English is subject–verb–object).	ESL children have difficulty using articles, negation, noun–verb agreement, and tenses. Word order might be incorrect (C. Mercer, 1987).	In Black English, the speakers tend not to use SAE subject–verb agreement, negation, articles, and tenses (e.g., they often omit *a* and *am* in sentences such as "*I have coat*") (C. Mercer, 1987).	LD children may demonstrate difficulty in understanding sentences, negation, word order, and syntactic mood (Wiig & Semel, 1976; Wiig & Semel, 1984; Menyuk & Looney, 1972; Rosenthal, 1970). might be expressed academically in problems in reading comprehension.
These				
Semantics	Refers to the meaning of words and sentences.	Children are expected to understand simple word meanings and develop competency in using each aspect of language to communicate.	In the language form of children who speak ESL, the verbs *to be* and *to go* might be expressed differently (e.g., *he go to play*) (C. Mercer, 1987). ESL students have difficulties with multiple meanings and figurative language.	In Black English, the speaker also uses the verb *to be* differently (e.g., *he be busy*) (C. Mercer, 1987).	LD children may have difficulty understanding multiple word meanings and figurative language (Wiig & Semel, 1984). These also might be expressed academically in reading and listening comprehension.

*Note: The term "Standard American English" does not denote that other ethnic language variations in English are substandard or deficient.

and follow simple directions, they are able to function in a monolingual academic setting. These students often fall progressively below grade level in basic academic tasks (reading, writing, arithmetic) even in content areas such as social studies and science, which are heavily language based. A second-language learner who has achieved BICS may experience difficulty performing up to par academically with native speakers because he or she has not yet developed CALP, the type of second-language proficiency necessary to support higher-order cognitive tasks in the English language. Cummins (1984) argued that the result of not distinguishing between the two language proficiencies (BICS and CALP) and not recognizing that immigrant children or second-language learners require about five to seven years to approach grade-level norms in English academic skills, teachers inappropriately refer students for special education services, and school psychologists and educational diagnosticians misinterpret these children's performance on standardized tests.

SECOND-LANGUAGE LEARNING AND PSYCHOLOGICAL ASSESSMENT: COGNITIVE AND LANGUAGE PERFORMANCE

As discussed earlier in the chapter, the process of second-language learning brings about certain language patterns and linguistic behaviors that closely resemble those observed in monolingual children who are learning disabled. The United States Office of Education (USOE) in 1977 released under Public Law 94-142 regulations for defining and identifying definition learning-disabled students that are still currently being used by most school districts in the United States. This definition states:

> "Specific learning disability" means a disorder in one or more of the basic psychological processes involved in understanding or in using language, spoken or written, which may manifest itself in an imperfect ability to listen, think, read, write, spell, or to do mathematical calculations. The term includes such conditions as perceptual handicaps, brain injury, minimal brain dysfunction, dyslexia, and developmental aphasia. The term does not include children who have learning problems which are primarily the result of visual, hearing, or motor handicaps, of mental retardation, or emotional disturbance, or of environmental, cultural, or economic disadvantage (USOE, 1977, p. 65083).

When conducting a psychological evaluation of a youngster suspected of having a learning disability, the diagnostician looks for a number of characteristics or symptoms that have been accepted in the literature and identified in federal guidelines as constituting a learning disability. C. D. Mercer (1987) discussed a number of these characteristics indicative of a learning disability:

Academic and Learning Problems

Children who are learning disabled have difficulties achieving at grade level and learning at the same rate as their peers. These academic problems can be expressed in all areas of academic learning: reading (decoding and comprehension), math (calculation and reasoning), writing, and listening. Many second-language learners experience difficulty in various aspects of academic functioning due to their level of language proficiency.

Discrepancy Factor

A discrepancy between the student's estimated ability and his or her actual academic performance is considered a key component of and a common denominator in learning disabilities. This discrepancy may exist in all areas of academic functioning or only in one (C. D. Mercer, 1987). In LEP students, a discrepancy between achievement and cognitive potential can result if the student has not achieved CALP. Psychologists often look for a discrepancy between verbal (e.g., vocabulary, verbal abstract reasoning) and nonverbal abilities (e.g., visual spatial abstract reasoning) on standardized cognitive measures, such as the Wechsler Intelligence Scale for Children III, as a sign of a possible learning disability. However, such a discrepancy is common in students who have not yet attained verbal proficiency in the second language. A LEP student may even show a discrepancy when evaluated in the native language because exposure to enriching and meaningful linguistic experiences and activities in the native language has been limited. Therefore, level of proficiency in both languages must be undertaken to determine the presence of a learning disability.

Perceptual Disorders

This refers to a student's inability to recognize, discriminate, and interpret sensation. The student has difficulty deciphering and processing information at the perceptual level (e.g., visual discrimination and auditory memory). A LEP student may have difficulty differentiating symbols (e.g., letters) if they are unfamiliar or dissimilar to symbols in his native language (e.g., Arabic and Russian alphabets are very different from the English alphabet). Furthermore, if a student lacks literacy skills in the native language, he or she may find letters unfamiliar due to inexperience with sounds–symbol relationships.

Language Disorders

Language disorders are evident in students who have difficulty listening and processing meaningful language. A student with a language disorder may have problems following directions, and understanding sequence, sentence structure, semantics, and other aspects of language. A second-language learner may have difficulty following directions, understanding complex language, or simply processing language due to his or her level of proficiency in the second language.

Metacognitive Deficits

This term refers to difficulty in understanding how to learn. Baker (1982) indicated that metacognition involves two factors: (a) awareness of the skills, strategies, and resources that are needed to perform a task effectively, and (b) the ability to use self-regulatory mechanisms such as planning, evaluating effectiveness of ongoing tasks, monitoring one's level of effort, and remediating difficulties to ensure the successful completion of a task. Limited English-proficient students who have not achieved CALP tend to process language information slowly. In addition, if this youngster has a deficient educational background, he or she may exhibit learning difficulties because of a lack of preliteracy behaviors and strategies that are conducive to success in an American classroom setting.

Memory Difficulties

Children who have memory difficulties tend to experience problems recalling and retaining information taught by a teacher or following directions given in class. A LEP student may exhibit problems retaining and recalling information that he or she finds unfamiliar because transfer of information cannot occur. Because most of the information that is transmitted in a classroom is language based, a youngster who has limited proficiency in English may have difficulty remembering most of the information provided in class.

Motor Disorders

These include difficulties in coordination at the fine and gross motor levels. Children with motor problems might have difficulty writing, holding and controlling a pencil, buttoning, or zipping. At the gross motor level, the student may have difficulty running, skipping, walking. While language proficiency may not influence motor performance, cultural differences and lack of education can influence performance in this area. A student who is not experienced with using a pencil may show some weakness in graphomotor skills.

Socio-Emotional Functioning

Often, children who have learning disabilities show signs of low self-esteem and self-confidence because they have had very little academic success. These children compare themselves to their nondisabled peers and they begin to feel inadequate and frustrated by their academic failures. These feelings may lead to self-defeating types of behavior, such as learned helplessness that continues the cycle of failures. Some researchers have reported deficits in social skills and in the ability to read social cues that impact on a student's ability to form friendships and interact with peers and adults (Bryan, 1977). Also, LEP students who have been unsuccessful academically and unable to relate and communicate with peers may show signs of low self-esteem and low frustration tolerance. These students may even "act out" due to frustration.

Difficulty Attending and Focusing

Although attention deficit disorder (ADD) has not been added as a separate disability category under federal guidelines (IDEA-Act of 1995), the U.S. Department of Education issued a policy memorandum that indicated that students with attention deficit disorder who require special education intervention can receive services under existing categories. If attention deficit disorder is the primary disability, the student may receive services under the category of "other health impaired." If the primary disability is not attention deficit disorder, the student may qualify for services under such categories as "learning disability" or "emotional disability/behaviorally disordered." Children who have ADD exhibit difficulty controlling competing incoming stimuli from the surrounding environment. They are unable to focus on relevant stimuli, and are often characterized as distractible, limited in attention span, unable to complete assignments, and impulsive. In addition to the attentional problems, these students may also exhibit a high motor-activity level (e.g., finger tapping, excessive talking, fidgeting, and unable to remain seated). These behavioral characteristics make it difficult for these students to learn. A LEP student who is unable to understand what is transpiring in class may have difficulty attending to verbal stimuli that he or she does not comprehend. The LEP student might be distractible and fidgety. There are cultural differences in activity level.

In assessing a LEP student, the presence of many of these symptoms are not necessarily an indication of a learning disability, but rather may be a sign that the student is in the process of second-language learning. What can further complicate the ability to make a distinction between a natural second-language acquisition phenomenon and an intrinsic learning problem is the lack of literacy skills in the native language. A psychological assessment of a LEP student must include: (a) a thorough social, medical, and school history,

(b) analysis of language proficiency in both languages, (c) observation of a student's language usage in various settings and contexts, (d) determination of acculturation level in the home, and (e) determination of literacy level in the home.

SUMMARY

The process of second-language learning is a long, complex, and multifaceted undertaking that involves various stages (preproduction, early production, speech emergence, intermediate fluency, and advance fluency) and language patterns. These language patterns (interlanguage, fossilization, interference, and language loss) may produce idiosyncratic language forms that are a normal product of second-language acquisition. Two different types of language proficiency, BICS and CALP, have been identified as essential to understanding the difficulties that second-language learners may exhibit in the academic setting. Because many of the behaviors that emerge as part of the process of second-language acquisition are similar to those behaviors that are used as markers in determining the presence of a learning disability, it is imperative that teachers and school psychologists understand how second-language learning influences achievement in school.

► 4

Best Practices in Intellectual/ Educational Assessment

A BIO-ECOLOGICAL APPROACH TO INTELLECTUAL ASSESSMENT

The psycho-educational assessment of minority children has received much attention and discussion from educators and researchers (Armour-Thomas & Gopaul-McNicol, 1997a; Gopaul-McNicol, Black, & Clark-Castro, 1997; Oakland, 1977; Oakland & Phillipps, 1973; Samuda, 1975 and 1976; Mercer, 1979; Mowder, 1980; Tucker, 1980; Rodriguez-Fernandez, 1981; Vasquez-Nuttall et al., 1983; Vasquez-Nuttall, 1987). There has been an ongoing over-representation of linguistic, ethnic, and culturally different children in special education classes, which has been partially attributed to "the indiscriminate use of psychological tests, especially IQ tests" (Cummins, 1984, p. 1). The IQ test has therefore legitimized the labeling of many minority children as "mentally retarded" and their resulting placement in special education classes. This situation has become of even greater concern because educators are faced with an increasing number of culturally diverse pupils in the school system. The objective of this chapter is to examine from a practical standpoint some alternatives to traditional psycho-educational assessment for school psychologists.

The nature–nurture question has become one of the most polemical questions in psychology: To what extent are variations in intellectual performance due to genetic or environmental influences? Although there is little disagreement that genes and environment matter in intelligence, researchers are divided in terms of the degree to which it is heritable. But even if there were consensus regarding the heritability of intelligence, there are other far more troubling issues that continue to keep the nature–nurture controversy alive. One issue has to do with the interpretation of low scores on standardized tests of intelligence in terms of genetic inferiority, and the assumption that intelligence is a fixed and immutable characteristic. Despite the theoretical and empirical research evidence in support of the notion that intelligence is more than what IQ tests measure and that the trainability of cognitive capacities is indicative of intelligence, the genetic argument endures in some circles. The other concerns the use of IQ test data in making educational placement decisions. Low scores on these measures are used as "objective" evidence for placing children in special education, low-track, or general classes. Unfortunately, these judgments of low ability often parallel ethnicity, language, and class differences.

Although psychologists function as if the technology exists with respect to how culture is used in psycho-educational assessment, the empirical literature on culture in relation to psycho-educational assessment has yet to be embellished. Routinely, psychologists make diagnostic decisions without considering the possible effects of culture as mediating and intervening variables. Considering the effects of culture serves several purposes in assessment. First, it brings to the assessment robust knowledge of the family dynamics of the child, and it gives insight as to what the child is exposed to in his or her domestic environment. Thus, a child's potential is more readily assessed once the family background is understood from a clinical perspective, and once the child's cognitive learning style is ascertained. Second, observation of the child in various settings (Ceci, 1990), such as on the playground, offers interesting information. Thus, the insertion of context into the testing situation would add to the predictiveness of traditional tests (Ceci, 1990). In other words, intelligence is a multifaceted set of abilities that can be enhanced depending on the social and cultural contexts in which it has been nurtured, crystallized, and ultimately assessed. Ceci (1990) noted that when children were observed in familiar contexts such as their homes and in the company of familiar significant others, a heightened ability to perform the activity being assessed was found. The important point to note is that IQ is quite a labile concept and is quite responsive to a shift in context. Therefore, contextual influences on more complex tasks inevitably cast doubt on current conceptualizations of intelligence.

Armour-Thomas and Gopaul-McNicol's (1997a) bio-ecological approach to intellectual assessment is based on the work of Vygotsky (1978), Ceci (1990), and Sternberg (1986) who suggest a dynamically interactive relationship between cognitive processes and experiences nested within contexts that cannot be understood apart from each other. The authors take the position that cognition is, in part, a culturally dependent construct. This is because, as human beings, we are born with diverse capacities that predispose us to engage in activities within any given ecology. Our behavior may be described as "intelligent" to the extent that the nature and quality of experiences to which we are socialized require the exercise of these capacities in a given context. Therefore, the cognitive capacities required for intelligent behavior in one context may or may not be the same as in another context. The expression of these capacities through behavior may be different, because the socialization experiences within one context are psychologically different from the other context. Consequently, the expression of these capacities may reflect the context in which they were socialized. This line of thought has led the authors to conceive of intellectual behavior as an inextricable bio-cultural phenomenon and they argue for a bio-ecological approach to intellectual assessment (Armour-Thomas & Gopaul-McNicol (in press)). They propose a more flexible and ecologically-sensitive assessment system that allows for greater heterogeneity in the expression of intelligence. In short, they contend that other qualitative, nonpsychometric approaches must complement the quantitative psychometric measures of intelligence. Table 4–1 outlines this four-tier bio-ecological assessment system.

THE FOUR-TIER BIO-ECOLOGICAL ASSESSMENT SYSTEM

Psychometric Assessment

There is no single psychometric measure that taps the three interrelated and dynamic dimensions of intelligence—biological cognitive processes, culturally coded experiences, and cultural contexts. Therefore, any psychometric measure or an amalgamation of tests (inter-battery testing, the process approach to assessment, cross-battery testing) that emphasizes a score-oriented approach should be used in conjunction with nonpsychometric ecological measures, because they help to further gain an understanding of the child's potential intellectual functioning and his or her ability to function in settings other than the school.

Note that this assessment system gives pure psychometric assessment (biological explanation) only 25 percent of the entire weight for determining an individual's intellectual functioning. Psychometric potential, ecological assessment, and other intelligences are each weighted 25 percent as well. Thus, the bio-ecological assessment system relies more heavily (75%) on personal experiences nested within contexts to determine intelligence.

TABLE 4–1   The Four-Tier Bio-Ecological Assessment System

1. **Psychometric assessment**

2. **Psychometric potential assessment**
    This tier consists of four components:
        Suspending Time
        Contextualizing Vocabulary
        Paper and Pencil
        Test–Teach–Retest
This section reveals the child's potential/estimated intellectual functioning. If the child showed an improvement in his/her performance, the examiner should state so.

3. **Ecological assessment**
    This ecological taxonomy of intellectual assessment consists of four components:
        Family/community support assessment
        Observation to determine performance in the settings below (item/cultural
            equivalence)
    These components are used to assess the child in three settings:
        School (classroom, gym and playground)
        Home
        Community (church, playground and/or other recreational sites)
In this section, a child is observed in his or her ecology—home, community, school. Therefore, the examiner discusses all tasks that the child was able to perform in these settings, but what he/she was unable to do in the IQ testing situation, even under potential IQ assessment.

4. **Other intelligences**
    This tier consists of four components:
        Musical intelligence
        Bodily kinesthetic intelligence
        Interpersonal intelligence
        Intrapersonal intelligence

Given this percentage breakdown, one will expect that only 25 percent of the diagnostic power comes from standardized tests of intelligence. Prescription and intervention strategies are directly formulated from the information gained through potential and ecological assessment (Armour-Thomas & Gopaul-McNicol, 1997a & 1997b).

Psychometric Potential Cognitive Assessment

This measure consists of five procedures to be used in conjunction with the psychometric measure. They are used to provide supplementary information on cognitive functioning that goes beyond that provided by the traditional standardized measure of intelligence. A description of each procedure is as follows:

Suspending Time

The assumption that to be smart is to be quick permeates American society. Thus, many contemporary theorists (Brand & Deary, 1982; Carroll, 1993; Eysenck, 1982; Horn, 1991; Jensen, 1979; Woodcock Johnson, 1990) based their theories on individual differences in the speed of information processing, and considered speed to be a major correlate of general intelligence. This assumption also underlies the majority of creative tests for gifted children. Several researchers differed with these researchers' positions, arguing that there is still much uncertainty with respect to reaction time and psychometric intelligence (Carlson, 1985; Jones, 1985). Das (1985) noted that many American Blacks have surpassed Whites in the judicious use of their speed abilities especially in athletics and dancing, yet on speeded tests they do not do as well as Whites. The explanation must be in their familiarity, or lack thereof, of certain stimuli. Sternberg (1984) argues that although speed may be critical for some mental operations, "the issue ought not to be speed per se, but rather speed selection: knowing when to perform at what rate and being able to function rapidly or slowly depending on the tasks or situational demands" (p. 7). Sternberg (1984) also argues that although speed of mental functioning has been associated with intelligence testing, it is well known that snap judgments are not an important attribute of intelligence. Thurstone (1924) emphasized that a critical factor of intelligence is the ability to substitute rapid, impulsive responses for rational, reflective ones. Noble (1969) found that children can be trained to increase their reaction time by teaching them to do so. Jensen and Whang (1994) agreed with Noble, finding that "the more the retrieval process has become automatic through practice, the faster it occurs" (p. 1). Therefore the greater the speed, the greater the amount of practice. Baron (1981, 1982) also noted that with respect to problem solving, a reflective cognitive style is generally associated with intelligence. De Avila (1974) noted that assessing culturally different children via timed tests confuses the measurement of ability with the measurement of aspiration, because little regard is given to children who are not culturally trained to work under timed conditions. Gopaul-McNicol (1993) found that most Caribbean children have difficulty completing tasks under time pressures because this represents the antithesis of what their culture dictates. On the contrary, slow and careful execution of their work is highly valued, so that even if the child is aware of being timed, he or she may ignore the request by the examiner for a quick response, and, rather, will execute the work methodically and cautiously. As such, scores tend to be lower for such students on timed tests, which comprise most of the nonverbal subtests. Of course, people in some professions, such as air traffic controllers, must consequentially make quick decisions every day. Although speed may be essential in such situations, most daily life events do not require such quick decision making, as is typically allotted for problem solving on IQ tests. The important issue here is not one of total time spent, but of time distribution across various kinds of processing and planning events. Students ought not to be penalized for not completing a task in the allotted time. Instead, they should be credited for successful completion of the task. Again, two scaled scores can be tabulated to compare how they function under timed conditions and how they function when tested to the limit. Thus, this measure involves *the suspension of time* and the tabulating of two scores—one timed and one with time suspended.

Contextualization versus Decontextualization

Although McGrew (1995) found that vocabulary is only moderately influenced by American culture, Hilliard's (1979) question, "What precisely is meant by vocabulary?" is a valid one and one that advocates for IQ tests have not yet answered. Words may have different meanings in different cultures. For instance, the word "tostones" means a quarter or a half dollar to a Chicano, but it means a squashed part of a banana that has been fried to a Puerto Rican. Given such a situation, it is recommended that the child be permitted to say the words in a sentence to be sure that his or her understanding of the word's meaning is the same as that on the American IQ test. Armour-Thomas and Allen (1993) found that the vocabulary of 32 ninth-grade students was elevated when unknown words were presented in a contextually embedded situation. These findings were consistent with those of other studies that found individual differences in the acquisition of word meanings in contextually embedded situations (Sternberg & Powell, 1983; Sternberg, Powell, & Kaye, 1982; Daalen-Kapteijns, Van & Elshout-Mohr, 1981). Thus, most of vocabulary is contextually determined; that is, it is learned in everyday contexts rather than through direct instruction. Children accomplish this decontextualization by embedding unknown words in simple contexts (Sattler, 1988; Sternberg, 1985).

In the authors' (Gopaul-McNicol & Armour-Thomas, 1997a) private practice they have found that children who do not know word meanings in isolation are able to figure out the words when placed in a surrounding context. Of course, on traditional IQ tests children are asked word meanings in isolation. Although this may be acceptable for children who have had adequate educational opportunities in adequate social environments, for children who have had little formal schooling, word definition without the surrounding context may lead to invalid findings of their intelligence, in particular, knowledge acquisition. Gardner (1983) recommended against using formal instruments administered in a decontextualized setting, but recommended instead that assessment should be part of the natural learning environment and ought not be set apart from the rest of the classroom activity.

With the bio-ecological model, the examiner can contextualize all words by asking the child to say them in a sentence. For example, the examiner can say to the child, "Please say the word clock in a sentence." Potential credit is given only if the child says it in a sentence (not the examiner).

Paper and Pencil on the Arithmetic Subtests

Over the past two decades researchers have studied problem solving in mathematics from a cognitive information-processing perspective and have found that a primary source of difficulty in problem solving lies in students' inability to monitor and regulate the cognitive processes engaged in during problem solving (Artzt and Armour-Thomas, 1992). On most IQ tests, arithmetic taps skill, memory/attention, and speed. In the standard procedure, it is difficult to tell which is operating. Potential testing allows the examiner to rule out which factor is operating. For potential testing on the arithmetic subtest of the Wechsler scales, the examiner can say to the child who fails, "Please use this paper and pencil and try to solve the problem." This response will fall under a potential score.

Test–Teach–Retest Assessment Measure

Although Esquivel (1985) emphasized that "performance scales of standardized intelligence tests appear to have the greatest predictive validity for limited English-proficient students, and may provide a more accurate estimate of their actual abilities" (p. 119), the nonverbal subtests contrary to the claims that have been espoused are not culture-fair and are definitely not culture-free. In fact, it is "the information (direct experience) components of these tests that carry their culture bound characteristics" (Cohen, 1969, p. 840). That nonverbal tests also rely on one's ability to reason logically, it is in this logical thinking that the most culture-bound way of cognitive processing is carried out. In some respects nonverbal tests embody more analytic modes of abstraction than the quantitative information components. This is because at times the task requires the individual to extrapolate and relate to relevant parts of the test items. Thus, the manner of cognitive organization is relevant for successful performance on nonverbal tests. The block design and object assembly subtests of the Wechsler scales are highly influenced by the American culture, and American children exposed to such items will find the experience less novel, and thus their performances will be more automized. Hence the tests will not measure the same skills across cultures and populations. Most children who are from rural areas in "Third World" countries have had little, if any, exposure to puzzles and blocks. Sternberg (1984) emphasized that "as useful as the tests may be for within-group comparisons, between-group comparisons may be deceptive and unfair for nonverbal subtests" (p. 10). A fair comparison between groups would require equitable degrees of familiarity or novelty in test items, as well as comparable strategies.

Sternberg (1984, 1985, 1986) found in his study that the ability to deal with novelty was critical to measuring subjects' reasoning skills. Gopaul-McNicol (1993) found that in working with Caribbean children, other, more complicated, activities also measure nonverbal abstract reasoning and visual integration, as do the block design and object assembly subtests respectively. Because they are more relevant to the children's cultural experiences, they felt that these ought to be considered instead. The average child who comes from such countries is very handy—able to help in constructing buildings, making furniture, creating a steel pan, maneuvering a motor boat, or cutting grass with a cutlass—even though he or she has no formal education in these areas. These tasks are as or more complicated than putting blocks or puzzles together. Therefore, it would not be logical to label these children as delayed intellectually when they have honed other more complicated nonverbal skills. Evidently, their American counterparts are not labeled as deficient because they are unable to perform some of the previously mentioned activities that these children can so easily do. However, these skills are not measured on typical Anglo intelligence tests. Gardner (1983, 1993) noted that the performance gap between students from Western cultures versus those from non-Western cultures narrowed or even disappeared when familiar materials were used, when revised instructions were given, or when the same cognitive capacities were tapped in a form that made more sense within the non-Western context. Thus, nonverbal tests have not been freed from their culture-bound components. Clearly, the substantive information experiences are still culture bound. Besides, when testing the limits of culturally different children, on the nonverbal subtests it is quite common for students to get the more difficult items correct after they have passed their ceiling points or after time limits have been expended. It seems as if the children were learning as they went along, and that lack of familiarity may have been why they did not do as well on the earlier items. Unfortunately, by the time they understood how to manipulate the blocks and put the puzzles together, it was time to stop those particular subtests, because they had already reached their ceiling point. Of course, in keeping with standardization procedures, one does not receive credit for items passed after the ceiling point has been attained.

Feuerstein (1979, 1980) produced evidence of the plasticity of the human organism, which has made cognitive performance modifiable through mediated learning experiences (MLE). Through his Learning Potential Assessment Device (LPAD), Feuerstein found that a substantial reservoir of the abilities of Jewish children remained untapped when traditional assessment instruments were utilized to determine the intelligence of these children. This LPAD instrument, as the name implies, involved a radical shift from a static to a dynamic approach in which the test situation was transformed into a learning experience for the child. The focus was on learning rather than on its product, and on the qualitative rather than the quantitative dimensions of the individual's thought (Feuerstein, 1980, 1990). Many researchers (Budoff, 1987; Beker and Feuerstein, 1990; Feuerstein, Rand, Jensen, Kaniel, Tzuriel, Ben Shachar and Mintzker, 1986; Glutting and McDermott, 1990; Lidz, 1987 & 1991; Missiuna and Samuels, 1988) suggest that the best way to predict learning efficiency is to assess it in an actual learning and teaching situation. Thus, dynamic assessment links testing and intervention with the goal of enhancing a child's performance through a particular intervention. The thrust of this approach is to identify obstacles that may be hindering the expression of a child's intellectual functioning and then to specify the conditions under which the child's intelligence may be enhanced. In summary, the child's modifiability is an important outcome of this dynamic approach to assessment.

Unlike in standardized testing conditions where the examiner is neutral, the test–teach–retest approach proposed in the bio-ecological assessment system allows the examiner to be interactive, and these interactions are an integral part of the assessment process. The ultimate goal is to link the assessment findings directly to the development of individualized educational intervention programs.

The Test–Teach–Retest assessment measure (Armour-Thomas and Gopaul-McNicol, 1997a) is only to be administered if the examiner realizes that the child was not exposed to these types of items prior to the testing, that is, if the child never played with blocks, puzzles, and so forth. Then, the examiner is to teach the child, and afterward retest him or her. For instance, on the block design, picture arrangement, or object assembly subtests of the Wechsler scales, if a child fails the items on both trials, for potential psychometric assessment the examiner can teach and give the test again. Credit is only considered under potential if the child gets it correct after the teaching period. Exact procedures are followed, as in the standardized testing, except that time is suspended, teaching is done, and potential scores are given after the child passes the teaching items.

In addition, the examiner should try to answer the following questions:

1. How much did the child benefit from the training intervention?
2. How much training is needed to raise the child's performance to a basic minimum level?
3. How well does the child retains the skills learned in the training period?
4. How much more training is needed to ensure that the child retains what he or she learns?
5. How well does the child generalize to other settings (home) what he or she has learned?
6. How easily is the child able to learn difficult problems other than what he or she has learned in training?

ECOLOGICAL TAXONOMY OF INTELLECTUAL ASSESSMENT

An examination of the literature on the consistency between IQ scores and real-life attainments calls into question the isomorphism between these two situations. For instance, the types of skills required for success on the picture arrangement and similarities subtests of the Wechsler scales are similar to the deductive reasoning necessary when grocery shopping. Shoppers tend to match prices, comparing how similar or dissimilar items are, as well as to plan whether the volume of their purchases can fit into their refrigerators. As such, the goal is to allow for a few days of supply rather than a week. The previous examples confirm that there are many instances in which deficits in cognitive functioning disappear when the problem is couched in familiar terms or using familiar stimuli (Super, 1980). Therefore, cognition is indeed context sensitive and multiple cognitive potentials exist instead of one cognitive potential or one central processor. In essence, assessment of intellectual functioning should be mindful of the multifaceted influences of culture on behavior.

The *Ecological Taxonomy of Intellectual Assessment* (Armour-Thomas & Gopaul-McNicol, 1997a) attempts to measure skills and behaviors that are relevant to the context in which a child lives (real-world intelligence, not just academic intelligence). Therefore, the child is assessed in several settings—the school, the home, and the community. Observing a child's interactions with family and friends in a natural setting brings to the assessment robust knowledge of the family dynamics and cultural experiences of the child. The examiner should observe the way a child communicates and socializes, the activities engaged in and friendships he or she has, roles played, and respect, or lack thereof, that the child is given by family and friends.

Family/Community Support Assessment

The second component within the ecological taxonomy is the *family/community support assessment*. This questionnaire is designed to determine what support systems the child has at home and in the community, what the child's previous educational experiences have been, what language is spoken at home, and how the family can boost a child's intellectual functioning. Family assessment as part of intellectual assessment brings to the assessment robust knowledge of the family dynamics of the child. Therefore, parenting, childrearing practices, disciplinary measures, punishments/reinforcers, the language spoken at home, religious values, the family's relationship to the society at large, as well as the family's impact on the child that are indeed rich sources of knowledge for school psychologists are listed in the Family Community

Support Questionnaire developed by Armour-Thomas and Gopaul-McNicol (1997a).

Item Equivalencies Assessment Measure

The third component within the ecological taxonomy is *cultural/item equivalence*. Cummins (1984) points out that when referring to concept formation, evaluators must keep in mind that it is difficult for examinees to know similarities or differences in objects if they have had little or no experience with the objects themselves. An alternative would be to determine if these children can perform comparable skills typical of their native lands. They could describe in a more qualitative manner their strengths and weaknesses with respect to the skills they can perform in their native countries, showing the similarities between these skills and those found on the traditional type tests. For instance, question 4 on the Similarities subtest of the Wechsler Intelligence Scale for Children—111, reads, "In what way are a piano and a guitar alike?" Many children from "Third-World" countries may never have seen or heard a piano. Perhaps the cuatro, another string instrument could be substituted. Likewise, consider question 6, "In what way are an apple and a banana alike?" Apples are not grown in tropical climates. Perhaps "mango" could be substituted. The important issue here is that the child knows the concept of fruits of different kinds. This idea of matching items to a child's culture has been emphasized by Sternberg (1986) and Helms' (1992) cultural equivalence perspective.

This item equivalency assessment measure (Armour-Thomas & Gopaul-McNicol, 1997) attempts to equate a child's cultural experience in every item of every IQ test by matching the questions on the IQ test to the child's culture. As such, the child's broad base information repertoire is recognized. A caveat though is that it is not statistically possible to quantify cultural equivalence. However, powerful information can be obtained clinically. Thus, psychologists who consider themselves more than just psychometricians will still find this measure very helpful, because they can clinically create a cluster of items that form the construct of intelligence for a particular cultural group. This cultural equivalence approach certainly also falls under the rubric of potential assessment.

THE OTHER INTELLIGENCES ASSESSMENT MEASURE

The Other Intelligences Assessment Measure is the fourth tier of the bioecological assessment system. This tier supports Gardner's (1983, 1993) position that all children can excel in one or more intelligence. Gardner's theories of seven multiple intelligences share the view that the human mind is a computational device that has separate and qualitatively different analytic ways of processing various kinds of information. He maintains that there are many types of intelligences, not one as IQ tests claim. He holds on to the position that all children can excel in one or more intelligences. Gardner regards his theory as an egalitarian theory. What is most important to him is not whether one child outperforms another on some skills, but that all children's skills are identified. So, a child may have a propensity for interpersonal skills, and another may have a propensity for numerical reasoning. These propensities are not borne because the parent exposed the child to situations and activities involving these intelligences, but because children have "jagged cognitive profiles," somewhat akin to the learning-disabled child who does well in one area and poorly in another. Of all the theoretical positions, the other intelligences assessment measure developed by Armour-Thomas and Gopaul-McNicol (1997a) attempts to capture four of Gardner's intelligences. Therefore, asking the child, the parent, and the teacher questions to ascertain the child's musical intelligence, bodily kinesthetic intelligence, and inter- and intrapersonal intelligence—areas not represented on any of the commonly used standardized IQ tests—is critical to understanding the breadth and depth of a child's comprehensive intellectual abilities. Interviewing several different people (child, teacher, parent) is necessary to add reliability to the child's description of his or her other intelligences.

Summary

The American Psychological Association (1993) has offered culturally relevant suggestions for practice for providers who work with culturally diverse families. The suggestions therein ought to be strongly considered. School psychologists should also familiarize themselves with the psychometric and nonpsychometric measures assessment tools that address the multifaceted nature of intelligence. This bio-ecological model of assessment is recommended as a comprehensive assessment system for the understanding of a qualitative, quantitative, cognitive, social, emotional, cultural, and behavioral comprehensive assessment. While the recommended methods of administering and scoring these traditional tests may seem quite unconventional and not in keeping with standardization procedures, they are a guide for psychologists in tapping the potential of culturally different children. Reporting two IQ scores, one following standard procedures and one taking into consideration issues raised in potential assessment, may be the best way to understand these children's strengths and weaknesses. If school psychologists intend to serve children well, they should give greater attention to qualitative rather than quantitative reports that highlight all of a child's past and present cultural experiences.

In summary, this "assessment view" seeks to connect school activities with after-school activities with emphasis on the individual's strengths. In other words, this approach calls for a broader menu of assessment options. All of the information presented in this chapter should be incorporated in the report in a qualitative/descriptive manner (see Chapter 5 for a sample bio-ecological report).

EDUCATIONAL ASSESSMENT

The American Association of Colleges for Teacher Education (AACTE) has repeatedly endorsed cultural pluralism; merely placating and accommodating racially and culturally different students is not what cultural pluralism is about. Rather, cultural pluralism requires educators to take a serious look at their curricula, which has thus far only endorsed the principle of one "model American" and has not yet given intrinsic respect to every individual. Teachers should consider the strengths and learning styles of different children as remediation is offered. Dunn and Dunn (1978) and Dunn and associates (1990) emphasized that if a student does not learn the way the teacher teaches, it is incumbent upon the teacher to teach the student the best way the student learns. This is important because instruction in the typical American classroom is very visual, whereas many immigrant children are very auditory. Therefore, speaking rather than writing information on the board, or using audiotapes for instruction rather than visual aids, such as computers, may prove to be more successful approaches with these children. Another difference in educational style is the type of examinations that are given. Some immigrant children are more comfortable with essay tests, while multiple-choice tests are more common in the United States. It takes time for children to get used to the multiple-choice form of test. Some children actually feel that the teacher will not take scores on such tests seriously because, in their perception, essay tests truly test knowledge and multiple-choice tests are simplistic (Gopaul-McNicol, 1993). In addition, many immigrant children engage in a more cooperative type of learning, which fosters more dependence and sharing; in contrast, the American educational style is more independent. These differences in learning styles are critical; teachers must both respect these differences and, initially, they should allow sufficient time for students to adjust and adapt to the American style.

Curriculum-Based Assessment

Over the past five years there has been much discussion around a serious need to examine alternative testing models in the area of education for determining the educational placement of children. A major limitation of edu-

cational achievement tests is their content validity (Shapiro, 1987). The existing achievement tests fail to adequately sample the classroom curriculum.
Therefore, scores from these tests may not appropriately measure what the
child has learned. Shapiro (1987) found that there is a marked difference between the curriculum and the achievement tests, not only in reading, but in
math as well. Another concern is the relevance of the test information gathered from the traditional achievement tests in planning a child's educational
instructional program. The need for alternative assessment procedures to
help plan instruction is critical if we are to best serve children, in particular,
children with special needs. Besides, statutory laws such as the Protection in
Evaluation Procedures (PEP) guidelines in Public Law (PL) 94-142 (Section
615-5C) state that "procedures to assure that testing and evaluation materials
and procedures utilized for the purposes of evaluation and placement of
handicapped children will be selected and administered so as not to be
racially or culturally discriminatory." The call for a more individual-focus assessment procedure that is better able to address the specific educational
needs of all children has become crucial.

Curriculum-based assessment (CBA) has been proposed by Shinn (1989)
to redress some of the issues in this arena. It is built on the premise that the
measures are tied to the student's curricula in order to facilitate frequent administration by educators, and that it is inexpensive because CBA does not require the procurement of costly test materials. Another salient focus of CBA is
the ability of the examiner to engage in repeated measurement of a student's
performance as the curriculum unfolds. As it stands, traditional achievement
tests are normed referenced and rely on indirect measurement of student
skills. Curriculum-based assessment, on the other hand, is based on a cur-
riculum-referenced approach that indicates the student's level of competence
in his or her local school curriculum. Thus, the assessment of reading skills is
drawn from the student's basal reading series, and spelling is assessed via the
words that the student learned in the classroom. The relevance of curriculum-
based assessment for linguistically and culturally diverse children is one of the
reasons for the endorsement of this approach among educators. Obviously, it
is easier to measure growth and progress in a student's performance. Besides,
CBA can identify a student's curricular skills that may need further testing.

Another obvious advantage of CBA is that it is not necessary to give an entire battery merely to determine an aspect of the child's performance, as is typical of assessing children with criterion reference tests. Certainly, CBA is more
time effective and more content specific. Furthermore, CBA encourages the examiner to become familiar with the child's curricula at a given grade. Therefore, emphasis should be on an exclusive assessment of the task that students
have to learn. Teachers can then develop their own instructional materials
based on the results of the assessment (Hargis, 1987). In actuality, Gickling
and Havertape (1981) pioneered the current movement of linking assessment

to curricula in a model best conceptualized as an accuracy model. CBA is indeed significant for instructional planning purposes, rendering it more an intervention model than an assessment model.

Dynamic Assessment

Lidz (1991) captures Feuerstein (1979) test–intervene–retest format via dynamic assessment techniques. Feuerstein (1979) emphasized the importance of assessing children's potential through the Learning Potential Assessment Device (LPAD), which also included an intervention derived from a similar theoretical premise—a "structural cognitive modifiability." This allows the examiner to assess the child's potential as well as the relevance to the educational setting. This also involves teacher observation so that linkages can be made between the assessor's findings and the classroom teacher's reports. The assessor then develops a continuum of tasks that continually approximate actual classroom content (Lidz, 1991) and the child is given remediation (intervention) to ensure that he or she masters the content. The strength behind this pre- and post-intervention performance is an important dimension in assessing linguistic and culturally different children because mediated learning experiences (MLE) are assessed to represent the proximal instead of distal factors related to cognitive development.

Dynamic assessment, as opposed to static assessment, allows the examiner/teacher to work with children in their cultural cognitive style, in their cultural communicative style, to work at the children's pace, and to self-monitor.

Portfolio-Based Assessment

Wiggins (1990) proposed that keeping portfolios of children's performance serves two distinct purposes: (1) to provide documentation of the child's work, and (2) serve as the basis for evaluating the child's work.

Wiggins (1990) recommended keeping the following in a child's portfolio: a self-portrait, a self-selected journal entry, a reading log, a cumulative math assessment, a research project, and a fall and spring writing sample. This approach to assessment allows the teacher and the parent to monitor the child's progress via a daily or weekly evaluation criteria.

SUMMARY

An informal assessment involving behavioral observations in several settings—classroom, playground, the home, and, if possible, the community—will also help to understand the needs, strengths, and weaknesses of the child before a referral to special education is made. Some children are quite capable of performing basic mathematical skills in a grocery store and yet on a structured type test, they find themselves at a loss. Gopaul-McNicol (1993) noted that immigrant children who may not be as communicative in the classroom are able to negotiate quite well for themselves in the larger community. They are often more articulate on the playground in spite of the taciturnity noted in the classroom. When placed in a context such as on the playground, they utilize words that they often have difficulty defining or expressing in the traditional testing situation. As such, assessing children in a multitude of settings is advised, in particular, children from diverse backgrounds.

► 5

Report Writing for Linguistically and Culturally Different Children: Utilizing the Bio-Ecological Assessment System

Surber (1995) noted that in "probably no other profession or specialty do leg-islative regulations have such an important effect on the information pre-sented in a written report" (p. 161). The purpose of the psychological report has traditionally been to address the reason the student is having difficulty in learning, behaving, and so forth, and to determine what services or class placement the child may need. A tremendous void in most reports is the con-version of the assessment data into specially designed, tailored interventions that fit the child's needs, thus leading to improved student performance in the areas of concern.

This chapter will first demonstrate how the bio-ecological assessment system can help school psychologists to write more culturally sensitive re-ports, rather than narrowly focused reports that are endemic to psychome-tricians or "tester-technicians" (Tallent, 1993) who restrict their reporting to test results only. When the psychologist's role is expanded to that of a diag-nostician or a clinician, the approach to report writing is more prescriptive and relates more to educational implications for classroom practice. Hence, the second purpose of this chapter is to assist school psychologists in developing interventions that can help the teacher and the parent to reduce the discrepancy between the child's current functioning, as assessed by classroom-type tasks, and the child's potential functioning, as assessed by this comprehensive bio-ecological assessment system and writing a bioecological psychological report (Gopaul-McNicol & Armour Thomas, 1997b).

To best address the purpose of this chapter, a review of a traditional psychological report and a bio-ecological report conducted on the same child will aid the examiner in detecting how the differences in assessment and report writing can lead to differences in recommendations.

Name: Miguel   **Date of Testing:** 5/21/94

School: JHS   **Date of Birth:** 8/19/81

Grade: 6th   **Age:** 12 years 9 months

Language: Spanish

Reason for Referral and Background Information

Miguel was referred for an initial evaluation by his teacher due to academic difficulties. Miguel arrived from Colombia in August of 1993 at age 12. His parents had migrated to the United States when he was seven years old. While in Colombia, Miguel was said to be a pleasant boy who related well to his aunts with whom he resided while his parents were in the United States.

The social history conducted in March 1994 by the school social worker revealed that since Miguel arrived in the United States, he has had serious difficulty adjusting to he classroom, not because of linguistic factors "because he is more proficient and more dominant in English since he attended English classes in his native country to prepare for his migrating to the United States." According to the social worker and the teacher, "Miguel clearly has no skills," and the school psychologist's report [see excerpts of the school psychologist's report from the first report that follows] revealed deficient intellectual functioning when tested with standardized tests of intelligence.

The social history revealed that Miguel lives with his mother, father, an older brother, maternal aunt, and grandmother. All family members present themselves as a cohesive unit with strong extended family ties and good family support systems. According to Miguel's mother, all developmental milestones were attained at age-expectant levels. However, there were reports of delays in reading even in Colombia, but "he was certainly able to read what was necessary to get by. He is definitely not stupid as the school is making him out to be."

Test administered and test results—Traditional school report
Wechsler Intelligence Scale for Children—111

Psychometric Assessment	Range
Verbal Scale IQ	Deficient
Performance Scale IQ	Borderline
Full Scale IQ	Deficient

Current Scale Score	Range	Current Scale Score	Range
Information	Deficient	Picture Completion	Borderline
Similarities	Deficient	Coding	Borderline
Arithmetic	Deficient	Picture Arrangement	Borderline
Vocabulary	Deficient	Block Design	Borderline
Comprehension	Deficient	Object Assembly	Borderline
Digit Span	Low average	Mazes	Borderline

Given the above findings, the teacher reports, and classroom observation, the following conclusions were drawn: "Miguel is said to be functioning in the mentally deficient range of intelligence" and even when tested to potential (extending the time limits in some of the nonverbal areas) he was at best borderline." . . . "He was unable to do basic math commensurate to his age and grade peers. He was deficient in his vocabulary skills, not knowing to define words such as 'nonsense, ancient and thief'." . . . When given the blocks and puzzles to manipulate he became noticeably frustrated stating "I do not know what to do, while pushing the blocks away.". . . On the general information subtests Miguel was unable to respond to basic questions such as 'name two kinds of coins'. . . . It is recommended that "Miguel be placed in a self-contained class where he receive special educational services in all areas to address his obvious delays in academic-type tasks and his overall intellectual deficiencies."

Behavioral Observation

Miguel, a pleasant young man, presented himself in a cooperative, compliant manner. He had a good disposition and was motivated to do all of the tasks assigned to him. Even upon completion of the testing, Miguel asked the examiner if he could do more. He was not fatigued and considered these types of tests as reinforcing to his self-esteem. In general, his response time was slow and he approached the testing in a cautious, reflective manner. When he clearly did not know the answer he still persisted, but became noticeably frustrated and embarrassed. He would sigh, frown his face, and seemed

Test administered and test results—Bio-ecological assessment system
Wechsler Intelligence Scale for Children—111

Psychometric Potential Assessment	Range
Verbal Scale IQ	Borderline
Performance Scale IQ	Average
Full Scale IQ	Low Average

Potential	Scale Score	Potential	Scale Score
Information	Deficient	Picture Completion	Low average
Similarities	Deficient	Coding	Borderline
Arithmetic	Low average	Picture Arrangement	Low average
Vocabulary	Average	Block Design	Average
Comprehension	Borderline	Object Assembly	Average
Digit Span	Average	Mazes	Average

Medical Examination—No Medical Difficulties

Ecological Intellectual Assessment Estimated Overall Functioning	Average

Other Intelligences Assessment	Bodily Kinesthetic (Soccer)—Advanced Artistic (Painting)—Advanced Musical Intelligence—Guitar—Advanced

Family Support Assessment—Adequate

Vineland Behavior Adaptive Scales—Parent Edition

	Range
Communication	Low
Social	Adequate
Daily Living Scales	Adequate
Social History	
Clinical Interview	
Parent Interview	
Teacher Questionnaire	
Language Dominance	English
Language Proficiency	

Vocabulary Subtest	*Proficiency Rating*
Spanish Expressive Vocabulary	Deficient
English Expressive Vocabulary	Borderline

upset that he did not know the answer to what he initially perceived as easy. All in all, it was a pleasure testing Miguel because he tried hard and was willing to please.

Language Assessment

Miguel's language proficiency was tested through the administration of the vocabulary subtest of the WISC-111 in both Spanish and English. He is clearly more dominant and more proficient in English. He spoke mainly in English, but on several occasions he requested that the examiner speak in Spanish. When he engaged in social play on the playground, he spoke in both languages. In general, his English receptive and expressive skills were better developed than his Spanish skills. It is possible that the English instruction he received prior to coming to the United States and the fact that his parents only speak in English at home aided in developing his proficiency and fluency in English. At this time, although Miguel can function well in a predominantly English-speaking class, the supportive environment of a bilingual paraprofessional may prove beneficial when faced with very difficult tasks.

TEST INTERPRETATION

Psychometric Assessment

On the Wechsler Intelligence Scale for Children—111, Miguel obtained a full-scale IQ score that placed him in the deficient range of intelligence. His verbal and nonverbal scores fell in the deficient and borderline ranges respectively.

Subtest analysis indicates considerable subtest variability both within the verbal and nonverbal spheres. In the verbal area (crystallized), Miguel was deficient in general information, suggesting that on this psychometric test, Miguel is not as alert to the social and cultural factors so typical of the American society as measured by the WISC-111. His deficiency in comprehension is also indicative of his limited understanding of the social mores here in the United States as assessed on the WISC-111. Miguel was also deficient in verbal abstract reasoning, suggesting that, on this test, Miguel has difficulty placing objects and events together in meaningful groups. In arithmetic and vocabulary, Miguel was also deficient. This is indicative of inadequate arithmetic skills as assessed by the standardized procedures of the WISC-111, as well as poor language development and limited word knowledge as defined by the WISC-111. In auditory short-term memory, Miguel was low average. Therefore, one can expect Miguel to be relatively good at rote memory and sequential processing.

In the nonverbal area (fluid intelligence), Miguel was borderline in identifying essential missing elements from a whole, suggesting delayed visual alertness and visual discrimination, and long-term visual memory on the Wechsler scales. In visual integration, Miguel was borderline, suggesting limited perceptual skills, poor long-term visual memory, and limited constructive ability commensurate to his peers nationwide on the Wechsler scales. However, Miguel was persistent and tried to put the puzzles together. There was a sense that he was unfamiliar with these items. As such, when he was taught how to connect the pieces, he tended to be more relaxed, although he continued to perform poorly. In visual motor coordination/motor speed, Miguel was also borderline, suggesting slow response time, poor visual short-term memory and limited visual acuity on the Wechsler scales. In nonverbal comprehension, Miguel was borderline, suggesting a delayed ability to anticipate the consequences of his actions, and to plan and to organize ahead of time on the WISC-111. In nonverbal abstract reasoning, Miguel was also low average, suggesting below average ability to perceive, analyze, and synthesize blocks on the Wechsler scales.

Psychometric Potential Assessment

When Miguel was tested to the limit, such as when time was suspended, and too, when item equivalencies were done, his scores were improved by fourteen IQ points in the verbal area, sixteen IQ points in the nonverbal area, and sixteen IQ points in overall intelligence. Thus, when the test–teach–retest techniques were implemented and time was suspended with the blocks and puzzles, Miguel went from borderline to average, displaying much confidence on these tests during potential assessment. Because block design is the best measure of nonverbal intelligence on the Wechsler scales, again, Miguel is of average potential in the nonverbal area.

Another important fact is that when Miguel was offered the opportunity to use paper and pencil, he was able to perform many of the mathematical tasks that presented difficulty under standardized procedures. For instance, he clearly knew multiplication, division, and even simple fractions. Thus, by allowing Miguel to use paper and pencil instead of relying on mental computations only, the examiner was able to determine that Miguel did master some arithmetic skills, but was unable to perform them without the aid of paper and pencil. Because one is usually allowed the opportunity to work with pencil and paper in real-life situations, one can expect that Miguel will be able to do basic calculations to function adequately well in his day-to-day duties. Moreover, although Miguel was unable to name two American coins on the psychometric test, he was able to correctly name and identify the "escudo" and the "peso," two monetary units from South America. Furthermore, when the vocabulary words were contextually determined, that is, when Miguel was asked to say the words in a surrounding context (Miguel said "I migrated to the USA recently," instead of asking the word "migrate" in isolation), Miguel went from deficient to average. He knew almost every word commensurate to his age and grade peers when allowed to contextualize them. Because vocabulary is the best measure of general intelligence, Miguel is of average potential in the verbal area. Incidentally, if the substitute test was used to tabulate his verbal IQ score instead of general information (the most biased of the verbal subtests), Miguel's verbal score would have been low average, albeit his overall IQ score would still have been low average.

Ecological Assessment

At home, on the playground, in school, and in the community, Miguel is described as "bright and promising" by his family and friends. According to his mother, Miguel helps with the groceries and assists with basic household tasks commensurate to his age peers.

Moreover, in observing Miguel on the community playground, it was clearly evident that he was able to perform several of the tasks found on the IQ test. For instance, although he was unable to put the puzzles and blocks together on the Wechsler scales, he was adept at fixing a car. On one occasion when his aunt's car was unable to start, he checked the carburetor and other car parts and deciphered the problem. His aunt mentioned that he is responsible for repairing any electrical appliances that malfunction in the home. Evidently, this activity involves the same visual motor coordination skills as putting puzzles together. Miguel's inability to reintegrate puzzle pieces on the IQ test even though he could assemble smaller, complex parts of a car suggests that cultural factors must be impeding his ability to perform such a similar task on the standardized IQ test. Clearly, he is at least average in his visual motor integration skills, albeit this was not evident on the psychometric measure. Also significant was Miguel's ability to remember a fourteen-item grocery list, although he was unable to recall as many as seven numbers on the Digit Span subtest of the Wechsler scales. Equally impressive was his ability to do arithmetic computations mentally in the grocery store, although he demonstrated deficient mathematical skills on the psychometric IQ test. Thus, in Miguel's ecology—that is, in a real-life situation away from the testing environment—he showed good planning ability, good perceptual organization, good mathematical skills, and good short-term memory. Unfortunately, none of these skills were manifested on the standardized traditional IQ test, albeit gains were noted when he was tested to his cognitive potential via the same IQ measure. Evidently, from an ecological perspective, in real-life situations Miguel's cognitive ability is approximately average.

Other Intelligences Assessment

Miguel's family and his gym teacher described him as "multi-talented." He is said to be very athletic, particularly in his ability to play soccer. His gym teacher described him as well-coordinated. He is artistic—he paints and draws all sorts of abstract images as well as cartoon-like figures. His art teacher described his artistic skills as advanced, and said that he was the best student in his class in all artistic-related fields such as painting, designing, architecture, and so forth. Thus, with respect to his bodily kinesthetic ability, Miguel was above average to superior commensurate to his age peers. Another intelligence that Miguel possesses is his musical ability. He plays the clarinet, and he formulates melodic and harmonic images with great fluency after only one year of playing the guitar. His mother stated that he also has an interest in other musical instruments, including the flute. An interview with his music teacher revealed that Miguel plays the piano "for fun" and composes songs and music so creatively that in the realm of musical intelligence he would be considered intellectually superior.

An interview with the after-school community director revealed that he is a "well-rounded, talented" young man who manifests accuracy, grace, speed, power, and great team spirit in all artistic and sports-like endeavors. He is said to have a well-developed sense of timing, coordination, and rhythm when playing music. The director also reported that he is able to remain composed under great pressure. Watching him play soccer, the examiner was able to observe his bodily intelligence in its purest form, with much flexibility and high technical proficiency. He is of superior ability in the area of gross and fine motor motions. The social feedback by the director should also be noted: "Everyone likes Miguel, both young children and his peers. Everyone wants him to lead the team. He inspires his peers to do their best." Interpersonal skills are described as excellent, because Miguel is a "warm, pleasant, and sociable young man."

DIAGNOSTIC IMPRESSION/EDUCATIONAL/ CLINICAL IMPLICATIONS

Intellectually, Miguel is functioning in the mentally deficient range on the WISC-111 psychometric test and low average range on psychometric potential assessment. Because Miguel attended school in his native country on a regular basis, he cannot be said to be educationally deprived. A diagnosis of mental retardation cannot be given either, because adequate functioning was noted on two sections of the Vineland Adaptive Behavior Scales. To be diagnosed as mentally retarded, low functioning in all areas of social adaptation ought to be evident. Only on communication skills was he found to be low, which was commensurate to his score on the WISC-111 psychometric test. Besides, after conducting a family assessment, it is clear that Miguel functions adequately in his community and is respected by his peers. Thus, in spite of communication delays, there are no overall social adaptive deficiencies to characterize him as mentally deficient. At this juncture Miguel's intellectual functioning best fits the diagnosis of "Learning Disabled Not Otherwise Specified." This category is for learning disorders that do not meet the criteria for any specific learning disorder, and may include problems in all three core areas of reading, mathematics, and written expression.

Given the obvious delays in several academic skill areas, and on the psychometric IQ test, one (such as the school psychologist) may be solely inclined to provide Miguel with intensive instruction in all academic cognitive skill areas on a daily basis in a small-classroom, special educational setting. Clearly, he does require the supportive environment of supplemental instruction. However, given his performance when assessed in other settings beyond the IQ testing environment, a less restrictive setting outside of the special education self-contained realm ought to be explored. For instance, Miguel should be encouraged to pursue music, especially the guitar. Likewise, he ought to be encouraged to embellish his athletic skills given his abilities in this area as well. As such, the typical special education, self-contained class in which there is little emphasis on honing one's career/occupational skills is not recommended.

Evidently, Miguel's obvious intelligence in music renders him a prime candidate for a scholarship at a music school. As such, opportunities for career-related academic skill development, which include essential work adjustment skills and direct work experience through daily practice in a music school, are needed for this young man to attain his potential and be self-supportive.

Clinically, Miguel was lacking in self-confidence and was noticeably frustrated when faced with demanding classroom-type tasks. However, when observed in the home and in his music and sports classes, no frustration nor anger was noted. Likewise, the after-school instructor reported that Miguel has a good sense of himself, the opposite to what his general classroom teacher had stated. It was indeed important that assessment of this youngster in various settings was done to ensure a more accurate diagnosis of his overall functioning.

SUMMARY AND RECOMMENDATIONS

Miguel is a 12-year-old young man who shows delays on both the psychometric and potential psychometric assessment measures in general information, comprehension, arithmetic, and verbal abstract reasoning. As a result, remediation should focus on exposure to a broad range of everyday facts and practical reasoning in social situations. Miguel should be encouraged to read

American literature or the newspaper on a daily basis, to gain more insight into world events and mainstream cultural views to help improve his general information. Other resources are museums, educational television shows, tapes, and film documentaries. Teaching same/different concepts should aid in improving verbal abstract reasoning. In addition, vocabulary skills can be enhanced by encouraging Miguel to learn new words by reading more. Teaching computational skills commensurate to his grade peers should aid in improving arithmetic skills.

Miguel can function in a monolingual class, although the supportive environment of a bilingual paraprofessional may prove beneficial when he is faced with difficult tasks.

The recommendation for Miguel also includes a referral to Operation Athlete, an organization in New York City that provides scholarships for gifted athletes. This organization has an after-school program whose goal is to recruit intelligent athletes who can become professionals in their areas of expertise. Miguel was recently offered a scholarship for soccer, but he has to finish high school while maintaining a passing grade in all core courses.

Miguel was also referred to Sesame Flyer, a Caribbean organization that teaches immigrant families to play various musical instruments.

Moreover, eight weeks of counseling aimed at increasing frustration tolerance surrounding his academic delays was offered.

A follow-up of Miguel's progress one year after the completion of the evaluation revealed a continued superiority in nonacademic tasks, such as sports, and a slight increase in academic areas. Miguel was taught to transfer his knowledge from his ecology to the classroom setting through various exercises offered by the examiner who continued treatment following the evaluation. Teacher and family consultation to assist those who work more closely with Miguel was offered on an ongoing basis. The most recent teacher report revealed "significant gains in reading, math, and spelling," and no frustration was evident when faced with difficult tasks. On the contrary, Miguel repeatedly stated, "This is my weak area, but I have many strengths." Miguel had learned to rely on his other intelligences—bodily kinesthetic and music—and hopes to pursue one of these vocational arenas.

Miguel ought to be monitored closely and tested next year to determine what progress he is making, and whether a more or less restrictive setting would be beneficial.

CONCLUSION

The linking of assessment/diagnosis to intervention continues to be one of the most challenging demands faced by school psychologists. It is important to note that assessment programs that fail to take into account the differences among individuals' cultural experiences are anachronistic. To take these variations into account, those in the formal testing enterprise must suspend some of the major assumptions of standardized testing, such as uniformity of individuals' experiences, and the penchant for one type of cost-efficient instrument. Surber (1995) emphasizes that incorporating a multimethod, multitrait approach to assessment and intervention can better ensure that the outcomes for students are nondiscriminatory. He suggests conducting more comprehensive assessments and writing more integrated reports. Indeed, such an approach allows the examiner to answer more readily the major question of what is interfering with the child's ability to learn. Such an approach expands the psychologist's role beyond that of a psychometrician who only administers standardized tests.

Psychologists in training should be taught about individual differences by being introduced formally to such distinctions. It will be quite difficult for students in training to arrive at such empirically valid taxonomies of differences in individuals on their own. Such exposure should occur during their professional training. Once exposed to different profiles in the course of their apprenticeships, it is easier for them to be more flexible in their assessment practices. Chapter 11 discusses issues in the training of psychologists.

Furthermore, it is equally important for students in training to be cognizant of their individual state regulations regarding bilingual/bicultural assessment. In several states, there are Chancellor's disclaimant statements for assessing bilingual children.

In summary, the most critical dimension to assessment is determining the strengths of a youngster and helping that child to feel a sense of empowerment and success in spite of any obvious academic deficiencies. Armour-Thomas and Gopaul-McNicol (in press) present several reports and case examples of wording the bio-ecological assessment report.

▶ 6

Best Practices in Personality Assessment

Although there is an incredible body of literature on the topic of psychopathology among people of African-American ancestry, considerably less literature exists on its cross-cultural manifestations. In mental hospitals, anxiety has been reported as the most frequent complaint among children and adolescents, and depression has been noted as the second commonly diagnosed psychopathology (Kashani et al., 1987). However, an intriguing paradox between immigrant status and mental health has been raised; although immigrants tend to report a high number of symptoms of psychological distress, when prevalence of psychiatric disorders is examined, immigrants tend to show lower rates of mental health difficulties than their U.S.-born counterparts (Burnam et al., 1987). Evidently, these apparently disparate findings raise concerns about the validity of Westernized diagnostic criteria for immigrants as a group. The Diagnostic and Statistical Manual of Mental Disorders–III-R, like its predecessors, assumes that across cultures and across populations, people manifest psychiatric distress similarly. However, evidence from cross-cultural studies of depression and other mental disorders suggests otherwise (Marsella et al., 1973; Tseng et al., 1986). The DSM-IV, unlike its predecessors, attempted to address specific cultural factors endemic to cross-cultural populations.

COMMONLY ACCEPTED PSYCHOPATHOLOGICAL DISORDERS AMONG IMMIGRANTS

While many disorders are seen in many cultures, the manifestation and acceptance of these disorders are dependent upon cultural values (Draguns, 1987). In general, mood and anxiety disorders are more prevalent and accepted than personality and thought disorders (Gopaul-McNicol, 1993). In most "Third World" countries, repression of one's sexuality creates difficulties that are seen in a more psychosomatic manner, such as vague physical aches, pains, dizziness, upset stomach, stomach gas problems, and nerves. Often these psychosomatic complaints are masking a depressive type of disorder that the individual for cultural reasons is unable to talk about. Most likely, this is because physical complaints are more accepted than psychological ones; most people around the world have not conceptualized psychotherapy in the same manner as Westerners have. In fact, physical complaints elicit much compassion, whereas psychological complaints result in a sense of weakness and failure, especially on the part of men. Thus, secondary gains are often achieved because the person is relieved of his or her responsibilities due to these ailments. Generally, the stresses include spousal abuse, marital tensions, infertility, the death of loved ones, querulous in-laws, defiant children, poverty, and the "evil eye" of family or friends. The response is usually in the form of physical and psychological symptoms that result in psychosomatic ailments, such as heart weakness, bodily aches, digestive problems, sleep disturbance, psychic dissociation, and hysteria. A classic example is captured in the vignette that follows:

Case Example
Mary, a 15-year-old high school student, originally from Barbados, West Indies, was failing four of seven courses. She tried to no avail to explain the situation to her parents. They refused to respond to her concerns that the courses are difficult and, instead, they said that she did not try hard enough. Suddenly she developed many ailments that were diagnosed as "nerves." She was given valium to address the "physical problem." This resulted in complaints of stomach aches, dizziness, and the inability to carry out the usual household chores and school assignments.

Mary's parents were forced to address these physical ailments and were more sensitive to her academic failings. Mary, through these psychosomatic complaints, got her parents to respond to her needs and to be less harsh on her when she did not pass her courses.

Thus, any cross-cultural study on psychopathological disorders should attempt to answer the following questions: Can a direct causal relationship be drawn between an individual's culture and his/her symptoms? If the relationship is not causal, is there some other way in which the culture influences the maintenance and elimination of symptoms? The former question is difficult to answer, because it has always been a compelling task in psychology to state with a high degree of certainty that one variable causes another. When an individual presents for treatment, the therapist is confronted with many aspects of the latter question. For example: In what ways have cultural norms influenced when a person decides to seek treatment? What indigenous treatments exist to deal with the pathology in question? Before addressing these questions, it is necessary to examine the risk factors that can lead to mental stress.

RISK FACTORS FOR THE DEVELOPMENT OF MENTAL DISORDERS

Immigration

Risk factors are those variables or situations that have the potential to make an individual or group of individuals vulnerable to developing a particular disorder. One potential source of stress for the immigrant client is immigration. For some, the very reason for leaving their countries and the means by which they had to leave results in traumatic reactions. The components of stress come from having to flee one's native country because of persecution, often abruptly, possibly with no chance to say good-bye to loved ones, with no opportunity to plan, no means of bringing belongings on the trip, and living in constant fear of discovery.

Another considerable source of stress for immigrants, regardless of their reason for migration, is leaving family members behind. Sometimes anxiety symptoms are not even present until after the family is reunited. Having lived through separation in the past makes any future separation, real or imagined, a very toxic issue (Brice, 1982).

Once an entire family or individual has successfully left the immigrant, made connections in the United States and established a home, other risk factors must be considered during evaluation and therapy. Adjustment disorder with anxious mood is a consideration when assessing reactions to a new home, a new physical environment, strange foods, or unfamiliar and brutal cold weather.

Dressler (1985) has posited another risk factor for stress associated with immigrant status. He suggests that the immigrant's exposure to the American or Western lifestyle without adequate means to access that lifestyle can make one vulnerable to the development of symptoms. In his study he tests the hypothesis that the greater the gap between the lifestyle the immigrant is exposed to and the immigrant's ability to attain that lifestyle, the higher the level of belief in witchcraft and the supernatural. His hypothesis was supported empirically in two of the three groups he examined.

Family Role Changes

Unlike in Western societies, such as the United States where nuclear families operate independently (Saeki & Borow, 1987; Sue & Zane, 1987; Triandis, 1987), among many immigrant families the nuclear family is part of the extended family. To a large extent, relationships with neighbors and institutions such as the church and the school are perceived in a collective, family-like manner, rather than in individualistic terms (Triandis, 1987; Thrasher & Anderson, 1988; Gopaul-McNicol, 1993). Likewise, whereas in Western societies egalitarian structures of power are nurtured and individualistic pursuit of happiness and fulfillment is emphasized (Kim, 1985; Sloan, 1990; Gushue & Sciarra, 1995), often with immigrants, individual desires are suppressed for those of the family and even for the society. In many "Third World" countries, relationships are hierarchical and power is dependent upon age and gender (Gopaul-McNicol, 1993). Parents and elders are highly respected in these societies, unlike in North America where youth takes precedence over the aged. Loyalty and respect for one's elders are emphasized to the extent that it is disrespectful to discuss negative feelings about one's parents to a stranger. Moreover, children are socialized to have a relational community orientation that focuses more on societal commitment than individual development (Brice, 1982; Gopaul-McNicol, 1993). An individual who pursues his or her own personal interest and forsakes the family's goals is perceived as self-centered and avaricious. Thus, the self is defined more with respect to the roles the individual plays in the community and the family, and is less conceived of in individualistic terminologies. Because of this, interpersonal and intrafamilial boundaries are not as clearly defined as they are in North America, and the need for privacy is seen as selfish.

Family therapists often get referrals when the family has been reunited. Such reunification calls into question family roles and family loyalty. Minuchin (1974) has stressed the importance of maintaining optimal family structure. Every family has a structure that provides family members with a blueprint for how to behave and knowledge of what is expected of them. It specifies gender roles (male and female) and generational roles (grandparents, parents, children). Minuchin and other structural family therapists contend that when a structure is altered (i.e., boundaries between generations get blurred or members of one generation assume the duties of another generation), this gives rise to anxiety in the family. The precipitator for the change in structure, the gradualness or abruptness of the change, and the family's accommodation to it are just some of the factors that may influence who becomes the symptom carrier (i.e., the family member who develops a clinical disorder).

Racism

Another risk factor is the experience of racism (Brice-Baker, 1994; Gopaul-McNicol, 1993). Racial discrimination is something that immigrant and African-American people share; however, there are some differences. Immigrant people of color have always been the racial majority in their countries of origin. They did not experience the lynching, the hosings, or the Jim Crow laws that characterized the Black experience in the United States. What both groups have experienced is a definition of who is Black, which has been imposed on them by Whites (Gopaul-McNicol, 1993). For the immigrant, a considerable emphasis is placed on skin color because one's "degree of brownness" has been so inextricably linked to social class. It is shocking for the immigrant on the lighter end of the color continuum to come to the United States and be "relegated" to the lowest rung of society. Anxiety can run high when one realizes that having a lighter shade of skin will not afford him or her any protection from discrimination.

COMMON MISDIAGNOSES AMONG IMMIGRANTS

Cultural factors play an important role in personality assessment. At the clinic of one of the authors, Multicultural Educational & Psychological Services, P.C., there were several incidents in which children's language was misinterpreted. One example is a child who referred to an "eraser" as a "rubber," the term used by the English immigrant to describe an eraser; the school psychologist said the child was being sexual and promiscuous in the testing situation. In another example, an immigrant child said "I can beat him"; the school psychologist did not realize that the child meant "I can win the race," and described the child as aggressive and violent. In assessing the emotional adjustment of immigrant children in the schools, it is necessary to examine the normal acculturation problems that any immigrant child can experience upon entry into the U.S. school system. In making a healthy adjustment to a new school, immigrant children will first tend to draw on their cultural background as a form of reference in the same way that kindergarten students draw on their home experiences. Many immigrant children, when they first arrive, are readjusting to their parents after several years of separation, because children are often left behind with relatives while the parents get established. During this period, children become quite attached to their caretakers, whom they come to know as their parents. When these children are reunited with their natural parents, conflicts arise around such issues as family relations, discipline, and culture. Conflicts also emerge when children are at different adaptation phases than their parents. Immigrant children can face overwhelming problems in school as they contend with the cultural clash between the norms of their country and the expectations in the host country (Goldstein, 1990). In addition, immigrants typically come from homogeneous nations; they are accustomed neither to racial and ethnic diversity nor to the flagrant racism found in the United States. Consequently, it is common for them to experience confusion and cultural conflict. As a general practice, mental health workers ought to conduct culturological assessment of immigrant clients to avoid misdiagnosis.

Several areas of misdiagnoses can result because of these cultural clashes. Anxiety disorders, especially post-traumatic stress disorder, depression, and schizophrenia are the most commonly found misdiagnoses (Gopaul-McNicol, 1993) and, therefore, will be highlighted in this chapter.

Post-Traumatic Stress Disorder or Emotional Disturbance?

Due to natural disasters such as hurricanes and ongoing political unrest in many "Third World" countries, many children enter the United States traumatized. Thomas (1991) has discussed the children's responses to trauma. In summarizing the literature, she stated that "the intrusion of memories and thoughts connected to the traumatic event can cause the child to be distracted from an academic task" (p. 5). Ronstrom (1989) found that some children become hysterical at the sound of loud noises. Thus compounding the already stressful process of migration, these children are faced with memories of violence and death. The behaviors exhibited by children in reaction to these stressors can range from withdrawal to aggression.

Mollica, Wyshak, and Lowelle (1987) emphasized that in spite of the profound stress that these traumatized victims experienced, they have difficulty articulating their trauma-related symptoms because the expression of these trauma-related symptoms can significantly increase their emotional distress. The result can be poor academic work, behavioral problems in school, and more difficulty in acculturation. Unfortunately, these behaviors can be misdiagnosed as emotional disturbance. It is vital that psychologists allow children the time to acculturate, and that they assist in directing families to supportive centers where they can receive educational and psychological services to aid in the cultural transition.

Adjustment Disorder or Depression?

Recently school psychologists have noted an increase in referrals of immigrant children due to "depression." While it is important to be concerned about such symptoms as a lack of interest in social activities, feelings of worthlessness, and depressed mood, it is equally important to bear in mind the DSM-IV criteria for a diagnosis of depression and the stages of acculturation that immigrant children go through. Many culturally diverse children who are referred by the school for therapy because of depressed mood are quite social at home and in their communities. In most countries around the world, children are taught to be quiet in the classroom; North American school officials often misinterpret their respect for the classroom setting as withdrawal, shyness, depression, and so forth. Many immigrant children say that they are amazed at the liberties that are accorded children in the American classroom. It takes time for them to get used to this liberal, unstructured approach. Simply observing these children on the playground should aid in ruling out shyness and withdrawal. A more appropriate diagnosis might be adjustment disorder with depressed mood, since many of these children do not continue to show signs of "withdrawal" for more than six months (according to the DSM-IV, an adjustment disorder cannot have a duration of more than six months). With such patients, as opposed to those with serious depression, the experience is transient and suicidal ideation (if it exists at all) is likely to be anxiety producing. Helping the client cope with the anxieties, and giving practical recommendations for adjusting to life in the United States tends to have good results without resorting to pharmacological treatment. In addition, reassuring clients that their symptoms are probably transient and can be treated by the therapist and the client together is useful.

Pathology or Real-Life Community Experiences?

Another common misdiagnosis is made when examiners are unable to differentiate true experiences told by children given their cultural exposure from symptoms of pathological behaviors. Many children reside in high-risk areas and are exposed to all sorts of violent activities. When such stories reflecting actual experience appear on projective tests, examiners tend to confuse them with pathological signs.

The Community Assessment Measure is an assessment tool that allows the examiner to determine what is important to the members of a particular community or what members of a particular community are exposed to on a continuous basis. So, children who relate many stories of violence and aggression, but are exposed to such violence and hostility in their communities on a daily basis, would not be considered as "having violent ideations" merely by examining their stories on projective tests. This is a reality for these children and, as such, these experiences must be considered before such a diagnosis can be made. In like manner, children who are exposed to drug pushers on a daily basis in their communities and relay stories of drug usage may not really be using drugs themselves. The Community Assessment Measure that follows helps to delineate or differentially diagnose real-life experiences from true pathology.

The Community Assessment Measure

What has been the child's real-life experiences with respect to:

    a. drug exposure?

    b. crime exposure?

    c. natural disasters such as hurricane, floods?

    d. civil wars?

    e. guns and other weapons?

Religious Belief and Its Impact on Personality Assessment

In attempting to understand the causes of mental illness, many immigrants, especially those from Eastern cultures and immigrant islands, rarely invoke psychological explanations. On the contrary, mental illness is attributed to some form of spiritual restlessness meted out to the individual via a vengeful spirit. Many cultures believe in some form of witchcraft that can be worked on someone by an enemy to cause various forms of harm, usually out of envy, or to take revenge. Folk belief says that when a person is "possessed," a spirit enters the individual's body, so that the behavior of the person becomes the behavior of the spirit. It is felt that the more suggestible a person is, the more likely he or she is to become "possessed."

Philippe and Romain (1979) found that females are more likely than males to become "possessed." Folk beliefs are deeply embedded in the culture and can exert a profound influence on people's lives. Many individuals, women and children in particular, wear a guard (a chain with a large cross on it), receive spiritual baths (herbal bath with holy water), and have a priest or minister bless the home, or even throw salt around the house to protect themselves from these evil forces. These beliefs are accepted by most sectors of society, transcending race, class, age, and gender.

Over the past ten years, we have seen several of our clients go to a spiritist while simultaneously seeking psychological help. For example, a woman had sought therapy because her sons had suddenly begun to misbehave "as soon as my mother-in-law had moved into the house." Because her mother-in-law had never accepted her, she attributed the children's misbehavior to her mother-in-law's "evil eye." She talked openly about her suspicions, assuming that the therapist not only understood but would be able to help her in exorcising the children. When the role of a psychologist was explained to her, she was very disappointed that the therapist would not even be able to accompany her to the spiritist. She felt that the problem with her sons was not a psychological one, but a spiritual one. Given the intensity of her belief, it was recommended that she seek the counsel of a spiritist first and then resume therapy later if the negative behavior of her sons continued after the "bad spirits" were removed from them. She was receptive to this idea and more trusting of the psychological treatment process after she had taken the children to the spiritual healer.

Thus, a therapist who hears a parent say, "My child is not conforming because an evil spirit is on him," and then sees the child wearing a guard, should not be alarmed. Similarly, when a woman from a Caribbean country attributes her husband's infidelity or lack of familial interest to someone who "gave him something to eat that has him tottlebey [stupid]," she is expressing a cultural assessment of her husband's behavior.

The individual who says "I see the evil spirit in my house" or "the evil spirit talked to me," is not necessarily hallucinating. Likewise, someone who says "God came to me and told me to give up my job, so I did" is not necessarily delusional. If mental health professionals are not aware of the folk culture system, they may misdiagnose a client or devalue or demean folk culturological behaviors. The major challenge for therapists in assessing psychiatric problems in immigrant families is to try to determine the difference between "being possessed" and true mental illness.

Differential Diagnosis: Spirit Possession or Schizophrenia

When dealing with immigrants, the area of most confusion is in the accurate assessment of schizophrenia, particularly paranoid schizophrenia. To make a differential diagnosis, it is first necessary to do a thorough historical assessment of the individual's psychosocial, behavioral, and cognitive functioning. Schizophrenics often exhibit dysfunctions in thought, form, perceptions, affect, sense of self, interpersonal functioning, and psychomotor behavior. To be given a diagnosis of schizophrenia, at least two of the following elements must have existed for at least six months: delusions, hallucinations, incoherence or marked loosening of associations, catatonic behavior, or flat or grossly inappropriate affect. In addition, functioning in such areas as work, self-care, and social relations must be markedly low. Lefley (1979) found that the responses of "possessed" victims reflected little of the impulsiveness, lability, and free-flowing emotionality that characterizes schizophrenia. In fact while "their consciousness is altered, it is not dissociated in the form of a split personality" as is commonly seen with schizophrenics (Lefley, 1979). Schizophrenia is generally treated with antipsychotic drugs, which are useful for eliminating delusions and hallucinations, and alleviating thought disorder.

Many immigrants, while acculturating, may exhibit psychotic symptoms due to situational stress. Folk beliefs are patterns of learned social behavior (through constant exposure from childhood) that people have been conditioned to believe. These beliefs are culturally sanctioned and are even considered to be spiritually uplifting experiences. "Possession is not abnormal, it is normal" (Wittkower, 1964). For people who endorse the spiritual unrest view, the duration can range from one day to several years. Many people from culturally diverse backgrounds believe a spiritist can remove the evil spirit and free the individual from an "evil force." Therefore, whereas schizophrenics have difficulty eradicating the psychosis, the "possessed" ought not do so.

▶ 7

Teaching Linguistically and Culturally Diverse Children

Many educators believe that children learn better when students' learning styles and teachers' instructional styles are matched. Current research has documented that when students are taught in environments and with strategies that match their learning styles, they achieve statistically higher test and aptitude scores and demonstrate better behaviors than when their styles are mismatched with the environment or teaching strategy (Hickson, Land, & Aikman, 1994). Learning styles refers to the manner in which each individual absorbs and retains information or skills (Dunn & Dunn, 1978); the way a person perceives, thinks, solves problems, learns, and relates to others (Hayes, 1992). Knowing that learning differences in the educational environment can enhance student success in schools can have an impact on reducing referrals to special education, improving low achievement, and lowering the high drop-out rate among culturally and linguistically diverse students (Hickson et al., 1994).

It is clear that the education afforded to linguistically and culturally diverse students is ineffective when one considers the high drop-out rate, grade retention, and the overrepresentation of these students in special education classes. The overall dropout rate for African Americans in 1988 was 12.6 percent, and for Hispanics/Latinos, it was 32.2 percent in 1986 (Gay, 1993). In addition to social conditions that may foster poor school achievement, cultural discontinuity is also believed to be a major factor. Most teachers do not teach culturally and linguistically diverse students how to survive and succeed in school; for example, they do not know how to study across cultural learning styles, how to adjust their talking style to accommodate school expectation, and how to identify and adjust to the procedural rules for functioning in different instructional classrooms (Gay, 1993). Frequently, the culture of these children does not reflect the culture of the school. Cultural diversity is one of the most important factors on which teachers should focus, because it has a significant influence on how students approach the learning process (Shade & New, 1993). The work of researchers such as Boykin (1982), Tharp and Gallimore (1988), and Heath (1983) revealed a subtle interplay between a school's ways of knowing, talking, thinking, and behaving and those of students from diverse cultural and linguistic backgrounds (Viadero, 1996).

This chapter will examine the learning styles of culturally and linguistically diverse students and the teaching strategies that have been successful with this population. Learning styles are greatly influenced by cultural beliefs and values, and these influences are visible in the classroom in several areas: communication, behavior, information processing, and social interaction. All of these are important components to what we call learning styles. To understand the impact of incompatible learning and teaching styles on student achievement, we must first understand the expectations of a typical American classroom.

AMERICAN CLASSROOM EXPECTATIONS

In most classrooms throughout the United States, teachers have clear and definite expectations of how students should behave, dress, learn, communicate, and socialize. These expectations, or norms, are culturally determined, and they are reinforced by society. A Eurocentric orientation provides the framework for these expectations or norms, and the influence of this orientation is also apparent in the school curriculum, instructional strategies, and instructional materials used by American teachers.

Behavioral Styles

In describing the code of behavior and norms of a typical American classroom, Hickson et al., (1994) indicated that school culture requires conformity, passivity, quietness, teacher-focused activities, individualized orientation, and competitive noninteractive participation of students. The classroom environment is generally structured, controlled, fast-paced, and sedate. For example, teachers expect their students to sit quietly and attentively, to follow directions, to raise their hands if they have questions, to complete assignments on their own or with minimal teacher assistance, and to be motivated by their own success or through competition with their peers. Students who do not conform to these norms stand out as deviant. They are frequently punished, chastised, suspended, labeled, placed on behavioral management programs, referred to special education, and viewed negatively by teachers and school principals. Behavioral styles that differ from those of the mainstream culture are often misunderstood, and the incompatibility between the behavioral style of the school and that proscribed by the student's culture interferes with the learning process and the student's social and emotional adjustment in school. Educators have been slow to recognize and accept that their own cultural background and the culture of the school have a bearing on learning (Viadero, 1996). Moreover, educators frequently do not think of culturally and linguistically diverse students as having a culture that is distinct and valid; they view these students as deficient (Viadero, 1996).

Shade and New (1993) submit that teachers generally described African-American children as not conforming to the behavioral norms of the schools. In a survey of teachers nationwide, Shade and New (1993) found that many teachers subscribe to the following beliefs about African-American students: (a) They have difficulty remaining in their seats and are constantly moving around the classroom talking with their classmates. (b) They seem to lack self-control, because they often fail to raise their hands to answer questions. (c) They are unable or unwilling to complete class assignments without direct teacher assistance. (d) They are excessively active (Shade & New, 1993). These findings are not surprising when one considers that many self-contained special education classes throughout the United States are filled with African-American boys classified as "emotionally disturbed/behaviorally disordered."

Boykin's (1982) work in an African-American community identified a vibrancy and a centrality of physical stimulation that he called "verve." Boykin (1982) defined verve as a particular receptiveness to relatively high levels of sensate stimulation. For example, African-American homes are packed with stimulation: The television is going while music is playing; there is movement all around with people talking loudly, playing, dancing, and cooking. According to Boykin (1982), African-American children generally are raised in environments that teach them to expect a variety of environmental interactions and stimulation with constant change of focus and interest (Shade & New, 1993). They perceive the school environment as monotonous, and thus interject some variety by ceasing to work and by looking and walking around the classroom (Shade & New, 1993, p. 319). When African-American children are provided with varied tasks, they do better (Boykin, 1982). Richardson (1993) emphasizes that the African-American culture exists as a significant socializing force for

African-American children, and because culture is learned, it is essential to investigate the nature of teaching and learning styles associated with that culture.

Communication Styles

In a typical American classroom, teachers speak to their students in a rather moderate volume, and to many non-English speakers, American teachers speak rapidly. Teachers expect their students to know how to listen, to decipher nonverbal messages, and to follow directions independently. Approval is demonstrated by either patting the child on the head or back, smiling with the child, or by verbalizing (e.g., "good job," "excellent work"). Additionally, the traditional school culture expects some distance between communicants and direct visual contact when speaking to each other (Shade & New, 1993).

Teachers and students must be able to effectively communicate so that instruction can lead to learning. Students must be able to both understand the teacher's verbal messages as well as the nonverbal ones, and teachers must do the same when communicating with their students. If the messages received and provided by both parties are inaccurate, misunderstandings occur. Teachers from White middle-class society may assume that certain behaviors or norms of communicating are universal and hold similar meaning for everyone. This belief is central to many difficulties that teachers report when working with linguistically and culturally diverse students. Dunn et al. (1990) emphasizes that communication styles are strongly correlated with race, culture, ethnicity, and gender. They include such behaviors as eye contact, gestures, tone, inflection, and posture, which may enhance or negate the content of a message (Sue & Sue, 1990). Sue and Sue (1990) believe that communication styles are manifested in nonverbal communication, and they concentrated on four aspects of nonverbal communication: proxemics (interpersonal space in social interaction); kinesics (bodily movement in communication—smile, eye contact, hand movement); paralanguage (vocal characteristics in communication—volume, pauses, rate, inflection, silence, turn-taking); and high–low context communication. Communication that relies on words or the verbal content of messages is called low context; communication that relies less on verbal messages and more on nonverbal messages is called high context.

Goldman (1980) observed that in the United States individuals seem to become uncomfortable when others stand too close, rather than too far away. When individuals feel that their personal space has been violated, it generates feelings of anger, flight, and fear (Baron & Needle, 1980). How much space is appropriate between individuals is determined by culture. For example, Latinos tend to prefer little distance between individuals. When interacting with a Latino student, a teacher could misinterpret the student's close stance as an invasion of personal space and may feel that the student is aggressive, pushy, or socially inappropriate. Parents socialize their children based on cultural practices and teach them when to make eye contact, for how long, and with whom, or even teach them when to smile. For example, in mainstream American culture, many positive attributes are associated with individuals who smile (e.g., good personality, pleasant, warm, intelligent); however, many Asians believe that smiling may suggest weakness or feelings of embarrassment, discomfort, or shyness (Sue & Sue, 1990). Sue and Sue (1990) pointed out that in the Asian culture, silence is traditionally a sign of respect for elders, a sign of politeness, and not an indication that the speaker no longer wishes to speak. Teachers of linguistically and culturally diverse students may interpret reticence in speaking out as a sign of ignorance, lack of motivation, or ineffective teaching when, depending on the student's cultural upbringing, he or she may be showing proper respect (Sue & Sue, 1990).

Even such factors as volume and intensity of speech in conversation are influenced by culture (Sue & Sue, 1990). In some cultures, individuals speak loudly, and this may not indicate that they are angry; conversely, in other cultures individuals speak softly, and this does not indicate that they are shy or have a speech impediment (Sue & Sue, 1990). However, if teachers are not aware of these cultural differences, they may misjudge the behaviors of their students. They may feel fearful or threatened by students who speak loudly or stand too close to them. For example, a group of African-American students enrolled in a predominantly White school were confused and angered by the frequent suspensions they were levied for talking loudly and moving around on the school bus (Viadero, 1996). When the students were taught to converse in a manner that did not appear to White teachers and students as if they were arguing, their suspensions ceased (Viadero, 1996). Teachers and students can behave in very different ways, and these behaviors communicate distinct messages. Because the communication process is paramount to teaching and learning interaction (Shade & New, 1993), teachers must be aware of the communication styles of their students so that they do not misinterpret their messages, and to provide a pedagogical atmosphere where students are comfortable.

Learning Styles

Cultural factors impact on how students from different cultural milieus prefer to function, learn, concentrate, and perform while completing academic tasks (Hickson et al., 1994). Unfortunately, in most classrooms throughout the United States, teachers have not incorporated instructional strategies that recognize and accommodate differences in learning styles. Differences in learning styles refers to the distinct individual and group preferences for learning under certain environmental conditions, instructional strategies, and cognitive and processing medium. For example, some children prefer to work with other children, while others are more comfortable with the teacher's direction. Students express individual and group needs for bright or soft illumination, warm or cool temperatures, seating arrangements, mobility, or grouping preference in the classroom (Dunn et al., 1990). Identifying learning styles as a basis for providing responsive instruction is even more crucial now as teachers meet the educational needs of a linguistically and culturally diverse student population (Dunn et al., 1990). Unfortunately, the current practice in most classrooms is that learning style preferences are rarely considered in a systematic way (Hickson et al., 1994). Scholars in this area do not recommend that instruction be guided primarily or solely by learning styles, but rather that teachers should make decisions regarding units within which style differences can be incorporated.

LEARNING STYLES AND CULTURAL INFLUENCES

Learning styles overlap significantly with cultural background and gender, and although not every member of a cultural or gender group learns in the same manner, patterns exist in how members of different groups tend to approach tasks (Grant & Sleeter, 1989). According to Grant and Sleeter (1989), these patterns are the product of such factors as childrearing practices, cultural beliefs and norms, and the role proscriptions that children are expected to fill as adults (Fennema & Peterson, 1987; Hale, 1982). However, the idea of identifying learning styles and recognizing their ties to cultural backgrounds should not be generalized (Grant & Sleeter, 1989), because significant differences occur within each culture, socioeconomic strata, and gender (Dunn et al., 1990). Learning styles can also be defined as the range of instructional strategies through which an individual typically pursues the act of learning (Dunn & Dunn, 1978). It must be noted that purposeful mismatching of students' learning styles and teachers' teaching styles can be positive under certain circumstances. For example, Smith and Renzulli (1984) reported that when impulsive children are placed with reflective teachers, children can become more reflective. However, this type of purposeful mismatching should be done with caution and good planning. Grant and Sleeter (1989) discussed several patterns used by students when approaching learning:

Working Alone versus Working with Others

Dunn et al. (1990) posited that the influence of students' social preference affects their achievement in school. There are students who work best cooperatively with a partner or in small groups; others prefer to learn by themselves with appropriate resources; and others work best directly with their teachers

(Dunn et al., 1989; Grant & Sleeter, 1989). For example, research in this area seems to support the view that African-American students improve greatly and derive significant social and academic benefits under cooperative learning conditions (Haynes & Gebreyesus, 1992).

Cognitive Processing and Perceptual Modalities

Students respond more readily and positively to material when their preferred mode of reception is used in presenting information to be learned (Shade & New, 1993). Two types of perceptual styles are discussed in the research: field-dependence and field-independence. Field-dependent learners are those who are able to see details only in relation to the whole (Chamberlain & Medinos-Landurand, 1991). Field-independent learners are those who can draw out specific details from complex patterns regardless of the whole; they are relatively uninfluenced by the surrounding field (Smith, 1992). This type of learner performs better when allowed to develop their own strategies in nonsocial problem-solving domains. Field-dependent learners, on the other hand, tend to view things more globally, interact more cooperatively, and pay more attention to the social context in which tasks are framed (Zanger, 1991). These individuals are primarily influenced by their surroundings (Hayes, 1992). Research suggests that field-dependent learners prefer to interact with the teacher, and learn better when some structure, mediation plans, or strategy is provided for them (Hayes, 1992). Researchers have found that many African-American students tend to be field-dependent learners; Mexican Americans and Hmong or Laotian immigrants have also been found to be field-dependent learners (Shade & New, 1993; Hvitfeldt, 1986). Many Native-American students, however, tend to be field-independent (Utley, 1983). This processing framework has been challenged by others (Ovando & Collier, 1985), but it is worth mentioning because research in this area has been inconclusive.

Cognitive processing refers to how individuals interpret and learn new information. Two cognitive processing styles have been identified: verbal/analytic processing (descriptive-analytic) and visual/holistic (inferential-categorical). In the verbal/analytic processing style, the whole is revealed through the unfolding of the units (Tharp, 1989). This type of learner prefers to split stimuli into discrete entities and to respond to them as separate units (Hayes, 1992). In the visual/holistic cognitive style, the pieces derive their meaning from the pattern of the whole (Tharp, 1989). These learners tend to group stimuli on the basis of inferences made about the stimuli that are categorized as a whole, and classification is based on a broader or central concept (Hayes, 1992). For example, many scholars have observed that African-American students are raised in an environment where they are taught to be flexible and adaptable in their use of language, and to use creative verbal play that includes metaphors and similes (Shade & New, 1993; Hanna,

1988; Kochman, 1981). Moreover, these students are taught to analyze a physical object or information holistically rather than as an accumulation of attributes or units; however, these skills are neglected or dismissed by the instructional strategies used in most American schools (Shade & New, 1993). Children who learn via a learning style other than verbal/analytic will not only be poor achievers early in school, but they will also become worse as they move to higher grades (Hale-Benson, 1982, p. 31). According to Hale-Benson (1982), schools not only reward the development of the verbal/ analytical style of processing information, but the overall ideology and environment reinforces behaviors associated with that style (p. 34)—to remain seated for long periods of time, to concentrate alone on stimuli that might be culturally irrelevant, and to observe and value organized time allotment schedules (Cohen, 1969, p. 830).

Competition versus Cooperation

Teachers often use competition to encourage and motivate students to do their best. However, in many students' cultural traditions, cooperation is valued over competition. For example, in the Navajo cultural tradition, as in many Native Americans', individuals do not compete with each other; rather, they measure themselves against their own performance (Smith, 1992). Consequently, a child in a race may slow down to allow others to catch up; children have also been observed to misspell words in a spelling bee in order to help the other child save face (Smith, 1992). Most competition-oriented incentives often used in American schools are counterproductive, because the Navajo culture does not reward winning at the expense of one's peers (Smith, 1992; Swisher & Deyhle, 1989). Similarly, many other cultures are not particularly motivated or encouraged by competition. For example, African-American, Hispanic/Latino, and Hawaiian students often seek achievement in a context and for the purpose of family and peer-group solidarity and acceptance, rather than for their own sake or personal gain (Gallimore, Tharp, Sloat, Klein, & Troy, 1982). Because some children are cooperatively oriented, some are competitive oriented, and some are individualistically oriented, teachers must change the manner in which school activities are typically structured by adding the option of cooperative activities to basic learning experiences, in addition to individualistic and competitive activities (Zanger, 1991).

Structured versus Nonstructured

Some students work best once they are provided with structure. They need a framework in which to operate, otherwise they have difficulty making sense of information or completing their assignments. Other students prefer to create their own structure (Grant & Sleeter, 1989), finding structured work nonchallenging. Teachers must be able to identify the needs of their students and make appropriate instructional accommodations.

Passivity versus Mobility

Dunn and Dunn (1978) argue that one element of learning styles is the need for physical activity or movement. In some students, physical activity enhances learning. Other students prefer passivity. In fact, no amount of persuasion can change certain students' interest in movement (Fitt, 1975). The need for mobility in some students can lead teachers to refer these students to psychologists because they suspect attention deficit disorder. However, these students do not exhibit all the clinical behaviors associated with true attention deficit disorder; they simply have a propensity to move around the classroom while they learn. In reviewing the research on discipline and ethnicity, it becomes clear that culturally and linguistically diverse students get referred more often for disciplinary actions than White children (Lorion & Filner, 1986). Differences in behavioral styles can lead to misinterpretation of a child's behavior. Morgan (1980) suggests that some African-American children are able to quell their motor responses; however, those who are not able to do so are usually in lower-income levels, are labeled disruptive, and are placed in classes where cognitive expectations are low.

As discussed earlier, Boykin (1983) noted that African-American homes provide an abundance of stimulation, intensity, and variation. This type of stimulating home environment produces greater psychological and behavioral "verve" in African-American children than in White children in a middle-class setting. According to Boykin (1983), African-American children have an increased behavioral vibrancy and an increased psychological need for stimulus change and intensity (Hale-Benson, 1982). They strive in academic settings that are dynamic and interactive, and need to move about in the classroom and prefer to learn using a variety of modalities. Boykin (1983) indicated that African-American children may learn better with instructional strategies that incorporate body movement into the learning process and when a variety of stimuli or formats are used.

EFFECTIVE TEACHING STRATEGIES FOR CULTURALLY AND LINGUISTICALLY DIVERSE STUDENTS

Tharp (1989) recognized that the typical mainstream American classroom primarily employs a whole-class organization, with rank-and-file seating, and a teacher who instructs the entire class. This is followed by individual practice, and then teacher-prepared assessment. This strategy has not been found to be the most effective for students from culturally and linguistically diverse backgrounds (Tharp, 1989) because it is not sensitive to students' experiential background and learning styles. Research suggests that accommodation of learning style preference through complementary instructional approaches or skills training can improve student achievement, attitudes toward learning, and retention of information taught (Grimes, 1995; Dunn & Dunn, 1978; Mickler & Zippert, 1987). When children are allowed to learn academic skills through their preferred learning modalities, they tend to achieve statistically higher test and attitude scores than when instruction is incompatible with their preferences (Dunn et al., 1989). Research investigating effective instructional strategies for culturally and linguistically diverse students has identified a number of interventions that have demonstrated some success: cooperative learning, comprehension development, language development and support in content areas, whole-group mastery learning, learning strategies, computer-assisted instruction, remedial programs with a tutorial component, and culturally familiar instructional materials.

Cooperative Learning

Slavin (1988/1990) conceded that there is wide agreement among researchers that cooperative methods usually have positive effects on student achievement. At the elementary and middle schools level especially, cooperative learning strategies that incorporate group goals and individual accountability accelerate student learning significantly. Cooperative learning has even demonstrated consistently positive effects on intergroup relations, and it improves the social acceptance of mainstreamed students with special needs (Slavin, 1988/1990). In addition, cooperative learning methods can also increase self-esteem, attitude toward school, time spent on school assignments, and attendance (Slavin, 1988/1990). Cooperative learning is a way of organizing small groups in a class setting to facilitate learning (Slavin, 1988). In this instructional strategy, students learn as they work together and assume responsibility for their own learning and the learning of their classmates in the group (Haynes & Gebreyesus, 1992). Three concepts are central to cooperative learning approaches: team rewards, individual accountability, and equal opportunities for success (Slavin, 1988). Student Team Learning (STL) is a cooperative learning approach developed by Slavin (1990) and his colleagues at Johns Hopkins University. STL has demonstrated impressive success in helping improve classroom participation and achievement of many groups of students in various settings (Levine, 1994). This approach employs a number of instructional techniques in which students work in four- or five-member learning teams and receive recognition based on the extent to which all team members complete and master a common set of skills (Levine, 1994). Slavin

(1990) and Levine (1994) noted that studies of STL have shown positive results in reading, mathematics, social studies, and science when implemented well. Other cooperative learning approaches that have also shown a promising degree of success include Team-Assisted Individualization (TAI) and Cooperative Integrated Reading and Composition (CIRC).

Comprehension Development

The development of strong, higher-order comprehension and thinking skills is conducive to good achievement in school (Tharp, 1989). A number of instructional techniques have been developed and refined to effectively develop comprehension and thinking skills of students whose performance has been unsatisfactory in reading, history, mathematics, science, and other areas (Levine, 1994). These instructional strategies include use of semantic webbing and mapping, inferencing and prediction techniques, summarization guidelines, and graphic organizers (Levine 1994). Review of research employing these strategies to improve higher-order comprehension and thinking skills has yielded favorable results that document impressive gains in the performance of students, particularly that of low-achieving students' (Levine, 1994).

Language Development

Communication skills are essential to school achievement; oral language facility is prerequisite to success in reading and writing (Soldier, 1989). Educational research is revealing the interrelatedness of language, thinking, values, and culture (Tharp, 1989). Language development at all levels is imperative, and must be a goal for the entire school day (Tharp, 1989). Students must be provided with the type of linguistic support that facilitates comprehension of material even in the content areas. To strengthen students' linguistic skills, teachers should:

1. Adjust the language demands of the lesson by modifying speech rate and tone, using context clues and models, and relating instruction to students' experiences (Parker, 1987; Northcutt & Watson, 1986)
2. Incorporate second-language acquisition principles with traditional teaching methodology to increase understanding of lessons (Krashen, 1982)
3. Bridge the gap between teachers' own language abilities and the listening skills of their students by preteaching vocabulary (Watson, Northcutt, & Rydell, 1989):
   a. Words used to explain the lesson
   b. Words necessary to understand the content of the lesson

4. Use lesson format repeatedly, so the student can understand what is expected and how the teacher is presenting the information (Watson et al., 1989)
5. Engage students through the use of visuals and manipulatives that clearly illustrate the concept and bring the lesson to life (Watson et al., 1989)
6. Have students generate prediction questions, because by predicting what will happen next, students create models for understanding and become more engaged in their learning (Watson et al., 1989)
7. Make extensive use of contextual clues (Crawford, 1987)
8. Base content on students' communicative needs (Crawford, 1987)
9. Use cooperative learning strategies

Whole-Group Mastery Learning

Levine (1994) points out five steps that are important to the whole-group mastery learning approach:

1. Define a specific learning objective
2. Teach the understanding or skills embodied in the objective
3. Use a criterion-referenced test to assess mastery
4. Provide corrective instruction for underachieving students, and enrichment or acceleration for students who have mastered the objective
5. Retest those students who received corrective instruction

According to Levine (1994), gains in academic performance can be magnified when the whole-group mastery learning approach is combined with the following:

1. Enhancement of students' initial skills on concepts prerequisite to the instruction
2. Provision of appropriate cues and feedback
3. Emphasis on students' active participation
4. Work with parents to improve the home learning environment

When implemented appropriately, the whole-group mastery learning approach can produce large gains in student achievement, not just for mastery of factual information but also for higher-order learning (Levine, 1994).

Learning Strategies/Study Skills

Weinstein and Mayer (1989) broadly defined learning strategies as behaviors or thoughts that facilitate learning. Learning strategies are under the learner's control and can be modified through interventions (Pintrich & Johnson, 1990).

These strategies include study skills such as underlining a main idea, and complex thought processes such as using analogies to relate prior knowledge to new information (Weinstein, Ridley, Dahl, & Weber, 1989). Grimes (1995) suggests that the combination of learning style and learning-study strategy assessment can provide diagnostic, prescriptive information to assist in understanding the educational needs of students. One effective learning strategy attempts to create a meaningful connection between what they already know and what they are attempting to learn (Weinstein et al., 1989). This strategy is called elaboration, and it uses what the student knows (e.g., prior knowledge, experiences, attitudes, beliefs, and values) to help make sense of what the student is trying to learn (Weinstein et al., 1989). Elaboration can be accomplished by creating analogies; paraphrasing; summarizing in one's words; transforming the information into another form such as a chart, graph, or diagram; applying the new information; using compare-and-contrast methods; drawing inferences or conclusions; and trying to teach what one is learning to a classmate (Weinstein, et al., 1989).

Computer-Assisted Instruction

Researchers have explored the possibility of using computers and other modern technologies to improve thinking skills and comprehension among students from culturally and linguistically diverse backgrounds (Levine, 1994), and they have identified the following guidelines and practices that can help educators accomplish this goal (p. 48):

1. Concentrate on comprehension and meaning
2. Place some emphasis on writing and publishing
3. Select software that is interesting and challenging
4. Examine and analyze text structures
5. Use content from a range of subject areas
6. Link reading to writing
7. Ensure cross-grade continuity
8. Provide massive staff development to build teacher commitment to and skill in introducing technologies
9. Have teachers attend computer laboratory classes with their students
10. Provide individual help to make sure students use the technology properly

Remedial Programs

Although supplementary and remedial programs, such as those provided in special education, show very little effectiveness, remedial tutoring programs do show evidence of effectiveness (Slavin & Madden, 1989). The most effective remedial programs involve one-to-one tutoring; use intensive, systematic and structured instructional materials (e.g., teacher's manual, lesson guides, supportive materials); and frequently assess student progress and adapt instruction to students' needs (Slavin & Madden, 1989).

Familiarity with Instructional Material

There seems to be a difference in the quality of comprehension when readers are more or less culturally familiar with the text (Smith, 1992; Johnson, 1982). In 1990, Pritchard found differences in the strategies employed by proficient readers when the text was more culturally familiar. Pritchard (1990) concluded that when reading culturally unfamiliar materials, readers lack the relevant experience to fully comprehend the material, resulting in fewer connections to prior knowledge and greater ambiguity. The classroom must reflect students' culture through the display of pictures, books, articles, and other materials consistent with their home lives (Soldier, 1989). Hoover and Collier (1989) caution teachers when selecting instructional materials. They stressed that teachers must be aware of potential biases that may exist within both printed and graphic material. Lemlech (1984) identified several issues that must be considered when determining whether potential bias exists in educational material: (a) stereotyping cultures or ethnic groups, (b) religious and gender bias, (c) expression of diversity, (d) specific material about culturally and linguistically diverse groups, and (e) portrayal of the interrelationship among diverse groups. Teachers must strive to obtain a match between instructional materials and the experiential and cultural background of the students.

SUMMARY

Cultural beliefs, practices, and values help mold and shape students' learning styles. The learning, behavior, and communication styles of culturally and linguistically diverse students often conflict with those of the classroom that is influenced by the mainstream culture. Research has identified a number of instructional strategies that have demonstrated some measure of effectiveness with linguistically and culturally diverse students: cooperative learning methods, language development, learning strategies, intensive remedial tutoring programs, and familiarity with instructional materials.

▶ 8

Issues in Counseling Immigrant Families

When counseling immigrant families, it is first necessary to examine several cultural issues that may impact on treatment:

1. The concept of mental illness and psychotherapy among immigrants
2. Therapeutic alliance
3. The effects of family-role changes and disciplinary practices on acculturation
4. The obligations of children to their parents
5. Language/communication patterns and their impact on acculturation
6. Legal status
7. Ethnicity
8. The race, gender, and culture of the therapist
9. Whether the family has acculturated or is in transition

CONCEPT OF MENTAL ILLNESS AND PSYCHOTHERAPY AMONG IMMIGRANTS

Due to a lack of exposure to and familiarity with the field of mental health in their home countries, many immigrants generally do not readily accept psychotherapy. They tend to seek the help of a psychotherapist as a last resort. Another impediment to accepting psychotherapy is the social stigma attached to it. Most people from "lesser developed countries" believe that a person is either normal or "crazy," and only "crazy" people seek psychotherapeutic help. Few understand that there is a continuum of behaviors between these two points, and that belief that intervention may prevent things from worsening. For all these reasons, an immigrant family may not seek treatment from mental health workers. Only after all internal family measures and the help of ministers and/or spiritists have failed do they enter therapy, then feeling ashamed and conquered. The therapist must be sensitive to all of these issues if therapy is to be successful. The therapist can assist the family by demystifying the concept of mental illness, while at the same time respecting this deep-seated cultural belief.

THERAPEUTIC ALLIANCE

In a successful therapeutic alliance, one must begin exploring the process by examining the client's expectations of the therapist, and vice versa. Many people from culturally diverse backgrounds tend to perceive the therapist as an expert, a sort of problem solver who can guide the family in the right direction. The therapist, like the teacher and the medical doctor, is seen as an authority figure and is respected.

However, if the therapist does not fulfill the expectations of the family, he or she may lose their respect, and treatment may be terminated. In general, many families from "Third World countries" want a psychotherapist to be active and directive, yet personal, warm, empathetic, and respectful of the family's structure and boundaries. Being active and directive does not mean telling clients what to do or how to live their lives, nor does it mean being too blunt and insensitive; rather, it means taking initiative and directing the process of the session. For example, the therapist may give some direction as to which family member will speak first; in keeping with the traditional family structure, the husband ought to be addressed first, then the wife, and then the children, according to their ages. If the wife is doing most of talking, the therapist should attempt to assist the husband in commenting on her statements. If he is in agreement with his wife, the therapist can mention this to reinforce their unity. At times, the man's silence may be indicative of his quiet strength and the respect he has for his wife's ability to understand the problems of their children. If he disagrees with her, the therapist can point out the validity of different perspectives and different solutions, while attempting to address the problems.

In most countries, people rarely initiate therapy because of marital problems. Those who do so tend to be more acculturated to American society. Most families who seek help do so because of a child's problem for which a medical doctor was unable to find a physiological cause. The alliance with children in therapy depends on their ages. With adolescents, it is important to remember that they may have difficulty speaking in front of their parents, especially their fathers, particularly if the topics discussed include drugs, sex, home conflicts, and school problems. It is important and beneficial to hear the adolescent's concerns in private. It is equally important to convince the parents of the importance of doing this. Many immigrant parents will not automatically respect or even understand this need for confidentiality; for them confidentiality is neither a right nor a given. But if they believe that part of solving the problem involves the acceptance of this process, they will be conciliatory to the therapist's request that they leave the room. Some parents will feel betrayed, however, because, for the most part, they expect the therapist to assume a parental manner. The goal, of course, should be to help the adolescent to express his or her concerns to the parents and to find ways in which children and parents can forge a compromise.

In initiating and maintaining a relationship with a client, it may also help to make home visits, which personalizes the relationship and increases trust. Moreover, in establishing a successful therapeutic alliance, a bit of self-disclosure (but not too much) is helpful, because it gives the family some perspective on the therapist. This does not mean telling one's life story or becoming too casual; but if questioned, it may be helpful to reveal enough so the family sees the "human side" of the therapist.

It is important for the family to feel that they can disagree with the therapist. Because immigrants tend to confer much respect on a therapist once trust has been established, it is difficult for them to express anger or criticism toward the therapist, especially if the therapist has been helpful in resolving some family conflicts, because obligation was thus incurred. The therapist must be responsive to nonverbal cues, such as changes in facial expression, sudden silence, or changes in vocal inflection, all of which may be indirect indicators that someone is angry or not in agreement and is trying to suppress his or her feelings. Such suppression of feelings is also noted among lower-status individuals toward higher-status individuals in the family. It is likely that this reluctance to open up may result in the family's terminating treatment without even telling the therapist why.

In general, to establish a successful therapeutic alliance, it is necessary to explore the cultural strengths of the family, demonstrate a caring attitude, and be directive, warm, and "human," but not overly friendly. In addition, it is best to be flexible with respect to home visits.

Resistance: The Concept of Time and Family Secrets

In spite of all attempts to foster a therapeutic alliance, many immigrant families remain resistant to therapy. Two concepts, in particular, impact on resistance from the immigrant family—time and family secrets. Lack of observance of scheduled appointment times is a major concern in therapy with immigrant families, who do not have the same concept of time as North Americans. In fact, in many cultures, the people endorse the adages "better late than never." Besides, in many cultures, people often visit friends to socialize at any time, without having received an invitation or without calling. Because of the informality of their homelands, many clients miss appointments or appear at unscheduled times, expecting to be seen. It is important for the therapist to explain the process of treatment and that timeliness is important, because if they are not punctual they will have less therapy time for the same money that they are spending. This will be quite effective, because in spite of their tardiness, immigrants give priority to job demands and will not sacrifice work for therapy; they take very seriously the aphorism "time is money." However, such behavior does not necessarily reflect resistance to therapy. A therapist may, therefore, have to be flexible in scheduling treatment, so that therapy does not interfere with educational or work opportunities. If treatment results in the loss of money for the family or individual, they may become resistant and resentful.

Although immigrants may come to psychotherapy, sharing real family secrets is a different issue. Secrets are to be kept within the family unit. Every child is told very early, "Do not put our business on the street." Therefore, openly and freely discussing personal and family issues with a stranger is often very difficult. Many immigrant families also tend to deny family problems because they believe there is nothing that they cannot solve from within the family. They indulge in much circumlocution, especially in the initial stages of therapy. Thus, unless the therapist has clinical evidence that maintaining secrets is hindering the therapeutic process, the therapist is advised particularly in the initial stages to proceed on the assumption that keeping secrets may merely be a maneuver to keep boundaries in place. Pushing the family to tell their secrets too early in therapy may provoke mistrust and resistance, thus jeopardizing the therapist's position.

In general, immigrant families view the therapist as an expert or a teacher who is supposed to solve the problem quickly. Thus, short-term behavioral therapy is more effective with immigrant clients. In general, therapists are considered authority figures and are expected to play a significantly active role in the lives of their clients. They are seen as powerful, a sort of scholar, but are still expected to respect the cultural boundaries as they address the client's needs.

THE EFFECTS OF FAMILY-ROLE CHANGES AND DISCIPLINARY PRACTICES ON ACCULTURATION

In traditional cultures, interpersonal relations and interactions are determined primarily by expected roles, duties, and obligations. The role structure is hierarchical and vertical, determined by age and gender. Even if a woman is a professional, her role is primarily one of childrearing and caring for the emotional well-being of her family. Therefore, if a child is having psychological problems, the woman is held accountable. Her most important bond is with her children rather than her husband.

In most patriarchial cultures, the father is the financial provider and the disciplinarian when the mother "cannot handle the children." His strongest bond is usually with his mother rather than his wife. Due to the unequal power distribution between parents and children, there is always need for an intermediary, who may be a well-respected aunt or uncle, or even a "parental" child. The "parental" child is usually the caretaker for the younger ones when the parents are not at home.

The oldest son has many roles. He has to be an emotional support to his mother, and he is often an intermediary between his parents because, should the situation arise, he is expected to defend his mother against his father's abuses. He is also responsible for his younger siblings' educational development and is a financial contributor to his family.

The youngest child may, as an adult, be expected to stay at home with the parents. Because this child is the one likely to be the most acculturated to American ways, having migrated at the youngest age, he or she tends to be most vulnerable to familial conflicts due to cultural differences.

Changes in family roles markedly affect acculturation. Many cultures are patriarchial in nature, thus migration to the United States results in a loss of power for the males. A man may lose his decision-making power and may no longer be the family's sole breadwinner, possibly resulting in a loss of self-esteem. Sharing power with his wife (a discrepancy between U.S. cultural attitudes and that of many cultures) may make the man feel disrespected, and he may consider himself a failure as a man. The man may experience even greater displacement if he is unable to obtain employment, while his wife can, and he has to remain at home to care for the children. This shift in marital roles may not be as distressing for the man if the woman maintains a traditional perspective on family life. Usually, however, the wife feels more independent and becomes more assertive. If the wife becomes too assertive, challenges his authority, and reminds him who is bringing in the money, the husband may then feel emasculated; often this results in depression. If the man is unable to regain his position of dominance through the major means he was taught—employment, he may panic and attempt to assert his authority in an abusive manner. The result may be separation due to marital discord, caused by the feelings of helplessness and confusion about role change.

Likewise, women who are also employed outside the home no longer consider domestic life as their center and are no longer defined mainly by their roles as wives and mothers. Some even return to school, therefore advancing themselves educationally and professionally.

Children also go through periods of role change. They observe their American counterparts and are impressed with their assertiveness and independence. The children come to resent their parents' rigid controls, imposed structure, and authoritarian behaviors. They become angry and frustrated about their parents' traditional and "outdated" modes of disciplining them and solving family problems. For example, in an anecdote that highlights the high regard and respect some immigrant families have for teachers, one parent was so appalled at her son's defiance of a teacher that she publicly scolded and spanked him in the presence of his teacher, actually taking the child's pants down to spank him on the buttocks. The teacher was amazed at such "autocratic measures," claiming "this was a bit abusive." But this is not atypical among many cultural groups, even though more acculturated and assimilated immigrant families who are more familiar with the American social, legal, and political systems usually do not resort to such measures.

Payne (1989) administered a questionnaire to 499 Barbadians, excluding teachers and child-care workers, to determine their views on corporal punishment. This study found that corporal punishment was seen as a means of "teaching right from wrong, lessening the risks of law-breaking when older, training children to grow up in a respectable and decent manner" (p. 397). Payne (1989) also found that the majority (76.5%) endorsed flogging/lashing with a belt or strap as an approved method of punishment, with the buttocks most frequently identified as the part of the anatomy to which it should be administered. Slapping with the hand, spanking with a shoe, and hitting the knuckles or palm of the hand with a ruler were approved by 14.4, 14.2, and 5.4 percent respectively. Burning and scalding (traditional methods used to punish stealing) and lashing out at the child with any object at hand were the forms of corporal punishment most strongly disapproved of. Payne (1989) also noted the types of misconduct for which corporal punishment was considered most appropriate—disrespect to parents/elders, dishonesty, disobedience, stealing, indecent language, violence, deliberate defiance, disregarding the rules of the home/community, and laziness and neglect of chores. Although this study was conducted only in Barbados, West Indies, in general, the biblical maxim "spare the rod is to spoil the child" is the general sentiment shared by most cultures around the world. Therefore, mental health practitioners and researchers need to adopt a cross-cultural, dual perspective in conceptualizing and defining child abuse, neglect, and maltreatment among immigrant families. The tasks of the therapist, therefore, is to educate the parents to alternative ways of disciplining their children and to help mitigate the guilt, shame, and cultural conflict that children experience when they are spanked or reprimanded in the presence of their peers or teachers. Therapists must pay close attention to all these factors and familial roles, because these issues are all played out in therapy.

THE OBLIGATIONS OF CHILDREN
TO THEIR PARENTS

American culture emphasizes self-reliance and independence, with high value placed on the ability to "pull yourself up by your bootstraps" without relying on others. In contrast, many people from varying cultural backgrounds believe that people are who they are because of support from and relationships with many people, especially family members. Therefore, the concept of obligation and reciprocity is crucial, and is a dictum that everyone understands. This obligation is hierarchical in nature, such as parent/child, employer/employee, or teacher/pupil. This obligatory reciprocity also derives from the sacrifices made by individuals. Many immigrant families are known to work as many as three jobs to give their children an education. One woman illustrated the general attitude when she said, "If I have to be a slave in someone's kitchen, I will do it for my son to be a doctor. I do not think about it. I just do it." In the face of that kind of unflagging support, the greatest obligation children feel is toward their parents. Children feel they can never really repay such a debt, so they give respect to their parents at all costs, even if it means interrupting their own personal lives. It is important for a therapist to understand this obligation, because much difficulty may arise if a therapist tries to help an individual separate or individuate from his or her family. Giving adolescents assertiveness training without understanding this family ethic can be more problematic than beneficial. Thus, it may be more helpful to solicit the help of a significant and close family member, such as an uncle, aunt, or grandparents, who can convey to the parents what the child is experiencing. Detriangulating the most significant people who can aid in the assimilation process can begin the ripple effect of change throughout the rest of the family system.

Another area of concern is that children are expected to maintain loyalties to their parents' cultural values. Many parents expect their children to remain enmeshed with the family, because they are concerned that the children will get too Americanized and "get lost in the system." So the family closes its boundaries to the outside world, participating in few cultural events and using few support facilities. This fear of the new environment and a longing for the old one cause the family to isolate itself from the new environment. In attempting to cope, the child may disengage from the family and reject its values. The problem here is that both the child and the family may become vulnerable to an environment that neither knows how to fully negotiate. Children who are caught between conflicts of cultures may develop a negative sense of self and a poor self-image. The therapist needs to assist youngsters in integrating old values with newly learned ones, in respecting the values of the older generation while forging on and forming their own. An important factor is the sensitivity of the therapist to the preservation of continuities during this fragile process of change. To expect an individual, especially an adult, to become completely Americanized can create anxiety and a feeling of a loss of control. It may be beneficial to teach the adolescents to select the best of both cultures and incorporate them into their pool of coping skills (Gopaul-McNicol, 1993, 1997; McNicol, 1991).

LANGUAGE COMMUNICATION PATTERNS AND THEIR IMPACT ON ACCULTURATION

When clients find themselves having to repeat their answers because the therapist has difficulty understanding them, they tend to become very frustrated and feel that the therapist will not be able to assist them. In other words, they equate the understanding of their language with the understanding of their culture. Some families who are already skeptical about the treatment process use this as an opportunity to terminate therapy. Of course, the potential cultural barriers are reduced if the therapist can understand the language/dialect and the nonverbal language. The therapist ought to tune in to the client's use of cultural proverbs and nonverbal body language, such as eye contact. Direct eye contact on a continuous basis can be perceived as threatening; in the case of opposite-sex therapist/client relationship (especially if the therapist is a woman), it may even be perceived as a sexual overture. When the individual feels at liberty to express himself or herself, rapport may be established more easily and the possibility of a positive outcome may increase. Moreover, the therapist must be sensitive to topics that the client has difficulty discussing. For instance, discussing sexual matters creates discomfort, especially in older women. Talking about impending death is considered ominous and may be thought to be a sign of bad luck. Such matters should be broached only after a therapeutic alliance has been established.

LEGAL STATUS

To a large extent the legal status of clients or of school children determines whether they will feel comfortable opening up to a therapist. Therapists ought to familiarize themselves with the immigration laws (Gopaul-McNicol, 1993) to best service these families, since illegal immigrants tend to appear resistant to therapy by drawing little attention to themselves. The Center for Immigrant Rights in most metropolitan cities could prove beneficial to illegal immigrants for guidance in their immigrant status.

ETHNICITY

Racism presents serious problems for many immigrant families while accul-turating. Many immigrants in their native lands were not in the minority be-cause of the existing homogeneous societies around the world. Therefore, many immigrants of African heritage have difficulty endorsing such labels as "minority," "disadvantaged," and "oppressed."

THE RACE, GENDER, AND CULTURE OF THE THERAPIST

Because most cultures are patriarchial, vertical, and hierarchical in their fam-ily structure, many immigrants who come into therapy "tend to respond best to an older male therapist because this is syntonic with the cultural respect most feel for men and elders" (Brice, 1982, p. 130). Therefore, when working with immigrant families, an inexperienced therapist, especially one who is fe-male or young, may do well to solicit the support of a co-therapist who fits this image, or of extended family elders who can serve as intermediaries be-tween the therapist and the family. The latter course of action would show that the therapist recognizes and respects the value of elders in the family and society. Male/female team therapy is recommended in such a case. A caveat here is that, while clients may more readily take directives from a male, they may speak more easily to a woman about emotional matters, because women tend to handle such issues in the family. However, both men and women will respect a therapist whom they perceive as a knowledgeable expert.

A therapist from a different culture than the immigrant family being coun-seled may encounter difficulties. A therapist needs to begin by exploring his or her stereotypes, attitudes, and feelings about the culture in question. In general, a degree of cultural understanding helps. A therapist who has expe-rience with immigrant families has a greater chance of success when work-ing with clients from diverse cultural backgrounds. However, such a therapist must be careful of making overgeneralizations by assuming that all immi-grants will respond in a similar manner to a particular problem. Likewise, the therapist should not assume that a client of a different race from the therapist will have problems identifying with the therapist. Carter (1995) outlines issues of race in psychotherapy, and Chapter 11 also attempts to capture some of the salient issues raised by authors who believe that a race-inclusive model should be included in psychotherapy (Carter, 1995). A caveat, though, is that some culturally diverse clients of African ancestry have not conceptualized racism in the manner that African Americans in the United States have. This may be because in their native lands, there were no impassable barriers between the races that were upheld by institutional racism, as seen in the United States. By contrast, "the brutality of racism was softened and masked by the concept of social color" (Gopaul-McNicol, 1993, p. 52). Thus, a person's particular classification was determined more by his or her education, social position, and wealth, than by skin color. As a result, a therapist has to be careful not to make any assumptions about a client's feelings about him or her because that client is of a different race.

THE QUESTION OF WHETHER A FAMILY HAS ACCULTURATED OR IS IN TRANSITION

Individuals who immigrate experience several stages of cultural transition. The first is a physical transition requiring economic security, employment and educational opportunities, the ability to communicate in the host country, and the ability to understand the social and political differences between the host country and one's native land. The second stage is cognitive and affective in nature. In this stage, the family has to deal with the psychological pain of "letting go" and assimilating to the new country. In other words, physically arriving in the United States does not necessarily mean that one has emotionally arrived. The experience is like a person who wants a divorce, but is nevertheless pained having to sever ties with his or her spouse. This is the most difficult stage. The loss of family, friends, and culture, along with the change in family roles, the hope of "returning home one day," the state of uncertainty, and the expectation that one has to adapt and acculturate immediately can lead to stress and dysfunction. Some possible cognitive and affective responses or reactions are:

1. Grief at the loss of culture, family, and friends
2. Culture shock and disappointment at the discrepancy between expectation and reality
3. Frustration, anger, and resentment
4. Depression
5. Acceptance

Gopaul-McNicol (1993) outlines several factors that may influence the differences in the rates of acculturation among individuals:

1. Whether they are first-, second-, or third-generation Americans: The longer a family is in the United States, the easier the acculturation process tends to become. However, the number of years in the United States is not the absolute measure, because many immigrants attempt to preserve their culture by freezing traditions.

2. Whether they are children of mixed marriages: Inter-cultural marriages can ease the process of acculturation, because one parent is familiar with the workings of American culture.
3. Language: Fluency in English aids in the assimilation process.
4. Immigration status: Being in the United States legally makes for greater stability, more opportunities for scholarships, and higher-paying jobs.
5. Educational and professional backgrounds: Professional affiliations tend to open doors and help accelerate the acculturation process. Resources such as status and money increase their esteem among Americans.
6. Age at the time of migration: The younger the individual, the easier the assimilation process should be.

The ability to acculturate is a crucial indicator of one's willingness to change familial roles, a much needed aspect in cultural assimilation. Of particular importance is that, in most cases, migrants are separated from their families for more years than they had anticipated, because of the length of time required for them to become eligible to sponsor their families. Contact is maintained by mail and telephone, and migrants usually send goods and money home to their families regularly. Spouses tend to join the immigrants first, followed by the children. Often the children come at different times, depending on the immigrants' financial stability. Most immigrants continue to work more than one job in order to bring up members of their extended families. Thus, it is not unusual for an immigrant family to be comprised of the nuclear family, grandparents, aunts, uncles, godparents, and even friends. In a sense, this family structure is akin to a multigenerational type of household, with everyone playing a role in disciplining and caring for the children. So, when gathering information on a client, one may have to be patient if the biological parents are not forthcoming about the family background. Because of the prolonged separation of children from their parents, the parents may not be cognizant of many important stages in the child's development. The parents may not be aware of information such as medical inoculation, diseases, and other developmental milestones. Some therapists mistakenly view these parents as "uncaring" because they are ignorant of such important information. It is important, therefore, that when a therapist is developing social services for such families, he or she does not do so from the perspective of the traditional nuclear family, a constellation of biological parents and their children. Due to the prolonged separation, children may not view the parents as the primary caretakers and may continue to seek the guidance of their grandparents or significant others. The parent who so desperately wants to be the primary parent figure again may resent this, resulting in parent/child conflict.

Some of the conflicts center around cultural differences in disciplining, parents' unfamiliarity with age-appropriate behaviors for typical American children who are their children's counterparts, and parental unavailability to the children and to school personnel because they have several jobs. It is important to remember that a major concern of a family in transition is its need for financial security about the fundamental necessities of life—food, shelter, clothing, and so forth. Reestablishing the parent's role as the primary authority figure and the transition from one culture to the next are difficult processes, particularly because grandparents or other extended family members often intervene—sometimes unconsciously—in defense of the children. In addition, parents may feel that the many sacrifices they made and abuses they endured to create a better life for their children are not appreciated. These issues, coupled with changes in school, peers, environment, weather, and political climate, all exacerbate the tension for the culturally different family.

CURRENT MAJOR APPROACHES IN COUNSELING CULTURALLY DIFFERENT FAMILIES

Multicultural Counseling

Multicultural counseling has become a popular concept among practitioners and researchers because it is a way to acknowledge cultural diversity between therapist and client. Dillard (1983) includes in the definition of "culture" a shared belief system, behavioral styles, symbols, and attitudes within a social group. Assimilating to a particular culture is a slow process that involves the acculturation stage, that is, adopting some dominant social and cultural norms and possibly losing a sense of one's original cultural identity. In attempting to conduct multicultural counseling, the goal must be to assist the culturally different client to adapt to or reshape his psychosocial environment (Dillard, 1983). Sue (1981) examined the underlying principles in attempting to counsel the culturally different. His major point was the importance of therapists being knowledgeable about the client's culture and lifestyle in order to provide culturally responsive forms of treatment. Sue and Zane (1987) emphasized that changes had to do with the process of "match or fit." Treatment should match or fit the cultural lifestyles or experiences of clients in order to prevent premature termination and underutilization of services, which ultimately results in positive outcomes. Thus, knowledge of the culture, the formulation of culturally relevant and consistent strategies, credibility (the client's perception of the therapist as an effective and trustworthy helper), and giving (the client's perception that something was received from the therapeutic encounter) are all important and necessary in providing more adequate service to the culturally different.

Implicit in cross-cultural psychology is the notion of biculturalism. Many theorists view biculturalism as the healthiest identity resolution in the United States, although some view it as an abandonment of one's cultural heritage.

Pedersen (1985) sees biculturalism as an addition to one's original heritage, and examines the process by which cultural identity develops, because intercultural interactions influence one's behavior. Helms (1985) outlines the three stages of cultural identity:

Stage one, the preencounter stage, is the phase before the individual's cultural awakening. In this stage, the individual is so enmeshed in the Eurocentric view that he or she idealizes White culture while degrading his or her own culture of origin. The affective state associated with stage one is both poor individual and group self-esteem.

Stage two, the transitional phase, occurs when the individual realizes his or her lack of absolute acceptance by the White world. The individual goes through a period of withdrawal and cultural reassessment, ultimately deciding to become a member of his or her own cultural group. Dillard (1983) points out that in this stage, the individual sees his or her cultural systems as superior to other cultural systems. It is a stage of ethnocentrism. The affective state is one of euphoria, a sort of spiritual rebirth, as the individual tries to identify with his or her culture of origin. However, confusion and sadness results as the individual realizes that there has been some loss of cultural identity, because he or she cannot identify with all the values of the original culture.

The final, or transcendent, stage occurs when the person becomes bicultural and uses the experiences from both cultural groups to best fit his or her own circumstances. In this stage, the individual is more accepting of the flaws in both cultures and does not idealize either group. Affect is less tempered, and an identity resolution is experienced. Interpersonal relations are not limited by race, culture, gender, and so forth; a broader perspective is endorsed. Self-esteem is improved. This stage is attained after one experiences an identity transformation, via personal readiness and educational and cultural-socialization experiences requiring cultural flexibility. Recommendations for therapists regarding how to best treat individuals in these various stages are discussed later in this chapter.

Multimodal Therapy

The aim of multimodal therapy is to reduce psychological discomfort and promote individual growth by recognizing that few, if any, problems have a single cause or a single cure. Instead, the disquietude of people is multilayered, requiring a holistic understanding of one's interactions. Lazarus (1976) dissected human personality by examining the interaction among multiple modalities—behavior, affect, sensations, images, cognitions, interpersonal, and biological (BASIC IB). To make the acronym more compelling, it became BASIC ID; the biological modality was called "D" for "drugs," although it actually includes the range of medical interventions (e.g., nutrition, hygiene, exercise, medication). The multimodal assessment focuses on behaviors that get in the way of a person's happiness, and how a person behaves when he or she feels (affect) a certain way, as well as what the sensations (e.g., aches and pains) are and what bearings these sensations have on behavior and feelings. In addition, the goal is to examine one's perception of body and self-image, how one's cognitions affect emotions, and one's intellectual interests. The most important people in a person's life (interpersonal) and how they affect that person are also explored. Moreover, the focus is on a person's concerns about his or her state of health and drugs or medication used.

Educational Approach

Bowen's (1978) systems therapy, in which the therapist is portrayed as a teacher, who utilizes an educational approach to therapy, is compatible with the perspective of many culturally diverse people. This approach of securing and accepting help recognizes the value of education and research toward self-change. Bowen, also an advocate of the multigenerational perspective, focuses on transgenerational patterns. Thus, what has occurred in the past, and how the older generation feels about it, is important in Bowenian therapy. One goal of therapy is to increase differentiation of individuals within their families. Another goal is to decrease individual anxiety and emotional reactivity by diverting the focus from the "identified patient" to past and present family members. By doing this, the individual is allowed to think clearly and avoid the need for triangulation or emotional cutoff, which Bowen believes occurs when anxiety is high. He engages in couples therapy more than in family therapy, but he encourages couples to work on their relationships with their families of origin, based on the assumption that unresolved issues with one's original family affect current family relations. Therapy constitutes a cognitive reencounter with one's past as it is represented in one's present life. The focus is on facts and patterns, not feelings. He also establishes a leverage within the family system by discovering the most likely entry point (the person most capable of change, that is, the least-resistant family member). He then uses this least-resistant, most-motivated member to deal with the resistance of other family members.

His concept of the "coach" is applicable to working with immigrant families. Rather than meeting with the entire family, Bowen has the family member who came to therapy coach other family members into emotionally mature relationships with one another. This "coaching" approach has been found to be very helpful (Gopaul-McNicol, 1993), because it is very difficult to get an entire family to come into therapy. Because men are so resistant and tend to deny the therapist adequate entry, using a coach may be the next most effective approach. In addition, the term family therapy can be quite threatening to immigrant families who may surmise that the entire family is being seen as dysfunctional. Bowen's "coaching," which makes it unnecessary for the entire family to be present simultaneously, is also useful because immigrant parents often have difficulty engaging in discussions in the presence of their children, which is the typical mode of family therapy. By using this technique, members who may not have otherwise become involved in therapy may be treated. Gopaul-McNicol (1993) has found that the best coach is the eldest male child. Although the mother is traditionally the intermediary between the father and the children, in the final analysis, she is expected to side with the father, especially in the presence of the children. The eldest son, by virtue of being a male and an elder offspring, is the one who can gain the respect of the younger siblings (because he himself is still in cultural transition), as well as get the attention of his parents, especially his father, because of his seniority in the hierarchical family structure.

Structural Approach

The structural approach to family therapy is mainly associated with Minuchin (1974). The focus is mainly on boundaries, the patterns of the family, and the relationship between the family system and its wider ecological environment. An individual's symptoms are perceived as the result of a family's failure to accommodate its structure to the changing developmental and environmental requirements. These dysfunctional reactions to stress create problems that manifest themselves in family interrelations. The responsibility for change rests primarily on the therapist, who utilizes three strategies—challenging the symptom, the family structure, and the family reality. The therapist has to negotiate the family boundary in such a manner as to be given the power to be therapeutic. These boundary issues incorporate the concepts of enmeshment (some or all of the family members are relatively undifferentiated or permeable) and disengagement (family members behave in a nonchalant, distanced manner, because family boundaries are very rigid and impermeable).

While most families fall within the normal range, Boyd-Franklin (1989) stated that the cultural norm among Black families tends to fall within the enmeshed range. Aponte (1976), one of Minuchin's colleagues, discusses the issue of the power of some family members, who may or may not be in therapy with the identified patient. Aponte emphasizes that even if one conducts several therapy sessions with the identified patient and other family members, change may be sabotaged because of a powerful family member who did not become involved in the therapeutic process. These powerful members may influence the other members to terminate or continue treatment. Thus, the therapist is advised to explore as early as possible who the truly powerful family members are. The therapist needs to find out such information as who the client goes to before making a decision, which family member has the final say on most matters (in most societies around the world, it tends to be the father), who the client listens to most in the family, and who tends to disagree most with the client's decision. These questions can help in identifying the powerful figure who needs to be more directly involved in therapy.

Multisystems Approach

Boyd-Franklin (1989) emphasized that effective therapy with Black families requires from the therapist a flexibility that allows her or him to draw from different systems theories and incorporate them into an overall treatment plan. It also requires the therapist to intervene at a variety of systems levels, such as individual, family, extended family, church, community, and social services. Boyd-Franklin's multisystems approach has been quite challenging to traditional theories in the field of mental health. Many clinicians feel that working with social service agencies and churches is the task of a social worker, not a clinician. Many therapists feel overwhelmed by the complexity of this multisystem model.

However, in working with Black families, establishing rapport and building credibility are necessary and may involve intervening in numerous systems and at many levels. This model was built on the structural family systems model of Minuchin et al. (1967) and Minuchin (1974); Aponte's (1976) ecostructural approach; Aponte and VanDeusen (1981); and the ecological approach of a number of theorists, such as Auerswald (1968), Bronfenbrenner (1977), Falicov (1988), Hartman (1978), Hartman and Laird (1983), and Holman (1983).

The multisystems approach, which comprises two main axes, is based on a concept of circularity rather than linearity, as are most treatment approaches. Axis I, the treatment process, is composed of the basic components of the therapeutic process: joining, engaging, assessing, problem solving, and interventions designed to restructure and change family systems. Each component can recur throughout the treatment process at all systems levels. Axis I, the multisystems levels, is made up of levels at which the therapist can provide treatment, such as individual, family, extended family, nonblood kin and friends, church, community, social service agencies, and other outside systems.

THE INTEGRATION OF THE THREE APPROACHES

The three approaches—multicultural, multimodal, and multisystems (Gopaul-McNicol, 1993, 1997)—can be effectively combined in a treatment process when working with immigrant families. In our clinical experience with culturally diverse families, we have found that it is necessary to gain knowledge of the various cultures that impact on a child within his or her family system. Knowledge of a client's culture should help the counselor know how and when to intervene to promote healthy development.

The multimodal approach, which emphasizes therapeutic pluralism, utilizes a multilayered approach to address human discomfort. The goal is to assess the individual through several modalities, and then examine the salient interactions among them. Via this approach, a therapist is able to achieve a thorough understanding of the individual and his or her social environment.

Bowen's approach helps to clarify the power within the family and the process of multigenerational interactions. The focus is on facts and patterns of behavior rather than on feelings. This approach can be quite helpful, because in the initial stages of therapy many culturally diverse families can be quite unrevealing of their feelings.

The structural approach helps in restructuring the family that may be too enmeshed or disengaged. This approach is helpful with immigrant families who find themselves losing many of their boundaries during the process of acculturation.

The multisystems approach is useful with immigrant families whose experiences traditionally extend to support systems outside of the nuclear family—the extended family, nonblood kin and friends, and churches. Although the educational and legal systems were barely examined in Boyd-Franklin's multisystems model, they were discussed in great detail in Gopaul-McNicol (1993) because these two systems tend to be very significant as a point of intervention with culturally different families. In particular, the legal institution, specifically with respect to immigration status, constitutes an important systems level.

In summary, treating immigrant families requires the use of multisystems, knowledge of the culture of the family, and an understanding of how psychopathology is experienced and manifested. It is necessary to respect the family's belief in their cultural religious folk practices. Clearly, a review of the international literature on family therapy reveals how culture influences, defines, and shapes the family structure, family practices, family responsibilities, and roles. Likewise, culture determines how people conceptualize psychotherapy. Moreover, it is critical that the therapist be familiar with his or her own culture and cultural beliefs.

▶ 9

A Model for Treating Culturally Diverse Children

In general, treatment of immigrant families can be best understood via a comprehensive model—the multicultural, multimodal, multisystems (MULTI-CMS) approach proposed by Gopaul-McNicol (1993 & 1997). She emphasized that effective therapy with immigrant families requires from the therapist a flexibility that allows him or her to draw from different systems theories and incorporate them into an overall treatment plan. It requires the therapist to intervene at various levels—individual, family, extended family, church, community, and social services. This approach has been found to be most effective with immigrant families because it provides a flexible set of guidelines for intervention. This approach also recognizes that within the community, the idea that "it takes a whole community to raise a child" is fully endorsed by most people. Thus, empowering them to use all of the support systems available is crucial to the treatment process. The use of these systems can be implemented at any stage in therapy, but the families must be aware of all potential systems before therapy is terminated so that they can readily tap into them if the need arises. Encouraging the individual to embrace the support of their extended family and nonblood kin, and of churches in areas such as child care and education, may help in preventing personal difficulties.

Unlike many treatment approaches, which are based on linear models, the MULTI-CMS approach is based on the concept of circularity and is composed of four phases. Therefore, each component of each phase can recur repeatedly at various levels throughout treatment. So the therapist must be flexible, and willing to intervene at whichever phase and whatever level an individual is at in therapy. With this understanding, the flow of treatment for the multicultural/multimodal/multisystems approach (Gopaul-McNicol, 1993 & 1997) is as follows:

Phase I. Assessment Process
  Step 1. Initial assessment
    A. Explaining the process
    B. Establishing trust
  Step 2. Gathering information
  Step 3. Determining the stage of acculturation
  Step 4. Outlining the goals
Phase II. Educational treatment process
Phase III. Psychological treatment process
Phase IV. Empowerment treatment process

PHASE I. ASSESSMENT PROCESS

Step 1. Initial Assessment

The initial assessment stage, which occurs in the first therapy session, is broken into two phases: (1) explaining the process and (2) establishing trust. Because therapy is a relatively new phenomenon among many immigrants from "Third World" countries, and because most immigrants are taught to heal themselves within their own familial context, initially most immigrants are resistant to therapy. Consequently, immigrant families generally enter into treatment because they were referred by school personnel or child protective services due to difficulty with their children in school, or due to charges of child abuse or inappropriate ways of disciplining their children. In an effort to establish a relationship, the therapist must explain the therapeutic process as clearly as possible, because many immigrants view psychotherapy as a visit to a medical doctor. Many do not understand how merely talking about one's problem can bring about relief and an actual change. Many believe that therapy will be for only one session and that only the identified patient (in most cases, a child) will be involved. Most families, especially those referred by child protective services, do not believe they should be there; as far as they are concerned, their forms of discipline are appropriate. To the therapist this attitude may appear resistant, but from the clients' perspective, it is sensible. This is because in most of their countries of origin, corporal punishment is an acceptable form of discipline. Therefore, it is important that the therapist not degrade the disciplinary measures they have used in the past, but, rather, explain alternatives to corporal punishment. It is also necessary to point out that a therapist works with "normal, healthy" people who are simply experiencing adjustment difficulties, not just "crazy" people, as they tend to believe. The therapist should explain that therapy sessions usually last approximately one hour, and at times it may be necessary to see the entire family, not only the identified patient. Thus, the first few minutes of therapy involves clearing up the misconceptions about psychotherapy and explaining the process of treatment.

The next stage of this initial assessment process is the establishment of trust. This can be done through Sue's concepts of credibility and giving. According to Sue and Zane (1987), credibility refers to the client's perception of the therapist as a trustworthy and effective helper. Giving is the client's perception that something was gained from the therapeutic encounter. For immigrant families, a therapist is credible if he or she implements culturally relevant techniques, skills, and empathetic understanding. It is important to remember that with this model, from the inception of therapy—and within minutes of the first session—the therapist is engaging in some form of intervention and some type of problem solving.

Questions can include the following:

1. Why are you here? Given their response, help alleviate any guilt or anger via empathetic understanding. If their understanding of why they are there is different from that of the referral source, the therapist should mention the discrepancy only if it will not hurt the therapeutic alliance. If there is denial on the client's part, it can be addressed later in the session.
2. Were you ever in therapy before? If they were not, explain the therapeutic process.
3. What are your thoughts about a psychotherapist or about psychotherapy? Address their misconceptions or anger about being in therapy.
4. What do you think you can gain from therapy? In other words, what does the client want the therapist to address immediately? Addressing what the family views as most pressing will help to build the therapist's credibility as well as empower the family.

It might also be important to note:

1. The seating arrangement of family members—who sits next to whom?
2. Who is the powerful figure in the family?
3. Who speaks on behalf of the family?
4. Are the children allowed to speak?
5. What significant family members are missing?

The next stage of this initial assessment process is the establishment of trust. This can be done through Sue's concepts of credibility and giving. Credibility, according to Sue and Zane (1987), refers to the client's perception of the therapist as an effective and trustworthy helper. Credibility can be ascribed or achieved. Giving is the client's perception that something was gained from the therapeutic encounter. For most culturally diverse families, a therapist's credibility is based on his or her ascribed status in keeping with three cultural factors, age, gender, and education. In most societies, the youth is subordinate to the elder, the female to the male, and the less educated individual to the more educated authority figure. A lack of ascribed credibility may be the main reason such clients resist therapy.

Credibility can also be achieved (instead of ascribed) based on the therapist's culturally relevant techniques, skills, and empathetic understanding. A lack of achieved credibility may be the reason clients terminate therapy prematurely. This is why the first session is so important in establishing credibility. Generally, clients will trust and view the therapist as more credible if he or she conceptualizes the problem in a manner consistent with their cultural experiences and beliefs. So it may be more beneficial, for example, if the therapist appears to understand (not necessarily support) how a parent can spank a child. Conversely, a therapist who tells a child to be very assertive toward his or her parents may lose credibility.

With this model, the assessment process (as is the therapeutic process) is ongoing and cyclic. From the inception of therapy, the therapist is engaging in some form of intervention, some sort of problem solving, because the client's fears, misconceptions, and confusion are being alleviated within minutes of the first session.

Step 2. Gathering Information

Therapists need to be aware that with most immigrants, copious note-taking can be intimidating and distracting, because families may feel the therapist is not paying attention. Thus, note-taking should be kept to a minimum so that trust can be established in the initial stage of treatment. The genogram, a tool derived from anthropology but quite commonly used in psychology, is a sort of family tree. This can prove to be quite useful to the therapist working with culturally diverse families because of the many family members and friends who are directly or indirectly involved. If nothing else, it will allow the individual or family to visually represent their support systems. It can be equally beneficial simply to record the information without the use of a tree, using such questions as: Who raised you? and Who did you live with prior to coming to the United States? Once a picture has been drawn, the therapist can encourage the family to bring in some or all of the family members who are impacting on the life of the identified patient.

Boyd-Franklin (1989) mentioned that information gathering on Black families often occurs later in the treatment process. She attributed this to the process of building trust, which must be established before extensive information gathering can take place. Although this may also be applicable to some immigrant families, most individuals want to do whatever is necessary so that they can be finished with therapy. Therefore, the therapist must determine whether the family is ready to engage in data collecting in the first session. It is important to keep in mind that with many immigrants, a therapist can establish credibility in the first few minutes of the first session merely by ascribed status.

Step 3. Determining the Stage of Acculturation

Although it is important to keep in mind that not all families need therapy because of acculturation stressors, with immigrant families, difficulties in acculturation can be a major contributing factor to their family problems. Determining if there is any transitional conflict via Helms's (1985) three stages of acculturation is important in helping immigrant families. A caveat, though, is that not all families are unable to negotiate the acculturation process. Some families need therapy for the same reasons American families need therapy, for instance, the teenage rebellion typically found in any culture. In any event, once it has been determined which stage of acculturation the individual or family is in, it will be necessary to outline the goals for therapy based on the acculturation stage or any other transitional conflicts.

Step 4. Outlining the Goals

To further establish credibility, it is necessary, before the end of the first session, to outline concisely what the individual or family will gain; that is, the goals of therapy should be highlighted. This is to ensure that there is no discrepancy between the client's goals and the therapist's, because this can affect the therapist's credibility. As a matter of practice, at the end of every session, it is wise to reevaluate progress and see if the goals are being accomplished. Of course, even as the goals are being outlined, therapy can begin. Here, again, is a reminder that one advantage of this comprehensive model is that therapy can begin even while assessment is still in progress because of the cyclical nature of this treatment approach.

PHASE II. EDUCATIONAL TREATMENT PROCESS

When working with immigrant families, much of therapy may be educational in nature, because many adjustment difficulties may be due to cultural differences, or a lack of knowledge about the host country's educational, social, and political systems. Gopaul-McNicol, Thomas, and Irish (1991) explore basic educational and social issues of which immigrant families need to be aware and the facilities that are available to help them in the process of adjustment. Understanding the American school system, particularly the special education process (a concept foreign to many immigrant families), was examined by Thomas and Gopaul-McNicol (1991). Gopaul-McNicol (1993) suggested that if, after the assessment process, it is determined that the family members lack knowledge about these basic systems that they have to deal with every day, they may have to be educated about them. This stage of therapy may also involve a lot of homework, such as reading (bibliotherapy), to gain an understanding of the various systems. As can be seen, effective therapy with immigrant families requires flexibility, the use of a circular model, and even the removal of some traditional rigid boundaries. Therapists must be willing to explore the impact of the educational, social, legal, political, and social conditions of the families they treat. To attempt to treat these families without addressing these systems could impair the therapist's credibility.

Regarding the legal system, the next treatment stage for clients who are in this country illegally is to educate and empower them. This may involve such things as helping them find an immigration attorney, or explaining their rights with respect to their children's education. This means that the therapist must know the various systems, be willing to establish contact with the different providers in these systems, and, if necessary, include these providers in therapy sessions.

If the assessment shows that the child is embarrassed by his or her parents (a common problem many immigrant families face) because of their accent, clothes, foods, and so forth, therapy has to focus on both the parents and the children. Parents generally feel rejected, frustrated, angry, and confused. In this stage, therapy has to focus on teaching parents the social/emotional adjustment stages that children go through. The goal of therapy is still educational at this point, because the therapist needs to assist the parents in understanding the following issues:

1. The causes of childhood misbehavior and the principles and concepts underlying the social learning of such behavior
2. The cultural differences in values and discipline as they affect their children's adjustment
3. The emotional stress and fears that emerge in a child as a result of migration and adjustment to a new family, and the difference between an emotional disturbance and cultural adjustment
4. The differences in the school structure, and school expectations
5. The criteria used by the school system in placing children in special programs and their parental rights

6. How they can build positive self-esteem and self-discipline in their children via a home study program, so that their children will be empowered to maintain a positive self-image in this race-conscious society
7. How to communicate more effectively with their children and to be critical without affecting their child's self-esteem
8. The impact of peer pressure and how it can be monitored

At this juncture, therapy will be both educational and psychological, because the child ought to be taught:

1. To understand the sociocultural differences between their native country and the United States (educational)
2. To cope with peer taunts about their accents, mode of dressing, foods, family, and so forth (psychological)
3. To communicate more effectively with their families (educational and psychological)
4. To acquire the social skills and assertiveness skills needed (psychological)
5. To improve study skills and to understand cultural differences in test taking, school structure, school expectations, and language factors (educational)
6. To cope with the emotional stress and fears that comes with migration (psychological)
7. To understand the psychology of being Black in American society (psychological)
8. To understand the concept of self-esteem; its relation to performance and success; and the sources, institutions, and images that affect self-esteem (educational and psychological)

The assessment may reveal that the child is in Helms' stage two, the transitional phase in which the child realizes his or her lack of absolute acceptance by the White world. The individual withdraws from the dominant culture and tries to identify with his or her culture of origin, immersing himself or herself in the values and lifestyle of that culture. This is when many adolescents begin to wear the dreadlocks, to rebel against their parents' Eurocentric view, and talk emotionally of their "Mother Country," such as "Mother Africa." In other words, they do not necessarily have a true understanding and a true appreciation of their history; they identify out of rebellion, due to a loss of culture, feelings of rejection, and a need to grasp anything left of their cultural pride. This is the most difficult stage for both parents and children. They all have to acknowledge racism and discrimination. The main effect is one of frustration and anger, and behavior is generally militant. Interpersonal relations tend to become limited mainly to one's own cultural group. Therapy has to be both extensive and intensive, tapping many modalities—affective, interpersonal, educational, behavioral, cognitive, structural, system, and community.

If the assessment shows that the child is in the final or transdescent stage of acculturation, the client may not need psychological therapy as such (at least not for acculturation matters), because he or she has become bicultural and uses the experiences from both cultural groups to best fit personal circumstances. As can be seen from the above, Bowen's systems educational therapy, which views therapy as a self-change process and which portrays the therapist as a teacher (as described early in the previous chapter), is quite compatible with the needs of immigrant families.

PHASE III. PSYCHOLOGICAL TREATMENT PROCESS

The greater the cultural difference between therapist and client, the greater the challenge to maintain the relationship. These cultural differences can dominate the therapeutic relationship and affect therapeutic progress. With an immigrant family, the therapist's efforts to "cross over" may have to be more than a family with similar values and customs as the therapist's. Gopaul-McNicol (1993, 1997) found that the combination of Lazarus's broad-based, multimodal approach, Minuchin's structural approach, and Bowen's family dynamics approach are the most helpful in addressing the psychological problems faced by immigrant families and in easing the "joining" or "crossing over" process. As demonstrated earlier, the initial stages of therapy with immigrant families tend to be very educational, unless there is a crisis due to some traumatic incident. However, once the individual or family is familiar with the various systems, and if the problem persists (at times therapy with immigrant families may be merely educational), then a more psychological approach to treatment is needed.

Applying Multimodal Therapy with Immigrants

Multimodal assessment with its multilayered approach focuses on behaviors that are impeding happiness and acculturation of immigrant families. The therapist will observe and ask what makes an individual sad, frightened, angry, anxious, timid, and so forth. He or she will observe what type of behaviors the individual displays when feeling these emotions—is the individual avoiding, violent, and so forth?

Generally, when maladaptive behaviors are present, behavior therapy will be implemented. Thus clients will be taught to practice prescribed exercises such as relaxation, meditation, assertiveness training, modeling, and so forth. Behavioral contracts would be set up, whereby the client is rewarded for compliance and deprived of privileges for noncompliance. The works of behaviorists such as Skinner (1974), Bandura (1969), Wolpe (1969), Meinchenbaum (1977), and Jacobson (1938) can all be applied, depending on the nature of the problem. Likewise, exploring how thoughts influence emotions and behavior, the therapist may try to examine the client's belief (cognition) systems. Examining the client's belief that his or her child "should, ought to, must" do well may help shed some light on the undue pressure that some parents sometimes place on their children, albeit unintentionally.

PHASE IV. EMPOWERMENT TREATMENT PROCESS

The empowering of the family via a multisystems approach is the final stage of treatment. Boyd-Franklin (1989) examines the importance of intervening at various levels—individual, family, extended family, church, community, and social services. There is little doubt that this approach can be quite effective, because it provides a flexible set of guidelines for intervention with immigrant families. Encouraging individuals to embrace the support of their extended families and nonblood kin in areas such as child care and education may help in preventing personal difficulties. The use of the church in therapy with immigrants is also very relevant, because of the importance religion plays in the life of most immigrant families. The church can serve as a valuable social service in times of crisis, particularly for single parents. The therapist should suggest the church as a support system and even seek permission from the family to talk to the priest or minister in attempting to ascertain what role the church can play in the therapeutic process. Of course, it is also important for the therapist to recognize the significant influence of the folk beliefs in many religious societies. Leininger (1973) recommended using both indigenous practitioner skills and professional practices. We do not believe it is necessary for the therapists to conduct spiritual counseling or to even have a referral list for practitioners of witchcraft, since one has to be knowledgeable to venture into this form of treatment and comfortable with this procedure to make such a referral. However, therapists must understand that their opposition to the family's seeking the help of such practitioners may impede the psychotherapeutic process. We have always provided emotional support to our clients who felt they were victims of bewitchment, and have asked them to keep us abreast of what happened after their visits to the spiritists.

It is critical that the therapist help the family find out what afterschool programs exist in their communities, since allegations of neglect are sometimes brought against working parents whose young children are at home alone after school. The families need to be taught that this is frowned upon in American society and that child-care programs can be used. Boyd-Franklin

(1989) recommended that therapists should keep a file on these different services so they can mobilize them when necessary. This tapping of available resources is sometimes the single most important interaction in facilitating the possibility of treatment.

In addition, the therapist needs to be knowledgeable about the legal system as it applies to immigration policies and to be familiar with at least one immigration attorney, because of the illegal immigration status of many immigrant families. The American Immigration Lawyer's Association can provide a list of names to help in obtaining the name of an attorney from the individual's cultural background. Knowing about immigration laws is important both in order to be sensitive to the family's fears surrounding their immigrant status and also to be able to help them with specific information. For example, they should be aware that in the United States children cannot be denied a public education because of their immigrant status.

The MULTI-CMS approach also recognizes that within communities, the idea that "it takes a whole community to raise a child" is fully endorsed by many people around the world. Immigrant families are generally not aware of the various support systems available to them (educational, legal, community), and empowering them to use all of these systems is crucial to the acculturation process. The use of these systems can be implemented at any stage in therapy or after therapy is terminated, but first families must be made aware of them.

In general, when using the MULTI-CMS approach to treating immigrant families, a therapist can explore a broad spectrum of techniques to address the needs of this population. The following case example demonstrates how this comprehensive approach can be practically implemented.

CASE SAMPLES WITH THE MULTI-CMS APPROACH

The following case example is a practical illustration of the MULTI-CMS approach to therapy with a family from the English-speaking Caribbean.

The Matthews family was referred for therapy by the school psychologist due to the academic and behavioral problems of their two sons, Michael and Kendall, ages 7 and 9 respectively. The eldest child, Taiesha, age 13, was also having academic difficulties, because she was failing all courses except gymnastics. Mr. Matthews is originally from Jamaica, and Mrs. Matthews is from Trinidad and Tobago. They had met in Jamaica, where Mrs. Matthews spent two years after completing high school in Trinidad. They have been married for 14 years, although eight years after they married Mrs. Matthews migrated to the United States "for a better life and to give my children the chance to get a good education." The children lived in Jamaica with their father and paternal grandparents. Michael was one year old when his mother left home, Kendall was three, and Taiesha was seven. Because Mrs. Matthews had come to the United States on a holiday visa, but had decided to stay on doing domestic work, she had lived for three years illegally in this country. During that time, she was unable to visit her children in Jamaica because she would not have been allowed reentry into the United States. She was later sponsored by her employer and obtained permanent residency (approximately five years after leaving home). She immediately sponsored her family, who are now in the United States. Although they are not legal permanent residents yet, she expects them to become so within the next few months. When the family had joined Mrs. Matthews the children were then 6, 8, and 12. Currently, the household is comprised of the nuclear family, a maternal aunt and uncle, and the maternal grandmother. The children have not seen the paternal grandparents with whom they lived since they left Jamaica.

These background data were sent by the school psychologist along with the referring information. In addition, there are allegations of possible child abuse and educational neglect due to the children's excessive absences from school. School officials are strongly considering placing both boys in special education due to emotional disturbances and Taiesha in special education due to a learning disability. However, they agreed to withhold special education placement until psychotherapeutic intervention occurred.

Initial Session

As had been agreed on the telephone, all members of the nuclear family came in for the first session. The therapist, having greeted the family, began the treatment process by asking the parents to discuss the problem as they understood it. Mrs. Matthews looked frustrated because Mr. Matthews was very angry that the family "had to be seen as crazy and abusive." He sat away from the rest of the family and did not say anything for the first 15 minutes. Mrs. Matthews explained much of what was mentioned in the referral, and the children were generally quiet. The therapist (who was a young, female clinical psychologist) initially found it necessary to address some of the family's misconceptions about the range of clients who seek counseling. The therapist also agreed with Mr. Matthews that many families are labeled abusive when in fact they are using culturally sanctioned ways of disciplining their children. At this juncture, Mr. Matthews "joined" with the therapist by sharing his frustration with this system. By conceptualizing the problem in a manner consistent with the family's cultural experiences and beliefs, the therapist gained credibility with Mr. Matthews. The therapist also used this session to enlighten the family about some basic social and cultural differences, such as sleeping arrangements, educational neglect, and the meaning of child abuse in American society. Sensitivity to the children's presence was taken into consideration, because the therapist wanted to respect the hierarchical order of family life structure and not reveal too much in the presence of the children. Both Mr. and Mrs. Matthews said at the end of the session how much they had learned about educational, social, and cultural differences. The therapist had given to the family a "gift," and the family had already seen the therapist as "credible" after the first session. The therapeutic process was explained, and the family agreed to give therapy a chance for at least one month.

Gathering Information, Outlining Goals, and Empowerment

Both the first and the second sessions were spent gathering information, as well as engaging in the treatment process. The Comprehensive Assessment Battery (Gopaul-McNicol, 1993) was used as a guide. The second session was quite enlightening, with several issues revealed as problems within the family:

1. Mr. Matthews' unemployment
2. the children's feeling that they did not belong in the school and that their parents did not understand them
3. Taiesha's embarrassment about her parents' accent and cultural values
4. the maternal grandmother's attitude toward her son-in-law because her daughter was now the breadwinner (working two jobs)
5. the spanking of all the children by extended family members
6. the parents' belief that Taiesha "had gotten rude"
7. the endorsement of the folk belief that "it is possible someone in Jamaica envied us because they heard we were doing well and put something on the children"
8. the fear that the children "will be deported home if they continue to give trouble in school"

The therapist continued to engage in the treatment process by explaining the educational and legal rights of the family. At the end of the session, the family was also given homework—reading two handbooks for immigrants on the educational and social systems and on special education. At the end of this session, some goals were outlined, which included empowering the family to use the educational support systems in their communities in order to help the children in math and reading. The therapist also supported the family's decision to visit a spiritist by asking to be kept abreast of the results of their meetings with the obeah practitioner. In the meantime (during session interim), the therapist sent a letter to the school explaining to the principal that supplemental instruction in English language (SIEL) might prove to be beneficial for all of the children. Goals also involved teaching all adults in the household alternative ways of disciplining children, as well as examining the effect of family role change on the family's stability.

Empowerment through Extended Family and the Implementation of the Educational and Psychological Treatment Processes

There was much resistance to coming in for treatment by members of the extended family because they did not think that the problems with the children were caused by them. Therefore, the therapist suggested making a home visit for the third session of family therapy. As agreed, the entire family was at home upon the therapist's arrival. The family was more responsive to therapy being conducted in the home. In addressing the resistance, the therapist did not agree or disagree with the extended family's attitude that they did not need therapy, but, rather, spoke of contributions family members could make in helping to solve the problem. Resistance was diminished considerably, because each family member explored ways in which he or she could be of more assistance. The aunt and uncle agreed to help in the areas of remediation and in spending more time with the children. This session also focused briefly on what constitutes child abuse. Extended family members recognized that they had been unaware of the legal ramifications of engaging in corporal punishment. Subsequent sessions with the adults were also educational in nature; the focus was on the emotional stress that children experience as a result of migration and their concomitant shift in value orientation. The differences in the school structure and expectation, test-taking styles, and so forth were all examined.

By this time, the family had agreed to continue with therapy for another month, and the extended family members had agreed to come into the clinic. At this juncture both family and group therapy were being provided on a weekly basis. From the fourth session up to the end of therapy, Michael and Kendall joined a group for young boys, while Taiesha joined a group for teenage girls. In both groups, issues such as coping with peer pressure, social skills and assertiveness training (to assist with interpersonal relations), building self-esteem, understanding the educational differences in test-taking styles, and coping with their fears about acculturation were addressed. In addition, Michael and Kendall were taught self-control separate from the group, while Taiesha's embarrassment about her parents' accent and her father's refusal to treat her as a teenager were discussed in a family session.

Family therapy was held with the adults only to address the conflict as a result of family role changes. The children were asked to sit outside when marital issues were being discussed. Mr. and Mrs. Matthews both felt that having the children sit in on the therapy session would result in their knowing about marital conflicts. This wish was respected, but Mrs. Matthews' mother, who was also a catalyst in creating stress on Mr. Matthews, was expected to be in attendance. Rational emotive therapy explored their cultural beliefs about men being the sole breadwinners. In addition, the role conflict for children and parents was addressed in family therapy by helping family members to establish some individuation, but at the same time maintaining family cohesiveness. Group therapy for Taiesha also addressed how adolescents can prepare their families at each stage of the differentiation process. Furthermore, group therapy focused on helping Taiesha to understand her parents' perception of the hierarchies within the family and what it means in relation to respect.

In addition, the family was taught the principles of behaviorism, and how family members may have directly or indirectly reinforced negative behaviors in one another. A behavior modification program was set up at home, whereby the children were reinforced for good behavior and effort in school. After obtaining the parents' informed consent, the teachers were sent letters explaining what was being done and how it would be helpful for them to send home the daily behavior checklist so that the family could appropriately reward the children. The children were then further rewarded by the therapist during group therapy time.

Not until about the sixth family session was the issue of the children's not feeling loved by their family addressed. The children's feelings about their father's "abuses" and their mother's extended hours at work were also discussed. Kendall was particularly emotional as he talked about not feeling loved because his father never hugged him. This session focused on touching as a form of communicating, and everyone was asked to hug the person nearest them. Then everyone was told to hug whichever family members they so desired. Interestingly, no one reached to hug Mr. Matthews until it was pointed out by the therapist. At that point, he said he would like to hug everyone and proceeded to do so. From that session onward, homework involved daily tactile forms of communication. In the meantime, the issue of Mrs. Matthews' need to work to pay the bills was explored, but all family members decided they would assist in domestic matters so that she would be free to engage in family activities once she got home. Mr. Matthews, who had refused to cook before, agreed to do so, so that Mrs. Matthews would not have to get up early to cook before leaving for work. In addition, Mr. Matthews agreed to enroll in an educational program to obtain his high school diploma while still seeking employment.

The ninth session in treatment was educational again; family members were encouraged to establish contact with more social support systems. Taiesha joined a youth group that was monitored by West Indian adults in the community. She built a wonderful network of friends who had themselves gone through cultural conflicts while in transition. Mr. Matthews eventually agreed to join a Black male self-esteem group, which focused on such issues as "the invisibility syndrome" as it pertains to Black males and the psychology of being a Black male in this society. All family members agreed to become members of their local church. The therapist established contact with the pastor, who introduced the family to the congregation.

In the meantime, the children continued to show academic delays, but behavior problems had decreased considerably. The therapist visited the school with the parents and suggested at a school-based support-team (SBST) meeting with each discipline (psychologist, nurse, social worker, teacher) could be responsible for assisting these children. Although this was a difficult task given the bureaucracy in the education system, they did agree to refrain from placing the children in special education for at least two years.

The success of this case may be a result of the holistic approach to therapy. The MULTI-CMS approach, while demanding, covered all areas that caused distress within the family unit. In addition, the concept that it takes a whole community to raise a child certainly aided this family in arming and empowering themselves as they attempted to acculturate to American society.

▶ 10

Ethical and Professional Issues in Working with Culturally Diverse Children

Today, many professional organizations (i.e., American Psychological Association, Multicultural Counseling and Development, Council for Exceptional Children, American Speech-Language-Hearing Association, and others) have clearly recognized that professionals who work with children and families of diverse cultural and linguistic backgrounds must be trained and prepared to address and understand the special needs of all children and families in order to provide appropriate services. The American Psychological Association (1993) conceded that issues of language and culture do impact on the provision of appropriate psychological services. However, although most training institutions have been informed by accrediting institutions to include in their curriculums courses addressing multicultural and cross-cultural issues, a true acceptance of this basic fact continues to produce much debate and controversy. Still, many professionals who work with linguistically and culturally diverse populations have not received appropriate training, and continue to treat and test individual members of this population. It is an historical fact that changes in practices do not usually come voluntarily. Social climate is influential in determining what changes in practices are embraced and which ones are rejected. In this chapter, we will discuss several major litigations or court cases that forged new practices in the area of psychological assessment, placement of linguistically and culturally diverse students in special education programs, and ethical guidelines for the provision of psychological services (e.g., counseling) to this population.

LEGISLATION THROUGH LITIGATION

Prior to the 1970s, children who had special educational needs, who were limited English proficient, or who were of African-American descent were neglected and discriminated against by the American educational system (Salamone, 1986). The Civil Rights Movement of the 1950s and 1960s provided the framework and the venues that gave impetus to recognition of all citizens' rights, including disabled and bilingual individuals. The National Association for the Advancement of Colored People (NAACP), the Southern Christian Leadership Conference, and other organizations that led the sociopolitical climate in the United States were committed to ensuring the basic constitutional civil rights of African Americans (Kretschmer, 1991). Consequently, other groups, such as individuals with disabilities, were able to advance their causes. The Civil Rights Movement and its resultant call to action benefited linguistic minorities and individuals with disabilities (Kretschmer, 1991). Public school education throughout the country was built upon a segregational viewpoint that provided separate and unequal education to African Americans. The NAACP brought about a number of lawsuits culminating in a Supreme Court landmark decision. In Brown versus Board of Education (1954), the Supreme Court ruled that segregation by race in the public schools was a violation of the Fourteenth Amendment to the United States Constitution. Kretschmer (1991) noted that legislative acts and litigative actions were reactive—they reflected reactions against current practices and attitudes (p. 9). Court decisions have greatly affected assessment practices (Prasse, 1986) because they have generated federal laws and guidelines that changed the current practices. These laws were originated by parents of children with disabilities who advocated for legal redress (Wallace, Larsen, & Elksnin, 1992). Furthermore, the increasing demand for accountability in the process of educational assessment produced an emphasis on ethical concerns that established correct, appropriate, or competent actions of professionals conducting the assessment (Wallace et al.). Most of the litigations addressed several issues: (a) the administration and interpretation of tests by inadequately trained professionals, (b) making classification decisions based on the results of inappropriate tests, (c) provision of appropriate educational services, (d) stigmatization of students inappropriately placed in special education classes, and (e) involvement of parents in the assessment process (Helton, Workman, & Matuszek, 1982).

The 1970s stimulated an avalanche of significant court cases that shaped important federal education laws such as:

Education for All Handicapped Children Act—1975 PL 94-142: This law ensured that all school age children, including severely disabled students, received a free and appropriate education.

Section 504 of the Rehabilitation Act—1973: This civil rights law for individuals with disabilities established provisions relating to assessment (included in PL 94-142) in the employment and educational settings.

The Family Education Rights and Privacy Act—1974: This law stated that parents and all students 18 years of age or older had the right to examine all student's educational files or records, to object to any data in the files, and to indicate who can have and grant access to student's records. Parental consent was required before the district released any information in the student's file to other agencies (Wallace et al., 1992).

Carl D. Perkins Vocational Education Act—1984: This law intended to assure that students who were disadvantaged or disabled were adequately served by vocational educational programs; additionally, vocational planning and programming should be included in the Individual Educational Program, and the student with a disability must receive vocational assessment, counseling, and career development. Also, these students are entitled to special services such as adaptation in curriculum, instruction, equipment, and facilities (Wallace et al., 1992).

The Education of the Handicapped Amendments of 1986: This law was the first amendment to PL 94-142. However, it added several new mandates: services for children from age 3 through 5; preschool incentive grants for states already providing services to these children; and a new state grant program for infants and toddlers who were developmentally delayed or at risk (to include their families) (Wallace et al., 1992).

Americans with Disabilities Act of 1990 (ADA): The purpose of this law was to safeguard the civil rights of individuals with disabilities in private employment and guarantee them access to all public services, public accommodations, transportation, and telecommunication.

Education of the Handicapped Act Amendments of 1990 (PL 101-476): This law was the second amendment to PL 94-142. It changed the name of the law from Education for All Handicapped Children Act to Individuals with Disabilities Education Act (IDEA). It also established that transitional and technological services be incorporated into students' IEPs, transitional services be addressed in IEPs for students 16 years of age and older, the addition of two new disability categories—traumatic brain injury and autism, and the identification of special programs for children who were classified as emotionally disabled (Wallace et al., 1992).

Individuals with Disabilities Education Act Amendments of 1995 (IDEA): This law was the third amendment made to PL 94-142. This reauthorization of PL 94-142 was intended to build on the basic purposes of the law (State Education Department, 1995). Each student must be ensured a free appropriate public education, determined on an individualized basis, designed to meet his or her specific needs in the least restrictive environment, protected through due process (U.S. Education Department, 1995). This reauthorization focused on a number of key principles:

1. Align IDEA with state and local education improvement efforts so that students with disabilities can benefit from them.
2. Improve educational results for students with disabilities through higher expectations and access to the general curriculum.
3. Address individual needs in the least restrictive environment.
4. Provide families and teachers, those closest to students, with the knowledge and training to effectively support students' learning.
5. Focus on teaching and learning.
6. Strengthen early intervention to help ensure that every child starts school ready to learn (U.S. Education Department, 1995).

Several of the landmark litigations that shaped legislative action include Diana versus State Board of Education (1970), Covarrubias versus San Diego Unified School District (1971), Guadalupe versus Tempe Elementary District (1972), Lau versus Nichols (1974), Aspira of New York, Inc. versus Board of Education of the City of New York (1972), Larry P. versus Riles (1979), Lora versus New York City Public School Board (1977–1980, 1984), and Dyrcia S. et al. versus Board of Education of the City of N.Y. et al. (1979).

In **Diana v. Board of Education** the plaintiff's contention was that inappropriate placement of Mexican-American and Chinese students was based on discriminatory test results; this case established that testing be conducted in the student's primary language, the use of nonverbal tests, and the requirement to obtain extensive supporting data to justify special education placement (Kretschmer, 1991). Many facts that emerged from this case found their way into PL 94-142 (McMillan, Hendrick, & Watkins, 1988). Discriminatory testing procedures were also believed responsible for the inappropriate placement of Mexican-American and African-American students in EMR classes in the **Covarrubias v. San Diego Unified School District** (1971); the court allowed a consent decree where plaintiffs could seek monetary damages for misclassification (Wallace et al., 1992). In addition, it recognized the need to provide informed consent prior to placement. Another case that dealt with inappropriate placement of culturally and linguistically diverse students in EMR classes was the **Guadalupe v. Tempe Elementary School District**. Here, Mexican-American and Yanqui Indian students were misplaced in EMR classes. The decision included the following resolution: Intelligence tests must be administered in a student's native language, a student's home life and cultural background must be considered when making placement decisions, parents must not only consent to the evaluation process and subsequent placement, but the district must explain disproportionate numbers of culturally and linguistically diverse students identified as disabled in special education classes (Wallace et al., 1992).

In 1974, the **Lau v. Nichols** case secured language programs necessary to provide equal educational opportunities. The court decision was developed to foster guidelines, now called the Lau Remedies, which focused on the identification of linguistically diverse students, assessment of their language proficiency and academic performance, and their placement in appropriate educational programs with bilingual instructional strategies (Kretschmer, 1991). The **Aspira of New York, Inc. v. Board of Education of the City of New York** established the need to use proficiency tests to determine student's eligibility for a bilingual program.

The **Larry P. v. Riles** case has been called the premier case involving bias in intelligence tests and placing children in programs for the mildly retarded (Prasse & Reschly, 1986, p. 333). It was a class action suit filed in California on behalf of African-American students who had been inappropriately and disproportionately placed in EMR classes based on a standardized IQ test (Wallace et al., 1992). The decision was in favor of the plaintiff; it found that the school's methods of evaluating and placing students were inappropriate in two ways. Standardized tests were determined to be discriminatory toward African-American children, and the history of placement of African-American students in EMR classes pointed to unlawful, segregated intent (Prasse & Reschly, 1986). The use of standardized intelligence tests in California to place African-American students in EMR classes was prohibited. According to Prasse and Reschly (1986), to rectify these past practices, the court dictated extensive actions, including the following:

1. Warning against the use of standardized tests on African-American students for identification as EMR and placement in EMR classes
2. Requiring the use of nondisciminatory and valid assessment instruments
3. Providing data to support the use of certain assessment instruments
4. Eliminating many African-American students from EMR classes
5. Reevaluating every African-American student previously identified as EMR without using standardized intelligence tests
6. Developing and implementing an IEP for every student found to have been misdiagnosed

However, as McMillan and Meyers (1980) recognized, the injunction against the use of standardized intelligence tests had little effect on rectifying the disproportionate percentage of culturally and linguistically diverse students placed in classes for the mentally retarded. Furthermore, McMillan and Meyers (1980) noted that: (1) to point to IQ tests as the prime culprit for the inordinate number of culturally and linguistically diverse students in EMR classes was to overlook the true complexity of overrepresentation; (2) school failure and not solely IQ tests were the primary determinants of EMR status; (3) instead of emphasizing why large numbers of culturally and linguistically diverse students were referred for assessment, the court focused on the issue of biased testing, and this prevented the development of effective educational assistance and instruction for this population of students; (4) the use of a quota system to make sure that EMR population was representative of the general population of school-age children found opposition in many educators and scholars including McMillan and Meyers (1980) (p. 147); and (5) the fear of litigation made educators reluctant to place culturally and linguistically diverse students who really needed special education intervention.

The inappropriate placement of culturally and linguistically diverse students in EMR classes was not the only concern. **Lora v. New York City Public School Board (1977–1980, 1984)** shed light on the overrepresentation of African-American and Hispanic students in classes for students with severe emotional disabilities. The decision established that students must be assessed in their native language; assessment information must be gathered from a number of sources; parents must be informed of referral and of their due process rights; parents have the right to participate in evaluation and placement decisions; and structured observations of students must be conducted by a member of the multidisciplinary team (Wallace et al., 1992). Finally, in **Dyrcia S. et al. v. Board of Education of the City of New York et al.**, the decision established the right to timely assessment and placement procedures. Bersoff (1981) concluded that there were three benefits from legal interference in assessment practices: (1) Society had become more sensitive and aware of linguistic and cultural differences and the fact that testing may produce discriminatory results; (2) professionals had been made to confront and deal with the issue of accountability; and (3) the criticism leveled on standardized IQ tests has energized the field to develop improved and alternative means of evaluating cognitive abilities.

Prior to the 1970s, school psychologists and other educational diagnosticians accepted that standardized and norm-referenced tests represented the best methods for identifying students' intellectual levels (Podemski, Marsh II, Smith, Price, 1995). It was common practice to make a determination as to the presence of mental retardation based on the result of one IQ test. Additionally, it became even clearer that standardized intellectual tests were not always the best measure of cognitive abilities for all students, and that these tests could be discriminatory when assessing culturally and linguistically diverse students.

Many of these landmark cases generated court decisions that were translated into an amalgamation of federal dictates held in such Public School laws as 94-142 (i.e., the Individuals with Disabilities Education Act–IDEA–1995). Six principles formed the core of this legislation:

Nondiscriminatory Assessment

The law provides safeguards and guidelines to protect the rights of linguistically and culturally diverse students by dictating specific testing and placement procedures:

1. A student must be assessed in his/her native language.
2. Tests must evaluate what they were intended to evaluate (i.e., they must be valid).
3. Assessors or test administrators must be appropriately trained to administer and interpret specific tests.
4. Results yielded by the tests must be an accurate indication of a student's ability and achievement and not a reflection of sensory, manual, or speaking impairments unless the test is designed to assess one of these domains (Wallace et al., 1992).
5. Placement decisions cannot be made on the basis of any single factor. The decision must be made by a multidisciplinary team or group of educational practitioners.
6. Students must be evaluated in all areas of suspected disability, which includes academic achievement, motor ability, hearing, emotional, vision, social and emotional, and communicative skills.
7. Every student identified as having a disabling condition must be reevaluated every three years by reviewing existing evaluation data regarding the student and focusing on the student's present level of performance and educational needs. The reevaluation must determine if the child continues to have the impairment and needs continual special education services.
8. Initial evaluation should focus on instructional relevant information in addition to determining a disability.

Individual Educational Program (IEP)

Once the assessment has been conducted and the student is identified as having a disability, an IEP is developed based on criterion-referenced assessment rather than a norm-referenced test. The IEP is like a legal contract between the school district and the parent. It identifies the student's present level of performance or areas of strength and weaknesses, and provides instructional objectives and goals to improve several areas of functioning, such as the student's academic, social–emotional, and management needs. The IEP is tailored to the specific needs of the student.

Due Process and Parental Involvement

To ensure that parents have input into the assessment and placement processes, public agencies are expected to notify parents in writing when there has been a referral for assessment and to obtain the parents' written consent before conducting the assessment as well as for placement. Parents also have the right to participate in the decision process for placement and can request an independent evaluation. The parents must be notified of their rights in writing and they must receive an explanation of the results of the assessment. Parents have the right to inspect the records or files and to disagree with any information contained in that file, and request an amendment. Finally, the school district is responsible for protecting the right to confidentiality of the student's records or files. Parents have the right to be made aware of who has access to their child's records and to request copies of the records.

Free and Appropriate Education

This law guarantees a free and appropriate public education to all children with disabilities regardless of the severity or nature of the disabling condition.

Least Restrictive Environment

Each child with a disability should be educated whenever possible in the least restrictive environment with great emphasis on educating the student with his or her nondisabled peer.

Funding

The federal government was expected to provide to states the funding necessary to help ensure the success of the law. However, the government never funded the law to the degree initially expected (Patton, Blackbourn, & Fad, 1996).

ETHICAL CONSIDERATIONS

Many organizations (e.g., Council on Exceptional Children (CEC), American Psychological Association (APA), National Association of School Psychologists (NASP), and American Speech-Language-Hearing Association (ASHA)) have developed codes of ethical behavioral standards that address the special needs of culturally and linguistically diverse students and families. However, not all of these organizations have incorporated these standards into their general set of ethical standards of conduct. The standards that have been developed not only address the issues that are particular to assessment, but also issues in the area of counseling or treatment. In 1988, a task force was established by APA on the delivery of services to ethnic minority populations in light of the increased awareness about psychological needs associated with ethnic and cultural diversity (APA, 1993). This task force developed a set of general principles intended to be suggestions for psychologists working with linguistically and culturally diverse children and families (APA, 1993). These sets of principles were titled "Guidelines for Providers of Psychological Services to Ethnic, Linguistic, and Culturally Diverse Populations." Sue, Arredondo, and McDavis (1992) addressed the issue of cultural and linguistic diversity in the area of "Multicultural Counseling Competencies and Standards" in which they set forth recommended ethical practices. A review of these manuscripts yielded three major coordinating principles of concern: competency, intervention strategies, and respect for cultural differences. The following recommendations are made by APA (1993) and Sue et al. (1992):

Competencies

1. Psychologists should recognize the limits of their skills, training, and expertise in working with culturally and linguistically diverse children and families, and should seek appropriate training, guidance, consultation with experts or defer to other trained professionals.

2. When assessing individuals from culturally and linguistically diverse backgrounds, psychologists must understand the limits of the assessment instrument or procedures (i.e., validity and reliability) with particular culturally and linguistically diverse groups. The resulting data should be interpreted in light of the cultural and language factors impacting on most assessment situations. The psychologist must understand how cultural and linguistic factors impact on the assessment process.

3. If the client is bilingual or LEP, linguistic factors may present a barrier to the assessment or therapeutic situation. Consequently, the psychologist should interact in the primary or dominant language of the client or student. He or she must not only be able to understand the verbal messages but the nonverbal ones as well. If the psychologist is unable to do so, he or she must consider either using an interpreter or referring the case to another professional competent in the language of the student or client.

4. It is not only sufficient to understand how cultural and linguistic factors impact on the assessment and therapeutic process, but the psychologist must also document in the records cultural and sociopolitical factors.

Intervention Strategies

1. Psychologists should understand how cultural, linguistic, and religious practices influence the diagnosis and consider a differential diagnosis.

2. Psychologists should understand the sociopolitical aspects of student life (e.g., discrimination, racism, poverty, immigration, and acculturation) as well as the client's worldview, because it is the framework from which the student evaluates and sees society and him or herself.

3. Psychologists must be able to incorporate into the treatment the culturally held views about healer or spiritual leader, and be willing to use these healers if they help the client deal with his or her problem.

4. Psychologists must remain up to date with the research as it pertains to working with linguistically and culturally diverse children and families.

Respect for Cultural Differences

It is not sufficient for psychologists to understand merely that cultural and linguistic differences do have an impact, but psychologists must also respect the fact that they exist. Respect allows psychologists to safeguard the rights of their clients or students, to incorporate into their practice strategies that are sensitive to the cultural and linguistic needs of the student and family, and to recognize the limits of their skills and expertise. However, in order to understand and accept these differences, psychologists must have an understanding of how their personal cultural and sociopolitical background and experiences impact on psychological processes.

SUMMARY

Current practices in the area of assessment have been guided by legislation that emanated from court decisions intended to address issues of discriminatory assessment, lack of due process, and inappropriate placement of culturally and linguistically diverse students in classes for the educable mentally retarded (EMR) or emotionally disabled children. Out of the many efforts to rectify or correct common assessment practices which were discriminatory, PL 94-142 (the Education for All Handicapped Children Act) and the subsequent Individuals with Disabilities Education Act Amendment of 1995 were formulated to safeguard the rights of all children and to guarantee a free and appropriate education. Although several organizations have developed ethical standards for working with linguistically and culturally diverse children and families, incorporation of these standards into their general set of ethical standards has been slow.

In conclusion, Korman (1974) encapsulates the issue of ethics in the following statement:

> The provision of professional services to persons of culturally diverse backgrounds by persons not competent in understanding and providing professional services to such groups shall be considered unethical (p. 105).

▶ 11

Training Educators and Mental Health Professionals to Work with Linguistically and Culturally Diverse Children

One of the major challenges facing the field of psychology today is the training of therapists to address the psychological needs of the increasing number of linguistically and culturally diverse families in the United States (Barona et al., 1990; *Population Today*, 1985; Reid, 1986; U.S. Department of Commerce News, 1989). Because it is virtually impossible to have an equal number of trained specialists who are themselves from the variety of culturally diverse backgrounds as our client population, it is critically important to have therapists be knowledgeable about and be prepared to address the concerns of this new clientele. The goal should be to train all psychologists to be competent, sensitive, and knowledgeable of the critical factors related to issues of cultural diversity in order to best serve the culturally different. This knowledge, sensitivity, and awareness ought to be built into the existing graduate training programs.

Throughout this book many models were proposed for working with linguistically and culturally diverse children. Although these are all strongly recommended, other competencies, discussed in the sections that follow, are needed as prerequisites to best utilize all of these models.

OTHER COMPETENCIES NEEDED FOR CROSS-CULTURAL TRAINING

Therapist's Awareness of Own Cultural Biases and Values

Arredondo et al. (1996) suggested that all psychologists in training should explore their fundamental significant beliefs and attitudes. Furthermore, they should understand the impact of those beliefs on the psychological processes and on their ability to respect others different from themselves. They should be allowed to examine personal values that may impede their ability to respect others' values and beliefs. The adage "counselor know thyself" is critical in preventing ethnocentrism, a significant ingredient in effective cross-cultural counseling. Culturally competent psychologists ought to be trained to recognize in a teaching or counseling relationship, how and when their beliefs, attitudes, and values interfere with providing the best service to their clients. Likewise, training should allow them to recognize the limits of their skills and refer the client to receive more appropriate resources. Training should have at its heart the ability to recognize the sources of discomfort/comfort with respect to differences in culture, ethnicity, etc., and how these differences are played out in therapy. A culturally competent psychologist tries to avoid making negative judgments on clients with different worldviews and respects and appreciates their differences.

Competence in Understanding Interracial Issues

"Race is an elusive, perplexing, troubling and enduring aspect of life in the United States" (Carter, 1995). When a Black person introduces race into psychotherapy, it is often perceived as a form of defense or as an avoidance of a more profound issue. Given the United States' preoccupation with race in the socio-political world, it is imperative that students in training are exposed to a psychotherapeutic model that includes race (Carter, 1995), specifically covering issues such as whether the therapist should wait for the client to introduce questions of race, how race should be discussed once it has arisen, ways that racial factors may influence the course of treatment, and how one can distinguish between a racial defense and poor psychological functioning. Moreover, knowledge of racial oppression and racial discrimination should be examined in training, so that White therapists can recognize how they benefit from institutionalized and cultural racism. Carter (1995) proposed a race-inclusive model in psychotherapy. All students in training should be exposed to such a model to best understand the influence of race in psychotherapy.

Competency in the Ability to Work with Interpreters

In spite of every effort to secure a bilingual psychologist, sometimes it is impossible to do so given the paucity of bilingual psychologists, especially those who speak languages not commonly encountered. As such, it is necessary for psychologists to develop competencies in interpretation procedures. Some of these skills can range from establishing rapport with interpreters, respecting the authority of the interpreter (whether the interpreter is a teacher's aide/paraprofessional or a member of the Parent Teachers Association), knowing the kinds of information that tend to get lost during the interpretation procedure, understanding nonverbal communication clues, and recognizing the importance of securing accurate translation. Moreover, "the psychologist should demonstrate the ability to plan and execute pre-service and in-service programs to prepare interpreters for psychological work with children and to help interpreters follow ethical practices of keeping information confidential" (Figueroa et al., 1984, p. 138). It must be emphasized that, unlike in a legal context, psychological testing involves a more complex role for the interpreter. Nonverbal cues can be misinterpreted if the interpreter is not familiar with the client's culture. The psychologist must ensure that kinesthetic cues are not misinterpreted by the interpreter. Figueroa et al. (1984) recommended the use of audio or videotapes to address this situation, because a precise recording of the testing can be reviewed by the psychologist after completion of the testing.

Cross-Cultural Issues in Conflict Resolution

The Worldview Congruence Model (Myers, 1991) discusses how interpersonal conflicts are often a result of eight worldview dimensions: psychobehavioral modality, axiology, ontology, ethos, epistemology, logic, concept of time, and concept of self. Brown and Landrum-Brown (1995) illustrated how worldview conflicts affect the client/counselor/supervisor triadic relationship. These conflicts may result in mistrust and resistance. Thus, knowledge of one's view and that of the other party is beneficial in the therapeutic and supervisory relationship. It is necessary for the supervisor to help the counselor, and the counselor to help the client to identify the ways in which these conflicts affect therapy.

Awareness of Special Education Misplacement

During the 1995/1996 academic school year, as we conducted several trainings attended by many practicing psychologists and their supervisors, they repeatedly stated that even if children are not truly handicapped, they have to place them in special education in order to secure some of the services that these children need. Therefore, they diagnose these "borderline" children as learning disabled when, in fact, they do not have profiles of the typical learning disabled child. An even more disturbing issue arose—the sentiment that if special education no longer exists, special education teachers will become unemployed. As a result, the institution of special education is necessary, not only for the children, but for the teachers themselves. There seems to be a maintenance of this system whether it is needed or not. Of course, the fact that children in special education do not receive a high school diploma, thus hindering their chances to go on to college, does not seem to be a major concern for these professionals. To say the least, this is quite unethical and unprofessional. What is needed is a transitory placement for these borderline children, as well as training for special education teachers to see themselves more as preventive workers than treatment workers. Psychologists can play a significant role in this enterprise. They can serve as consultants to school personnel in assisting special education teachers to utilize their time in working with regular education "at risk" students to prevent their placement into special education. Thus, a mere paradigm shift can ensure the continued employment of special education teachers in another capacity (special education prevention specialists) (Armour-Thomas & Gopaul-McNicol, in press) and, simultaneously, avoid the massive misplacement of children in special education. Training ought to focus on the role of psychologists in expanding the role of special education teachers to the regular education setting.

Knowing the Bilingual Education Curriculum

Knowing what constitutes a bilingual instructional program for bilingual or limited English-proficient (LEP) children is essential in working with linguistically and culturally diverse children. There is still considerable debate as to whether an ESL or an English immersion program is best suited to meet the needs of bilingual children (Homel et al., 1987). Because this debate is expected to continue for years, psychologists should be knowledgeable of the available programs, and aware that some children may benefit from a certain type of program and others may benefit from another. In other words, just as there is no one single program for monolingual students, likewise, no one single program can fit all bilingual children. It is critical that this be understood by psychologists who serve as consultants to school personnel.

Ability to Empower Families through Community-Based Organizations

Competent psychologists must be able to direct their families to the community-based organizations that can support the school by utilizing their resources in working with handicapped children. After-school tutorial programs, day care centers, free lunch programs, and free clinic care are some examples of community supports that can be used to supplement needed services that the schools are unable to provide. Utilizing the churches, social service agencies, and other outside systems are ways of empowering the families. For example, after-school transportation services can transfer children to and from therapy sessions. Tapping these community resources "is sometimes the single most important interaction in facilitating the possibility of treatment" (Boyd-Franklin, 1989, p. 156).

In addition, if certain necessary services are not available in a particular community, assisting families in forming extended family-support networks should be part of the responsibility of school psychologists.

Knowledge of Pediatric/Health Psychology

Given the increase in the reported cases of asthma and lead poisoning in the New York City schools, particularly in some of the Bronx and Brooklyn school districts (Brody, 1996), it is critical that psychologists begin to explore the impact of these factors on a child's ability to learn and pay attention. Brody (1996) presents the findings of Dr. Herbert Needleman of the University of Pittsburgh, who found that high levels of lead in the bones of an individual are most likely to lead to aggression, attention difficulties, intellectual deficits, and other social problems.

The New York State Department of Education has already established a "Healthy School Project" in several suburban school districts. Con Edison has been part of this initiative by linking its health awareness program to this State Education Healthy School Project. All of these efforts are aimed at helping families detect, early in their child's education, any medical problems that may impede their child's ability to learn or function effectively in the school system. This is essential in the accurate assessment of a child's handicapping condition. Ruling out any medical problems is one way of preventing misdiagnosis and misplacement.

Knowledge of Parent Training

Mental health workers can play a major role in educating immigrant parents about the educational and social differences in the U.S. systems (Gopaul-McNicol et al., 1991). They can encourage them to attend PTA meetings, explain the issues of confidentiality regarding school records, and help them establish contact with community resources to assist in the acculturation process.

All mental health workers can teach parents alternatives to corporal punishment. Helping parents to understand the social and emotional adjustment difficulties their children are experiencing is of major importance in parent training.

Mental health workers also need to alert parents to the reality of special education and the need for them to question the motives of the teacher. Generally speaking, immigrant parents trust their children's teachers and allow placement in special education if the teacher recommends it. But they need to be taught about the special education system, since this is a rather foreign concept to most of them. Thomas and Gopaul-McNicol (1991) discuss this in detail. In general, assisting in the acculturation process involves nine important points:

1. Education about the differences in the education and social systems, with emphasis on alternative disciplinary strategies, the meaning of educational neglect, and the importance of attending parent/teacher meetings
2. Family empowerment, with emphasis on their legal rights
3. Understanding the family role changes and their effect on acculturation (see Chapter 8)
4. Improving communication between parents and children
5. Teaching parents how to build or maintain positive self-esteem in their children
6. Coping with racism
7. Teaching parents what support their children need at home and the importance of prioritizing their time
8. Teaching parents how to cope with rejection from their children due to the children being embarrassed by their parents' accent
9. Teaching immigrants how to endorse the concept of biculturalism, so that they will not have to live between two worlds

The question most often asked by parents is: "How can I really raise children without disciplining them? I only know the way I was raised at home." The answer involves not only teaching parents the principles of assertive discipline but, in addition, helping parents to recognize that because their children are the first generation of Americans, many of their traditional cultural values will be passed on to them. Expediting the process of "Americanization" in a radical way may leave the parents feeling stripped of cultural pride. Although it is necessary for parents to understand there are laws that govern them with respect to "child abuse," they must also understand that acculturation for first-generation immigrants is a different process from acculturation for second- and third-generation immigrants. Although some of the traditional values will be passed on, inevitably their children will not have the tremendous allegiance to their native countries that the parents do. Parents must understand that the strong cultural identity may dissipate over time, as each new generation becomes more Americanized. However, immigrant parents should not be expected to abandon all of their values, because this can create much anxiety and despair, leaving them very vulnerable and immobilized in a sometimes hostile environment. Instead, these parents need to be taught that the essence and beauty of their culture are traditional values and, to some extent, can be quite beneficial when helping children to cope. Culturally diverse children need to be taught how to take the best from both cultures as they attempt to assimilate in their new country.

TRAINING FOR PARENTS

Armour-Thomas and Gopaul-McNicol (in press) propose a guide for teachers and community leaders on how to assist parents to teach their children to enhance their children's potential at home. Structured and informal activities for the parent and the child, skilled maintenance and generalization to the community at large are offered.

Whitehurst, Fischel, Lonigan, Valdez-Menchaca, Arnold and Smith (1991) found that severe language problems in children can be ameliorated with a home-based intervention that uses parents as therapists. Parents were given seven standard assignments on a biweekly basis that lasted about 30 minutes for each visit. Role play and other behavioral interventions helped the children to increase their expressive vocabulary, which was generalized to other situations and maintained over time.

Rueda and Martinez (1992) proposed a "fiesta educativa" program whereby parents play an active role by participating in community programs that address the needs of their learning disabled youngsters. Essentially, many Latino families work in tandem to oversee the assessment process, the remedial services, and the overall mental health services. Educating parents on their children's educational rights was a critical component of this program. Strom, Johnson, Strom, and Strom (1992a) and Strom, Johnson, Strom, and Strom (1992b) found that schools can better serve communities when opportunities for growth are provided to both parents and children. The main point raised is that Latino parents can help to enhance their children's intellectual skills by encouraging their children to ask more questions and to experiment with problem solving in a more independent fashion. Allowing their children the freedom to engage in fantasy and play were also important characteristics for enhancing intelligence. In general, it was found that children's divergent/convergent thinking, memory, and creative problem solving were increased by teaching these skills through a four-week (each session being two hours in duration) parent curriculum, which was as follows:

1. The first session focused on the folly of defining giftedness via a single criterion. Then, a more comprehensive perspective (Gardner's multiple intelligences) was presented. Before the end of the session, parents were taught how to identify their children's other intelligences/skills/gifts.

2. The second session dealt with the kinds of activities that teachers can use in the classroom to enhance critical thinking. An individualized instructional plan for each child was shared with parents. Adequate time was allotted for questions and answers.

3. Session three allowed parents to identify their own strengths, to evaluate their ability to be tolerant of persistent and inopportune questions raised by their children, and their ability to be supportive of their children engaging in conversation with adults.

4. Session four gave specific handouts to parents on how to continue enhancing their children's intellectual potential. Guidelines for follow-up sessions were given out so parents could continue to be supportive to each other after the group had terminated through a sort of steering committee. We endorse programs such as the ones outlined above. However, we propose a longer training period for parents—an additional four more weeks whereby parents are taught in these sessions to enhance their children's intellectual skills by exposing them to tasks commensurate to the type of tasks found on IQ tests, and then generalizing this skill to the classroom (Armour-Thomas & Gopaul-McNicol, in press).

Cultural transmission from the home to the school is essential for optimal functioning (Boykin, 1983). So, if results reveal that a child has the understanding of one way that he/she learned at home, but the school ecology needs it to be reflected in another, then it is incumbent upon the parent and the school official to train that child to master the skill in the way the school desires. For instance, when a child can put a fan together and is unable to put pieces of a puzzle in a unified whole—tasks that are conceptually quite similar—then such a child can be directly taught through mediated learning experiences (Feuerstein, 1980; Lidz, 1991) how to transfer this knowledge from one context to another. Thus, children should be exposed to puzzles, blocks, and sequential types of tasks—such as story telling via pictures and games—that have different and similar features to help nurture abstract thinking. Parents should be encouraged to teach their children to remember in a rote manner their time tables (as is done in the British educational system) to develop the ability to do computations mentally. Gopaul-McNicol and Armour-Thomas (in press) offer a step-by-step practical guide to parents, teachers, and community members as to how best to nurture and enhance the intellectual abilities of children. Moreover, the "Guidelines for Providers to the Culturally Diverse" (American Psychological Association, 1993) has offered culturally relevant suggestions for practice. More community visits whereby contact is established with families, community leaders, and church representatives are critical in understanding the learning styles of children, and in using these systems as support to aid in the best assessment practices of children. In general, the research supports that children can be trained to think creatively and enhance their intellectual potential if the appropriate intervention is put in place.

TRAINING FOR TEACHERS

Teachers' implicit theories of children's intelligence help to shape the manner they respond to them in the classroom (Murrone and Gynther, 1991). The authors found that teachers were more demanding of children with above average IQ scores as measured by standardized tests of intelligence. As such, teacher attitudes and perceptions of intelligence test scores need to be changed through a re-education process. Maker (1992) emphasized that "not only do standardized tests not predict success in nonacademic settings, but they also are poor predictors of success in school." Maker (1992) also found that the intelligence of children can be enhanced by teaching them Tangram activities (logical mathematical reasoning) in an enrichment program.

Riley, Morocco, Gordon, and Howard (1993) examined what it takes for complex ideas to become rooted in the daily instruction of teachers. The authors explored how teachers could design their curriculum to include the needs and strengths of all students. They recommended analogue experiences (writing and reading in different genre, conferencing, and role-playing) to activate the children's higher cognitive abilities. They also recommended posing questions to children in a directive manner. Thus, children were always expected to develop their responses in more elaborative ways.

Armstrong (1994) expanded Gardner's (1993) ideas on multiple intelligences in the classroom and in so doing aided teachers in enhancing the varied skills of all children. The concern for proponents of the multiple intelligences theory is that traditionally, schools have focused on students' analytic, mathematic, and linguistic intelligence which comprise a general intelligence as measured by the IQ test and ignored their other intelligence. Contrary to this psychometric school of thought, the other intelligences of children are being nurtured as a form of recognizing, respecting, nurturing, and enhancing the holistic intellectual potential of all children (Armour-Thomas & Gopaul-McNicol, 1997a).

ATLAS (authentic teaching, learning, and assessment for all students) communities are comprehensive reform programs that combines the work of four organizations—The Coalition of Essential Schools, The School Development Program (Haynes & Comer, 1993), The Educational Development Center, and the Development Group of Project Zero. ATLAS emphasizes all of the initiatives of these organizations—personalized learning environment, home–school collaboration, active hands-on learning, and ongoing assessment through a curriculum-based approach that responds to the strengths of students.

Lee Katz (1991) spoke of the home–school connection. She spoke of "scripts" that we all acquire through our experiences and through various contexts. Many children are socialized in the home to a particular script, and when they enter the school setting the script is different. For example, the child who is taught to be emotionally expressive in his or her adult–child interactions at home who comes to a school where the interaction is emotionally cool needs to be taught a new script. This is commonly the case with many African-American children (Allen and Boykin, 1992) who are found to have more emotionally expressive experiences in their homes. School psychologists, teachers, and special education prevention specialists (Armour-Thomas & Gopaul-McNicol (in press)) can assist such children in understanding when one script is preferred over the other. The idea is not to inform the child that his or her script is inferior, but rather that in the school setting, he or she must recognize when to use which script. The child must be taught the various scripts to be used. This is analogous to a bilingual child who learns that in the classroom she speaks English, but can engage her peers socially in her native language. To improve learning for all children, teachers, parents, and other significant others must work in a collaborative manner to bring the scripts from the home, the community, and the school closer together.

Adams (1989) offers a thinking skills curricula which first includes ecologically valid materials such as real-world experiences, followed by more abstract materials typically found on psychometric tests. "The Odyssey: A Curriculum for Thinking" (Adams, 1989) focused on the foundations of reasoning, understanding language, verbal reasoning, problem solving, decision making, and creative thinking in a seven-part creative thinking program.

Armour-Thomas and Allen (1993) developed a cognitive training-intervention program based on Sternberg's triarchic theory of intelligence. The purpose of the program was to help teachers understand (1) the nature of cognition, in this instance, Sternberg's *Metacomponents, Performance Components and Knowledge-Acquisition Components*; (2) the function of these cognitive processes in students' learning, and (3) the importance of explicitness in the use of thinking processes in three major areas of teachers' work: instructional objectives, teacher–student interactions during instruction, and assessment.

Evaluation of the program revealed certain characteristics of teachers classified as high users of process. First, there was a consistency in their high use of process in all three stages of teaching. The objectives for their students were process-focused. Second, the interactions with students during instruction was also process-focused. The kinds of questions they asked and the quality of the feedback given to students demonstrated that not only did they model the process, but they encouraged student awareness and use of these processes as well. Finally, the emphasis on process was also apparent in the way they designed their assessment procedures: variation in the format, variation in the level of complexity of the tasks, and content equivalent to what students had learned in class.

A multidisciplinary approach to enhancing the performance of children has been touted as the new model of the millennium. Haynes and Comer (1993) recommend a theme concept approach to address the needs of children. At the Yale University Child Study Center, researchers and practitioners work closely with the home in a collaborative manner through the School Development Program (SDP) which emphasizes a holistic development perspective developed by James Comer, now known as the Comer Process for Reforming Education (Comer, Haynes, Joyner, & Ben-Avie, 1996). This model looks to the mental health team, the central organizing body in the school, to involve parents and teachers in a decision-making capacity to address the sociocultural needs of the child. This approach is one of collaboration rather than autocracy. Parents are selected by their fellow parents to represent their views on school planning. This indeed bridges the gap between the home and the school.

We endorse all of the above initiatives and, in particular, emphasize the importance of including people from the community in effecting these changes. We are increasingly mindful that the classroom is quite different from the context of the research lab, which is decontextualized and free of the ongoing activity of the typical classroom, and that while teachers are trying to include a more dynamic approach to tutelage, they are also dealing with the increase of student diversity, making teaching the most challenging vocation of our time. Increasing proficiency in cognitive competence in students will require much more than training in the use of process-based pedagogical strategies in planning, instruction, and assessment—the major areas of the teacher's work. In addition, teacher training programs would need to provide experiences for teachers to:

- appreciate the cognitive strengths that children bring to the classroom
- think of cognitive weaknesses as experience-specific and not as general person-specific deficits
- explore ways by which children's everyday cognitions could be applied to school tasks
- engage teachers in self-reflective practices in which they confront their beliefs about children whose cultural socialization may be different from theirs.

These experiences are likely to be rewarding because training programs forge more meaningful collaborations with the home and community to more fully appreciate the other cultural niches in children's lives. Also, they ensure that teachers are supported with extra resources in the classroom so that they may more effectively apply information gathered from the bioecological assessment system. We recognize the need to share the responsibility in the schools, and envision the psychologist as playing a prominent role in linking all of the disciplines in a multidisciplinary team approach as outlined in the next section.

PSYCHOLOGISTS' NEW ROLE AS CONSULTANT TO PARENTS, TEACHERS, AND SPECIAL EDUCATION PREVENTION SPECIALISTS

At present, in the school and clinical systems, many disciplines function as multidisciplinary teams, in that each discipline works almost as a separate unit, and comes together primarily at committee on special education meetings to decide on placement for the child. Our hope is that the various disciplines can begin to see the need to be more interdisciplinary than multidisciplinary (see Figure 11–1).

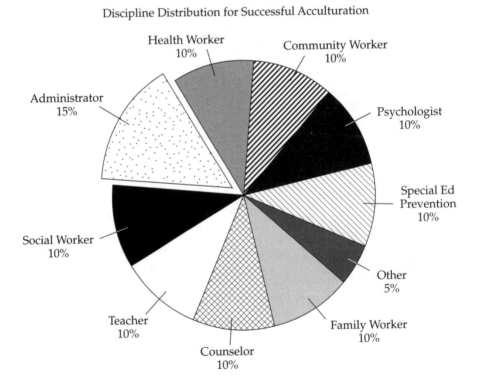

Discipline Distribution for Successful Acculturation

FIGURE 11.1   A Multi-System Interdisciplinary Model

Our vision is that administrators, such as psychologists, can serve as leaders in the school/community systems to bring these various disciplines together with the hope of enhancing the quality of education, and in particular, to bring about a reduction in special education placement. Thus, with a more interdisciplinary training, psychologists can link with health workers so that school officials will understand how health issues impede or enhance the child's functioning.

Likewise, psychologists can work with all school administrators to see how their assessment findings can be used in a prescriptive manner to assist the teachers in the classroom. At this juncture, special education teachers will intervene as special education prevention specialists. Therefore, with the help of these three subdisciplines, children will learn to use all of their strengths to work on their weaknesses. This should result in a reduction of special education placement.

Moreover, psychologists can liaison with the social workers and community resource people to develop a pool of resources outside of the school setting to best empower the child and his or her family. If the family is involved in any sort of treatment by a mental health professional, the psychologists can serve as a liaison to aid school personnel in understanding how the treatment program is enhancing or impeding the child's progress.

Finally, psychologists can work with guidance counselors in a consulting capacity, as mediators between the school and vocational organizations outside of the school setting. This will ensure that there is a connection between completion of high school and future job or advanced educational opportunities.

For school and child psychology to survive with dignity, a multimodal, multisystems approach is needed to address the needs of people from varying ethnic/cultural backgrounds. If such an interdisciplinary program is initiated, we envision this type of program becoming the model training program for the 21st century.

▶ 12

Implications for Policy Makers

Throughout this book, the authors have discussed a number of strategies in the areas of assessment, treatment, instructional, and educational intervention to improve the educational performance of culturally and linguistically diverse students. This chapter briefly recapitulates the approaches endorsed in light of their implications for culturally and linguistically diverse students, their teachers, school psychologists, and policy makers. The research has delineated pedagogical and assessment strategies that may provide a guide for the development of future educational policies, which would in turn lay a foundation for educational practices.

REASONS FOR FAILURE IN SCHOOL

The responsibility to adequately educate all children falls upon the shoulders of the federal government, local school districts, communities, teachers, and parents. However, it is clear that children who live in less affluent school districts of the United States attend schools that are overcrowded, with limited educational resources such as outdated text books, insufficient number of books per students, high student-to-teacher ratios in remedial and bilingual programs, inadequate level of services (e.g., remedial reading instruction in a large group once a week), inadequately administered programs, and dilapidated school buildings. As Cummins (1984) argues, policy makers must realize that the causes of school failure of culturally and linguistically diverse students are varied and complex. However, although no one factor can be identified as the sole culprit, research has identified a number of factors that operate together in such a way that predictions can be made (Cummins, 1984). Consequently, policy makers can create and fund programs that would prevent the failure of culturally and linguistically diverse students. Several factors have been identified as contributors to the school failure of these students.

Exit Criteria for ESL Programs

Limited English-proficient students are exited from the ESL programs based upon their scores on a language proficiency test. They are usually mainstreamed into a full English curriculum after two to three years in an ESL or bilingual program. Students who continue to score low on their language proficiency test are typically referred to special education. Research has found that when children have been exited from these programs, they usually have only achieved BICS (i.e., basic interpersonal communication skills) and not CALP (i.e., cognitive academic language proficiency), but educational policy has not changed to recognize this. It is not uncommon for LEP students who have been exited from ESL to continue to have learning problems because they have not achieved the type of cognitive language proficiency necessary for full comprehension and fast processing of academic facts in English. It is an accepted notion that it takes 5 to 7 years for LEP students to approach grade-level performance in English verbal academic skills (Cummins, 1984). However, children are still expected to function up to par with their monolingual English peers. Limited English-proficient students experience most of their learning difficulties in content-area courses, such as social studies and science, in which classes are heavily language based and use unfamiliar vocabulary. Policy makers must develop an extension to ESL programs (e.g., a transitional program) and interventions in which children are provided with academic and linguistic support to facilitate the development of CALP.

One such intervention is the Sheltered English Program, and its approach appears effective for teaching academic courses to LEP students (Watson et al., 1989). In this program, teachers incorporate second-language acquisition principles with traditional teaching strategies to increase the comprehensibility of the lesson for students (Krashen, 1982). Teachers make many adjustments; they preteach two vocabularies: the words necessary to understand the content of the lesson, and the words used to explain the lesson (Watson et al., 1989). Teachers use the same lesson format to provide a structure for learning, and this reduces the time necessary for the students to decipher how the teacher is presenting new material (Watson et al., 1989). Manipulative and visual techniques are used to illustrate the concepts. Cooperative learning techniques are utilized, providing the interactive aspect that brings lessons to life and enhances learning. Additionally, students are instructed on learning strategies or study skills—note taking, listening skills, and outlining (Watson et al., 1989).

Inadequate Educational Support

Limited English-proficient students are provided with either ESL or bilingual education, and in some cases they might be offered remedial reading in addition to ESL or bilingual education. Once children are exited from ESL or bilingual education, the only other support program available is remedial reading. However, strategies used in remedial reading are usually not effective, because they do not individualize instruction or target entry-level skills.

Policy makers should introduce educational legislative acts that endorse more individualized instruction in remedial reading. Research has found that the most effective remedial programs are those that provide tutorial or one-to-one instruction, and ones in which the students' skills are assessed and reassessed frequently (e.g., every 8 to 10 weeks) to readjust instructional goals and strategies.

Lack of Pre-Referral Services

When linguistically and culturally diverse students continue to experience difficulty in achievement, most teachers' first step is to refer them to special education. Although, the Individuals with Disabilities Education Act (IDEA) (1995) requests that the referring party document pre-referral interventions, teachers often consider ESL and bilingual education as a pre-referral intervention. Thus the present system has no structured procedure in place to determine the validity of a referral and provides very little incentive for preventing special education placement. In fact, teachers are encouraged by school administrators to refer low-achieving students to special education so that their scores on statewide or districtwide competency exams are not added to their school's overall performance. The undue pressure felt by school administrators to meet minimal competency standards set up by the State promotes a pressured, competitive classroom atmosphere that maximizes the risk of academic failure for students with potential academic difficulties (Cummins, 1984). This pressure encourages teachers to "teach to the test," giving them very little time or inclination to modify instruction or to accommodate the educational needs of at-risk students.

Armour-Thomas and Gopaul-McNicol (in press) argue that most special education students could be better served in a fully mainstreamed program if they were provided with greater attention to individual needs, if learning environments were adapted to accommodate diversity, if school personnel were trained and supported to respond to student diversity, and if efforts aimed at prevention were funded. In many instances, teachers (for lack of guidance as to how to provide pre-referral services and modify instruction) wait until students who exhibit minor gaps in achievement fall substantially below grade level to make a referral for special education. Otherwise, the student is referred a number of times until he or she qualifies (based on state criteria as to what constitutes a learning impairment) for special education services. During the "waiting" period, the struggling student is provided with little or no educational service to remediate the problem. These practices should be considered educational malpractice, and teachers and administrators should be accountable.

Although the current amendment to IDEA (1995) recognizes the need to fund prevention programs and include special education students in all assessment, most school districts have not been responsive in developing programs to address culturally and linguistically diverse students' needs. Federal and state funding formulas must help promote good practices in education, and this includes special education prevention programs (U.S. Education Department, 1995).

Traditional Pedagogical Strategies

If cooperative learning approaches have been found to be effective with culturally and linguistically diverse students who share a cultural worldview that embraces cooperative and noncompetitive values and lifestyles, then why are most teachers who work with this student population not implementing these strategies in their classrooms? Why is it that, if research supports the use of context in teaching language arts, most teachers still rely on decontextualized teaching strategies to impart their lessons? Moreover, the research is rather clear in terms of the benefits of using culturally relevant instructional materials and the use of context in learning new information, yet most culturally and linguistically diverse students are given instructional materials that are culturally alien. Consequently, children have difficulty connecting emotionally, cognitively, socially, and linguistically with the information, and this interferes with learning. Undoubtedly, many of the culturally and linguistically diverse students identified as "learning disabled" exhibit learning difficulties that are pedagogically induced (Cummins, 1984).

Policy makers should recognize the need for multicultural instructional materials, through executive orders, rules and regulations, or even public speeches or endorsements. This would in turn put pressure on the publishers of textbooks and instructional materials to develop multicultural educational materials that recognize the cultural heritage of students, and on local school districts to purchase these materials. Policy makers should take responsibility for promoting and transmitting an instructional model that has shown positive results with culturally and linguistically diverse students.

Lack of Appropriate Educational Planning for Overage Students

Unfortunately, an increasing number of immigrant students arrive in the United States with little to no educational background. These children present an even greater challenge to the public schools when they are overage (e.g., a seventeen-year-old 10th grader). These students are quickly frustrated by the educational system, so they drop out of school. Many times, the first course of action is to simply refer these children to special education in order to provide them with individualized or small-group instruction and remediation. However, most of these students are not disabled children in need of special education services. The lack of appropriate programming to address their needs seems to be the crux of the problem.

Individualized or small-group instruction appears to be the most effective type of educational intervention for overage students. In developing a program for these students, several components are essential: home/school connection to develop trust and a bond with the family; teaching study strategies; building self-esteem by including students in planning for their futures; vocational and career planning; work-study programs; cooperative learning strategies to reduce isolation so the student is able to bring his or her life experience to the discussion; using multicultural instructional materials; building basic literacy skills; frequent assessment to tailor instruction to students' needs; developing language skills; and using multiple strategies to illustrate and demonstrate concepts.

Lack of Comprehensive Assessment Models

Over the years professional organizations, such as the American Psychological Association and the National Council of Measurement in Education, have reflected concerns regarding discriminatory practices in intelligence testing through written bylaws, and ethical principles, and standards. However, these noble sentiments seemed to have had minimal impact on the construction of standardized tests or discriminary practices. As indicated in Chapter 3, interpretation and use of test results have been particularly inimical to ethnic and linguistic children, particularly those from low-income backgrounds. Test developers and practitioners seem to have been oblivious to the theoretical and empirical research regarding the situatedness of cognition over the last two decades, (Armour-Thomas & Gopaul-McNicol, in press) or to the influence of linguistic and cultural diversity in intelligent behavior. But, even more disheartening, they seem unaware of the devastating consequences of their judgments that place large numbers of children on educational paths that are neither enabling nor worth wanting. Indeed, the literature is replete with inequitable schooling of children placed in low-track classes or in unwarranted special educational programs (e.g., Kozol, 1991; Lipsky & Gartner, 1996, Oakes, 1990). Perhaps a list of principles and standards, no matter how well-intentioned, is insufficient insurance against discriminatory practices in standardized intellectual testing. What is needed, in our judgment, is greater democratic reciprocity in discussions among practitioners, test developers, and client representatives in the development of principles and standards with respect to intellectual assessment practices. Equally important is the need for enforceable principles that are truly reflective of our commitment to equity and cultural pluralism. Though not exhaustive, we submit the following questions for consideration:

- Do the principles and standards essentially and sufficiently accommodate multiple cultural perspectives?
- Do the principles and standards support multiple expressions of intelligent behavior?
- Do the principles and standards support the assessment of cognitive potential?
- Do the principles and standards support evidence of intelligence beyond the standardized testing context?
- Do the principles and standards provide clear implications for desirable competencies among practitioners, both psychologists-in-training and practicing psychologists/clinicians?
- Are there mechanisms for the incorporation of these competencies into accreditation criteria?

Legislative acts and statutes should specify and define what is involved in nonbiased or nondiscriminatory assessment. For example, legislative statutes must delineate that, as part of a nondiscriminatory assessment, school psychologists and educational educators must use testing strategies that modify standard testing procedures when necessary to accommodate bilingual and bicultural issues. Extensive background information should be gathered. This includes data about acculturation, immigration experiences, community lifestyle, religious affiliations and beliefs, academic background or school history, medical history, parents' educational background and ideas about education, social experiences in the country of origin, and language exposure.

Poor Training of Future Educational Practitioners at the University and College Levels

Very few university programs that train teachers, school psychologists, speech and language pathologists, and so forth, are not truly committed to preparing teachers that are ready to work with culturally and linguistically diverse populations. These educational practitioners do not understand the special issues that impact on this population: second-language acquisition, acculturation process, and historical events. More importantly, teachers' lack of understanding leads them to view culturally and linguistically diverse students as deficient, instead of being able to appreciate their differences and use them to enrich their learning. The failure to see the potential of these children results in the underestimation of their cognitive abilities, which limits their educational options.

Teachers, school administrators, psychologists, and other educational practitioners in training are required to take only one course in multicultural issues as part of their preparation. The implication here is that the understanding of multicultural issues is not viewed as important enough to warrant more required courses or adding a multicultural component to every course in their core curriculum.

Policy makers must allocate funding to universities and colleges to encourage multicultural and bilingual training programs that would prepare future educational practitioners to work with culturally and linguistically diverse students and families. Teachers, school psychologists, speech and language pathologists, and other educational practitioners should be certified to work with culturally and linguistically diverse students. Therefore, local school districts should be encouraged to provide in-service training or require further training of their school personnel by offering salary incentives or tuition reimbursement for additional training in this area, and to obtain certification to work with this population.

Accountability

Local school districts and policy makers must be accountable and responsible for providing an appropriate education to culturally and linguistically diverse students. This means that the local school district should be able to modify its already existing resources to accommodate the educational needs of these students. For example, current remedial reading services can be modified to accommodate culturally and linguistically diverse students by using instructional techniques that have shown positive results with this population. Policy makers can provide sufficient flexibility in their funding criteria that would allow local school districts to also service the needs of these students. According to Slavin (1987), in light of the increasing number of student failures, schools often blame parents, society, television, or the students themselves; although societal factors do make educating children a more difficult task, schools still hold the greater responsibility in ensuring that children attending their institutions succeed.

Slavin (1987) emphasized several areas in which schools have definite control:

1. *Focus on prevention.* From the onset, schools should ensure that every child learns to read by providing appropriate instruction (e.g., varied and culturally sensitive instructional strategies, emphasizing language development). Structured preschool and kindergarten programs provide the foundation children need when they are beginning to read in the first grade; moreover, it is in the first grade that intensive remedial programs should begin.

2. *Focus on Classroom Change.* The gains made by preschool and kindergarten educational experiences should be followed with appropriate instruction in the classrooms. This instruction should include the use of culturally sensitive instructional material and the use of varied manipulatives and visual techniques to illustrate educational concepts, as well as the development of language skills.

3. *Focus on the Appropriate Use of Remedial Programs.* The implementation of a remedial program after the student has fallen two to three grade levels below usually does not have a significant impact on reducing the gap. These programs should be used when they are most effective—when the child begins to show a lag in the mastery of basic academic skills. It is then that intensive remediation should be offered (Slavin, 1987).

Policy makers and local school districts should take a closer look at the manner in which programs are used and implemented in the schools so that they address the educational needs of all students. Policy makers should be accountable for relying heavily on quantitative indices (e.g., statewide and districtwide standardized competency tests) to determine minimal competency, because in so doing, they have ignored the quality of instruction in the classroom (Cummins, 1984), and this has contributed to the high rate of failure of culturally and linguistically diverse students in school. Most importantly, although research in second-language acquisition has supported the view that students' English and academic skills develop more rapidly and solidly in strong bilingual programs, policy makers have ignored the merits of this approach because bilingual classes are still a source of much controversy in the United States. Unfortunately, the controversy over bilingual education is not about the effectiveness of this program and instructional approach; instead, it is rooted in nationalistic concerns, and even prejudice.

Lack of Parent and Community Involvement

Parents and community involvement in school programs generate support for programs aimed at addressing the needs of these students not only at the local level but also in terms of political pressure to fund these programs. Additionally, parent involvement, such as school staff working with parents to establish an atmosphere in their home that is conducive to learning, is essential to children's success in school. Educators who can establish a relationship of trust and mutual respect with parents of culturally and linguistically diverse students will be able to involve parents in the process of building literacy skills in their children (Cummins, 1984). Teachers and parents must be partners in the education of children. Therefore, teachers must be knowledgeable of the cultural beliefs and practices of parents and community. They must know how to accommodate the cultural diversity that may exist, and be able to communicate with parents in their native language or with the use of an interpreter. Policy makers must encourage and provide the financial allocation so that local school districts may develop parent involvement programs.

ISSUES IN POLICY DEVELOPMENT

Dunn (1986) defines policy as the outcome of decision-making processes set in motion to respond to existing challenges. In educational policy making, an individual or group of individuals who hold similar beliefs and have similar needs want something from government or other agencies and build a coalition of influence to obtain it (Bransford, Goldman, & Vye, 1991). They strategize and develop tactics intended to provoke decision makers and those in power to pass laws and issue executive and judicial orders to address their needs and concerns (Bransford et al., 1991). The most critical issues impacting policy development are financing, state's rights issues or local control, planning and implementation, training needs (Bransford et al., 1991), and effectiveness of instructional strategies and educational programs.

Today, in light of the dwindling financial resources available to local school districts to develop effective programs aimed at addressing the educational needs of all children, cutbacks in funding from the federal government have been met with a certain hesitancy by local educational agencies expected to assume the cost, because they do not have the resources (Armour-Thomas & Gopaul-McNicol, in press). When the federal government shifts the responsibility of education to the state and local agencies, culturally and linguistically diverse students population are generally the first to feel the reduction in educational services. School districts in high poverty areas usually have the most needs and the least financial resources to address those needs, while more affluent districts do not have the number of culturally and linguistically diverse populations that would motivate them to create programs for these students. In either case, programs designed to answer the educational needs of culturally and linguistically diverse students are few.

There is an ongoing debate between the federal government and state agencies regarding the responsibility of educating the children of this nation. One of the main arguments used by states' rights advocates is that educating the children of America has long been recognized as the constitutional responsibility of the states and local school districts (Thompson & Hixson, 1984). They maintain that the U.S. Department of Education (1995) issues specific guidelines and statutes that usurp the power of the states and local school boards to determine educational strategies and curriculum policies. Bransford et al. (1991) argued that the lack of coordination between federal and state agencies in planning, implementation, and evaluation of programs has led to weak guidelines for program monitoring, wasted human and material resources, and a failure to address students' individual educational needs.

Cummins (1984) warned that changes in beliefs and attitudes among educational practitioners results only from the actual process of carrying out different approaches in which the evidence of their appropriateness is allowed to speak for itself. Moreover, at the level of policy making, parents' involvement in the community, school, and grassroots political organizations would place political pressures on policy makers to enact legislative acts whose goal is to strengthen and build the educational options of culturally and linguistically diverse students so that they can reach their fullest potential.

▶ 13

Implications for Future Research and Clinical Work

CROSS-CULTURAL RESEARCH

In addition to the ethical guidelines suggested for all mental health workers, the American Psychological Association (1993), Pedersen (1995), Ponterotto and Casas (1991), Tapp et al. (1974), and Wrenn (1985) outlined some ethical considerations in conducting cross-cultural research:

1. It is necessary to understand the prevailing psychosocial problems, identify the psychocultural strengths in each culture, and examine the community involvement in each culture.
2. It is important to avoid the dangers in defining everyone's reality according to particular cultural assumptions. In other words, it is important to understand the client's/culture's worldview.
3. It is important to check with colleagues in and out of the culture to help make good ethical judgments.
4. It is critical to attend to the technical problems of equivalent measurement across cultures. Failure to do so may result in inaccurate interpretations and potentially damaging consequences to the culture being studied.
5. Avoid overuse of a particular culture or a particular population.
6. It is worthy to note that the definition of private varies culturally. Therefore, what may be routine to a Westerner may be highly intrusive to the host culture. As such, behaviors that are public to a culture may not be intended for open and public discussion by noncommunity members.

7. The research should not only be beneficial to the researcher, but to the host community as well, so the population studied should be enhanced by the research.

The four-tier bio-ecological assessment system (Armour-Thomas & Gopaul-McNicol, 1997a) was developed in response to the authors' concern that standardized tests of intelligence provided an incomplete appraisal of children's cognitive functioning. Guided by the assumptions of the authors' emerging bio-ecological model, a number of cognitive enhancement procedures were used in conjunction with the traditional IQ measure—the WISC-111 to identify cognitive strengths and weaknesses of children. We are encouraged with the results that demonstrate that improvement on intellectual tasks is to be expected when children are:

- allowed the opportunity to contextualize words in sentences;
- given time, paper, and pencil to solve verbal problems involving memory and quantitative reasoning; and
- given time and opportunity to understand and solve spatial problems involving memory, understanding, and reasoning.

In addition, we have observed, as in Armour-Thomas and Gopaul-McNicol (1997a), that many children who perform poorly on standardized IQ tests are able to demonstrate comparable skills in their everyday lives. Consideration of these results from a bio-cultural perspective would suggest that a standardized measure of intelligence is insufficiently sensitive to discriminate which cognitions are well-formed from those that are still in an embryonic stage of development. These findings present some interesting challenges for researchers in the types of questions they may wish to consider regarding intelligence and its assessment as well as the kinds of research design and methodology that such questions would necessitate. We think, though, that the findings pose a more pressing challenge to those who set guidelines and standards for intelligence testing, particularly as these relate to nondiscriminatory practices for children from linguistically and culturally diverse backgrounds.

Perhaps as important, intervention studies should be longitudinal in design to allow sufficient time for reinforcement and generalizability of effects to other contexts. It may well be that Head Start and other intervention studies for improving intelligence showed few enduring results due to the brevity of the treatment. During the course of development of some children, threatening person–environment interactions may far outweigh the sustaining person–environment ones. To offset the negative impact of the former, longer and more enriching interventions are likely to produce more lasting cognitive change.

Several issues and questions that have been raised or implied throughout the course of this book need further investigation:

1. Further research is needed on the Black–White supervisory dyad that takes into account the level of racial identity of both supervisor and supervisee and looks at how this impacts on satisfaction with supervision.
2. Research also needs to recognize the complexity of the same racial dyad in which the race of the supervisor and supervisee may be the same but they may be from different cultures.
3. Rating scales for supervisors and supervisees should be developed to assess the quality of their experiences.
4. How can universities train mental health workers in a more interdisciplinary fashion, with the hope of enhancing their ability to provide psychological services?
5. Normative data should be collected on diverse cultural groups regarding their parenting practices.
6. The impact of parent–child separation due to immigration on parenting skills should be examined.
7. Determination should be made as to what extent, if any, acculturation strains parent–child relationships.
8. Studies should examine the impact of acculturation on discipline practices.
9. Do therapists make differential judgments about parenting skills based on culture/ethnicity/race/religion?

In general, all of the models and issues raised in Parts II and III of this book should be strongly considered for further research and clinical work. The use of the MULTI-CMS model for treatment should be examined in more detail in research studies. Likewise, the impact of second language or dialects such as Creole and Ebonics should be explored in light of the new findings that second-language acquisition dramatically affects learning. The suggestions proposed in Chapter 7 for teachers who work with linguistically and culturally diverse children should be implemented in a research program for the next decade. Possibly, one might witness an improvement in performance with this population if teachers themselves hone their cross-cultural clinical and educational skills.

The challenges set forth in this book in working with linguistically and culturally diverse children are tremendous, and certainly leave the interested researcher with a research agenda for the next decade.

References

Adams, M. J. (1989). Thinking skills curricula: Their promise and progress. *Educational Psychologist, 24,* (1), 25–75.

Adams, P. L. (1990). Prejudice and exclusion as social traumata. In J. D. Noshpitz and R. D. Coddington (Eds.), *Stresses and the adjustment disorders* (362–91), New York: Wiley.

Adebimpe, V. R. (1981). Overview: White norms and psychiatric diagnosis of Black patients. *American Journal of Psychiatry, 138,* 279–85.

Adler, N. E. , Boyce, T., Chesney, M. A., Cohen, S., Falkman, S., Kahn, R. L., & Syme, S. L. (1994). Socioeconomic status and health: The challenge as the gradient. *American Psychologist, 49,* 15–24.

Agbagani-Siewert, P. (1994). Filipino American culture and family: Guidelines for practitioners. *Families in Society: The Journal of Contemporary Human Services, 44,* 429–38.

Alba, R. (1990). *Ethnic identity: The transformation of White America.* New Haven, CT: Yale University Press, 1–15.

Al-Issa, I. (1982). *Culture and psycopathology.* Baltimore: University Press.

Allen, B. A., & Boykin, A. W. (1991). The influence of contextual factors on Black and White children's performance: Effects of movement opportunity and music. *International Journal of Psychology, 26,* 373–387.

Allen, B. A., & Boykin, A. W. (1992). Children and the educational process: Alienating cultural discontinuity through prescriptive pedagogy. *School Psychology Review, 21(4),* 586–596.

Allen, L., & Majidi-Ali, S. (1989). Black American children. In J. T. Gebbs and L. N. Huang (Eds.), *Children of Color* (148–78). San Francisco: Jossey-Bass.

Althens, Gary (1981). *Learning across cultures.* Washington, DC: National Association of Foreign Student Affairs, 63.

American Psychological Association (1993). Guidelines for providers of psychological services to ethnic, linguistic and culturally diverse populations. *American Psychologist, 48,* 45–48.

Anderson, P. P. (1989). Issues in serving culturally diverse families of young children with disabilities. *Early Child Development and Care, 50,* 167–88.

Angel, R., & Thoits, P. (1987). The impact of culture on the cognitive structure of illness. *Culture, Medicine and Psychiatry, 11*, 465–494.

Aponte, H. (1976). The family-school interview: An ecostructural approach. *Family Process, 15*(3), 303–311.

Aponte, H., & Van Deusen, J. (1981). Structural family therapy. In A. Gurman & D. Kniskern (Eds.), *Handbook of family therapy*. New York: Brunner/Mazer.

Aponte, J. F., & Barnes, J. M. (1995). Impact of acculturation and moderator variables in the intervention and treatment of ethnic groups. In J. F. Aponte, R. Y. Rivers and J. Wahl (Eds.), *Psychological interventions and cultural diversity*, (19–39). Boston: Allyn and Bacon.

Aponte, J. F., & Crouch, R. T. (1995). The changing ethnic profile of the United States. In J. F. Aponte, R. Y. Rivers, and J. Wahl, *Psychological interventions and cultural diversity*, (1–18). Boston: Allyn and Bacon.

Armour-Thomas, E. (1992). Assessment in the service of thinking and learning for low achieving students. *The High School Journal*, Vol. 75, No. 2, 99–118.

Armour-Thomas, E. (1992). Intellectual assessment of children from culturally diverse backgrounds. *School Psychology Review, 21*(4), 552–565.

Armour-Thomas, E. & Allen, B. (1993). The feasibility of an information-processing methodology for the assessment of vocabulary competence. *Journal of Instructional Psychology, 20* (4), 306–313.

Armour-Thomas, E. & Gopaul-McNicol, S. *Assessing intelligence: A bio-ecological approach*. Thousand Oaks, California: Sage Publications (in press).

Armour-Thomas, E., & Gopaul-McNicol, S. (1997a). A bio-ecological approach to intellectual assessment. *Cultural Diversity and Mental Health, Vol. 3, No. 2*, 25–39.

Armour-Thomas, E. & Gopaul-McNicol, S. (1997b). Examining the correlates of learning disability: A bio-ecological approach. *Journal of Social Distress and the Homeless, Vol. 6, No. 2*, 140–165.

Arredondo, P., Toporek, R., Pack Brown, S., Jones, J., Locke, D., Sanchez, J., & Stadler, H. (1996). Operationalization of the multicultural counseling competencies. *Journal of Multicultural Counseling and Development, 24*(1), 42–78.

Artzt, A. F. & Armour-Thomas, E. (1992). Development of a cognitive-metacognitive framework for protocol analysis of mathematical problem solving in small groups. *Cognition and Instruction, 9*, 137–175.

Aspira of New York, Inc. v. New York Board of Education, (Filed September 20, 1972). 72 Civ. 4002 (S.D.N.Y.)

Auerswald, E. (1968). Interdisciplinary versus ecological approach. *Family Process, 7*, 204.

Aver, J. C. P. (1984). *Bilingual conversations*. Amsterdam: John Benjamins.

Baca, L., & Bransford, J. (1981). Meeting the needs of the bilingual handicapped child. *Momentum*, 36–51.

Baker, L. (1982). An evaluation of the role of metacognitive deficits in learning disabilities. *Topics in Learning & Learning Disabilities, 2* (1), 27–35.

Bandura, A. (1969). *Principles of behavior modification*. New York: Holt.

Baron, J. (1981). Reflective thinking as a goal of education. *Intelligence, 5*, 291–309.

Baron, J. (1982). Personality and intelligence. In R. J. Sternberg (Ed.), *Handbook of human intelligence*. New York: Cambridge University Press.

Baron, R. M., & Needel, S. P. (1980). Toward an understanding of the differences in the responses of humans and other animals to density. *Psychology Review, 87*, 320–26.

Barona, A., Santos de Barona, Flores, A. A., & Gutierrez, M. H. (1990). Critical issues in training school psychologists to serve minority school children. In A. Barona, & E. Garcia (Eds.), *Children at risk: Poverty, minority status and other issues in educational equity* (pp. 187–200). Washington, DC: National Association of School Psychologists.

Baruth, G. L. & Manning, M. L. (1992). Understanding and counseling Hispanic American children. *Elementary School Guidance and Counseling, 27*, 113–22.

Beker, J. & Feuerstein, R. (1990). Conceptual foundations of the modifying environment in group care and treatment settings for children and youth. *Journal of Child and Youth Care, 4* (5), 23–33.

Benedict, F. (1959). *Race: Science and politics.* New York: Viking.

Bennett, C. (1981). A case for pluralism in school. *Phi Delta Kappan, 62,* (8), 589–91.

Bennett, M. J. (1986). A developmental approach to training. *Journal of Intercultural Relations, 10,* 179–96.

Bem, S. L. (1974). The measurement of psychological androgyny. *Journal of Counseling and Clinical Psychology, 42,* 155–162.

Bernal, M. E., & Padilla, A. M. (1982). Status of minority curricula and training in clinical psychology. *American Psychologist, 37,* 780–787.

Berry, J. (1980). Cultural universality of any theory of human intelligence remains an open question. *Behavioral and Brain Sciences, 3,* 584–585.

Berry, J. W. (1980). Acculturation as varieties of adaptation. In A. M. Podella (Ed.), *Acculturation: Theory, model, and some new findings* (pp. 9–25). Boulder, CO: Westview.

Berry, J. W. (1986). The acculturation process and refugee behavior. In C. L. Williams and J. Westerneyer (Eds.), *Refugee mental health in resettlement countries* (pp. 25–37). Washington, DC: Hemisphere Publishing.

Berry, J. W., Kim, U., Minde, T., & Mok, D. (1987). Comparative studies of acculturative stress. *International Migration Review, 21*(3), 491–511.

Berry, J. W., & Kim, U. (1988). Acculturation and mental health. In P. R. Dasen, J. W. Berry, and N. Sartorius (Eds.), *Health and cross-cultural psychology: Toward applications* (pp. 207–36). Newbury Park, CA: Sage.

Berry, M. (1981). *Teaching linguistically handicapped children.* Englewood Cliffs, NJ: Prentice-Hall.

Bersoff, D. N. (1981). Testing and the law. *American Psychologist, 36,* 1047–56.

Billingsley, A. (1974). *Black families and the struggle for survival: Teaching our children to walk tall.* New York: Friendship Press.

Boekestijn, D. (1984, September). Intercultural migration and the development of personal identity: The dilemma between identity maintenance and cultural adaptation. Paper presented at the XXIII International Congress of Psychology, Acapulco, Mexico.

Bowen, M. (1978). *Family therapy in clinical practice.* New York: Jason Aronson.

Boyd-Franklin, N. (1989). *Black families in therapy.* New York: Guilford.

Boyd-Franklin, N. (1990). Five key factors in the treatment of black families. In G. W. Saba, B. M. Karrer, & K. V. Hardy (Eds.), *Minorities and family therapy* (pp. 53–69). New York: Hawarth.

Boykin, A. W. (1983). The academic performance of Afro-American children. In J. T. Spence (Ed.), *Achievement and achievement motives* (pp. 322–371). San Francisco: Freeman.

Boykin, W. A. (1982). Task variability and the performance of black and white school children: Vervistic explorations. *Journal of Black Studies, 12,* 469–85.

Bracken, B. A. & Fouad, N. (1987). Spanish translation and validation of the braken basic concept scale. *School Psychology Review, 16*(1). 94–102.

Bradley, L., & Bradley, G. (1977). The academic achievement of Black students in desegregated schools: A critical review. *Review of Educated Research, 47,* 399–449.

Brand, C. R., & Deary, I. J. (1982). *Intelligence and "inspection time:" A model for intelligence.* Berlin: Springer Verlag.

Bransford, J. D., Goldman, S. R., & Vye, N. J. (1991). Making a difference in people's abilities to think: Reflections on a decade of work and some hopes for the future. In L. Okagaki & R. J. Sternberg (Eds.), *Directors of development: Influences on the development of children's thinking.* Hillsdale, NY: Lawrence Erlbaum Associates (pp. 3–23).

Brice, J. (1982). West Indian families. In M. McGoldrick, J. K. Pearce, & J. Giordana (Eds.), *Ethnicity and family therapy* (pp. 123–133). New York: Guilford.

Briones, D. F., Heller, P. L., Chalfant, H. P., Roberts, A. E., Aguirre-Hauchbaum, S. F., & Farr, W. I., Jr. (1990). Socioeconomic status, ethnicity, psychological distress, and readiness to utilize a mental health facility. *American Journal of Psychiatry, 147,* 1,333–40.

Brislin, R. W. (1980). Translation and content analysis of oral and written materials. In H. C. Triandis & J. W. Berry (Eds.), *Methodology: Handbook of cross-cultural psychology,* Vol. 2 (pp. 389–444). Boston: Allyn and Bacon.

Bronfenbrenner, V. (1977). Towards an experimental ecology of human development. *American Psychologist, 45,* 513–530.

Brody, J. (1996). Aggressiveness and delinquency in boys is linked to lead in bones. *New York Times, Health Section K,* p. 4.

Brown, D. H. (1987). *Principles of Language Learning and Teaching.* Englewood Cliffs, NJ: Prentice-Hall.

Brown, H. D. (1987). *Principles of language learning and teaching.* Englewood Cliffs, NJ: Prentice-Hall.

Brown, L. G. (1969). *Immigration: Cultural conflicts and social adjustment.* New York: Arno Press and *New York Times.*

Brown, M. T., & Landrum-Brown, J. (1995). Counselor supervision: Cross-cultural perspectives. In J. G. Ponterotto, J. M. Casas, L. A. Suzuki, & C. M. Alexander (Eds.), *Handbook of multicultural counseling* (pp. 263–286). California: Sage.

Bryan, T. (1977). Learning disabled children's comprehension and nonverbal communication. *Journal of Learning Disabilities, 10,* 501–06.

Budoff, M. (1987). Measures for assessing learning potential. In C. S. Lidz (Ed.), *Dynamic assessment: An interactional approach to evaluating learning potential.* New York: Guilford.

Burnam, M. A., Hough, R. L., Karno, M., Escobar, J. I., & Telles, C. A. (1987). Acculturation and lifetime prevalence of psychiatric disorders among Mexican Americans in Los Angeles. *Journal of Health and Social Behavior, 28,* 89–102.

Butcher, J. N., & Pancheri, P. (1976). *A handbook of cross-national MMPI research.* Minneapolis: University of Minnesota.

Canale, M., & Swain, M. (1980). Theoretical bases of communicative approaches to second language teaching and testing. *Applied Linguistics, 1,* 1–47.

Cardoza, D., & Rueda, R. (1986). Educational and occupational outcomes of Hispanic learning disabled high school students. *The Journal of Special Education, 20,* 111–26.

Carlson, J. S. (1985). The issue of g: Some relevant questions. *The Behavioral and Brain Sciences, 8*(2), 224–225.

Carney, C. G., & Kahn, K. B. (1984). Building competencies for effective cross-cultural counseling; A developmental view. *The counseling psychologist, 12*(1), 111–119.

Carroll, J. B. (1993). *Human cognitive abilities.* Cambridge: Cambridge University Press.

Carrow-Woolfolk, E. (1978). Reply to Rueda and Perozzi. *Journal of Speech and Hearing Disorders, 43,* 556–58.

Carter, R. (1995). *The influence of race and racial identity in psychotherapy.* New York: Wiley.

Casas, J. M., Ponterotto, J. G., & Gutierrez, J. M. (1986). An ethical indictment of counseling research and training: The cross-cultural perspective. *Journal of Counseling and Development, Vol. 64, January,* 347–349.

Cattell, R. B. (1963). Theory of fluid and crystallized intelligence: A critical experiment. *Journal of Educational Psychology, 54,* 1–22.

Ceci, S. (1990). *On intelligence: More or less.* Englewood Cliffs, NJ: Prentice-Hall.

Chamberlain, P., & Medinos-Landurand, P. (1991). Practical considerations for the assessment of LEP students with special needs. In E. V. Hamayan & J. S. Damico (Eds.), *Limiting bias in the assessment of bilingual students* (pp. 112-156) Austin, TX: Pro-Ed.

Chan, S. (1992). Families with Asian roots. In E. W. Lynch and M. J. Hanson, *Developing cross-cultural competence* (181–257). Baltimore, MD: Paul Brookes Publishing Co.

Cheung, F. K., & Snowden, L. R. (1990). Community mental health and ethnic minority populations. *Community Mental Health Journal, 26,* 277–91.

Chihara, T., & Oller, J. W. (1978). Attitudes and proficiency in EFL: A sociolinguistic study of adult Japanese. *Language Learning, 28,* 55–68.

Choney. S. K., Berryhill-Paapke, E., & Robbins, R. R. (1995). The acculturation of American Indians: Developing frameworks for research and practice (pp. 73–92). In J. G. Ponterotto, J. M. Casas, L. A. Suzuki, & C. M. Alexander (Eds.), *Handbook of multicultural counseling.* Thousands Oaks, CA: Sage Publications.

Cloud, N. (1991). Educational assessment. In E. V. Hamayan, & J. S. Damico. *Limiting bias in the assessment of bilingual students* (221-45). Austin, TX: Pro-Ed.

Cohen, R. (1969). Conceptual styles, culture conflict, and non-verbal tests of intelligence. *American Anthropologist, 71* (5), 828–857.

Comer, J., Haynes, N., Joyner, E., & Ben-Avie, M. (Eds.) (1996). *Rallying the whole village: The Comer process for reforming education.* New York: Teachers College, Columbia University Press.

Congress, E. P. (1994). The use of culture grams to assess and empower culturally diverse families. *Families in Society: The Journal of Contemporary Human Services, 46,* 531–40.

Corvin, S., & Wiggins, F. (1989). An anti-racism training model for white professionals. *Journal of Multicultural Counseling and Development, 17,* 105–14.

Covarrubias v. San Diego Unified School District (Southern California), No. 70-394-T, (S.D., Cal. February, 1971).

Crider, A. B., Goethals, G. R., Kavanaugh, R. D., & Solomon, P. R. (1989). *Psychology* (3rd Ed.). Glenview, IL: Scott, Foresman and Company.

Critoph, G. E. (1979). The contending Americas. In John A. Hague (Ed.), *American character and culture in a changing world* (pp. 143–145). Westport, CT: Greenwood Press.

Cummins, J., (1981). Age on arrival and immigrant second language learning in Canada: A measurement. *Applied Linguistics, 2,* 132–49.

Cummins, J. (1984). *Bilingualism and special education: Issues in assessment and pedagogy.* San Diego: College Hill Press.

Cummins, J. (1989). *Empowering Minority Students.* Sacramento, CA: California Association of Bilingual Education.

Daalen-Kapteijns, Van, M. M., & Elshout-Mohr, M. (1981). The acquisition of word meaning as a cognitive learning process. *Journal of Verbal Learning and Verbal Behavior, 20,* 386–399.

Dana, R. H. (1993). *Multicultural assessment perspectives for professional psychology.* Boston: Allyn and Bacon.

Das, J. P. (1985). Interpretations for a class on minority assessment. *The Behavioral and Brain Sciences, 8(2),* 228–229.

De Avila, E. (1974). The testing of minority children—A neo-Piagetian approach. *Today's Education, November–December,* 72–75.

Delgado-Gaitan, C. (1994). Consejos: The power of cultural narratives. *Anthropology and Educational Quarterly, 25(3),* 298–316.

Delput, L. (1995). *Other People's Children: Cultural Conflicts in the Classroom.* New York: The New Press.

Deutsch-Smith, D., & Lackasson, R. (1992). *Introduction to Special Education: Teaching in an Age of Challenge.* Boston: Allyn and Bacon.

Diana v. State Board of Education (1970). *Clearing House Review, 3(10).*

Di-Angi, P. (1976). Barriers to the Black and White therapeutic relationship. *Perspectives in Psychiatric Care, 14,* 180–83.

Dillard, J. M. (1983). *Multicultural counseling.* Chicago: Nelson Hall.

Dinges, N. G., & Cherry, D. (1995). Symptom expression and the use of mental health services among American ethnic minorities. In J. F. Aponte, R. Y. Rivers, & J. Wohl (Eds.), *Psychological Interventions and Cultural Diversity* (pp. 40–56). Boston: Allyn and Bacon.

Dohrenwend, B. P., & Dohrenend, B. S. (1981). Quasi-experimental evidence in the social causation-social-selection issue posed by class differences. *American Journal of Community Psychology, 9,* 128–46.

Dornic, S. (1979). Information processing in bilinguals: Some selected issues. *Psychological Record, 40,* 329–48.

Draguns, J. (1973). Comparisons of psychopathology across cultures. *Journal of Cross Cultural Psychology, March,* 9–47.

Draguns, J. G. (1980). Psychological disorders of clinical severity. In H. C. Triandis, & J. G. Draguns (Eds.), *Handbook of cross-cultural psychology: Psychopathology, 6,* 99–174. Boston: Allyn and Bacon.

Draguns, J. G. (1987). Psychological disorders across cultures. In P. Pedersen (Ed.), *Handbook of cross-cultural counseling and therapy* (pp. 55–62). New York: Praeger.

Dressler, W. (1985). Stress and sorcery in three social groups. *International Journal of Social Psychiatry, 31(4),* 275–281.

Dunn, R. & Dunn, K. (1978). *Teaching students through their individual learning styles: A practical approach.* Reston, VA: Reston Publishing Co.

Dunn, R., Gemake, J., Jalali, F., & Zenhausern, R. (1990). Cross cultural differences of elementary age students from four ethnic backgrounds. *Journal of Multicultural Counseling and Development, 18,* 23–33.

Dyrcia V. Board of Education of the City of New York. DCNY 557 F Supp. 1230.

Education of the Handicapped Act Amendments of 1986 (PL 99-457). (October 8, 1986). Title 20, U.S.C. 1400 et seq: U.S. Statutes at Large, 92, 2292–96.

Eisenstein, M. (1983). Native reactions to non-native speech: A review of empirical research. *Studies in Second Language Acquisition, 5,* 160–76.

Elbedour, S., Bensel, R. T., & Bastrieu, D. T. (1993). Ecological integrated model of children of war: Individual and social psychology. *Child Abuse and Neglect, 17,* 805–19.

Esquivel, G. (1985). *Best practices in the assessment of limited English proficient and bilingual children.* Bilingual School Psychology Program, Fordham University, New York, New York.

Esquivel, G., & Keitel, M. (1990). Counseling immigrant children in the schools. *Elementary School Guidance and Counseling, 24,* 213–21.

Everett, F., Proctor, N., & Cantwell, B. (1983). Providing psychological services to American Indian children and families. *Professional Psychology: Research and Practice, 14*(5), 588–603.

Eysenck, H. J. (1982). Introduction. In H. J. Eysenck (Ed.), *A model for intelligence.* Berlin: Springer-Verlag.

Falicov, C. (1988). Learning to think culturally in family therapy training. In H. Little, D. Breunlin, & D. Schwartz (Eds.), *Handbook of family therapy training and supervision* (pp. 335–357). New York: Guilford.

Faris, R. E. L., & Dunham, H. W. (1960). *Mental disorders in urban areas.* New York: Harper.

Fasold, R., & Wolfram, W. (1975). Some linguistic features of Negro dialect. In D. Stroller (Ed.), *Black American English: Its ways in the schools and in literature.* New York: Dell.

Fennema, E. & Peterson, P. L. (1987). Effective teaching for girls and boys: The same or different? In D.C. Benliner & B. V. Rosenshire (Eds.), *Talks to Teachers* (pp. 111–125). New York: Random House.

Feuer, C. H. (1985). The political use of Rasta. *Caribbean Review, 14*(4), 48.

Feuerstein, R. (1979). *The dynamic assessment of retarded performers.* Baltimore: University Park Press.

Feuerstein, R. (1980). *Instrumental Enrichment: An Intervention Program for Cognitive Modifiability.* Baltimore: University Park Press.

Feuerstein, R. (1990). The theory of structural cognitive modifiability. In B. Z. Presseisen (Ed.), *Learning and thinking styles: Classroom interaction* (pp. 68–134). Washington, DC: National Education Association.

Feuerstein, R., Rand, Y., Jensen, M., Kaniel, S., Tzuriel, D., Ben Shachar, N., and Mintzker, Y. (1986). Learning potential assessment. *Special Services in the Schools, Vol. 3, No. 1–2,* 85–106.

Fitt, S. (1975). The individual and his environment. In T. G. David & B. D. Wright (Eds.), *Learning Environments* (pp. 90–115). Chicago: University of Chicago Press.

Fohlen, C. (1965). *Les Noirs Aux Etats-Unis* (Blacks in the United States). Paris: Presses Universitaires de France.

Foster, D. V. (1988). Consideration of treatment issues with American Indians detained in the Federal Bureau of Prisons. *Psychiatric Annals, 18,* 698–701.

Fouad, N. A., & Bracken, B. A. (July, 1985). *Cross-cultural Translation and Validation of the U.S. Psychoeducational Assessment Instruments.* Paper presented at the Inter-American Congress of Psychology, Caracas, Venezuela.

French, L. (1989). Native American alcoholism: A transcultural counseling perspective. *Counseling Psychology Quarterly, 2*(2), 153–166.

French, L. & Hornbuckle, J. (1980). Analysis of Indian alcoholism, *Social Work, 25*, 275–80.

Friedman, E. (1982). The Myth of Shiska. In M. McGoldrick, J. K. Pearce, & J. Giordano, (Eds.), *Ethnicity and family therapy* (pp. 123–133). New York: Guilford.

Frisby, C. L. (1992). Issues and problems in the influence of culture on the psychoeducational needs of African American children. *School Psychology Review, 21*(4), 532–551.

Furnham, A., & Bochner, F. (1986). *Culture Shock: Psychological Reactions to Unfamiliar Environments,* 35–55. New York: Methuen and Co.

Gallimore, R., Tharp, R. G., Sloat, K., Klein, T., & Troy, M. E. (1982). Analysis of reading achievement test results for the Kamehameha education project: 1972–1979 (*Tech. Rep.* No. 102). Honolulu: Kamehameha Schools/Bishop Estate.

Garaway, G. B. (1994). Language, culture and attitude in mathematics and science and learning: A review of the literature. *The Journal of Research and Development in Education, 27*(2), 102–11.

Garcia, M., & Lega, L. T. (1979). Development of a Cuban ethnic identity questionnaire. *Hispanic Journal of Behavioral Sciences, 1,* 247–61.

Garcia, R. (1982). *Teaching in a pluralistic society: concept, models, strategies.* New York: Harper and Row, p. 23.

Gardner, H. (1983). *Frames of mind: The theory of multiple intelligences.* New York: Basic Books.

Gardner, H. (1993). *Multiple intelligences.* New York: Basic Books.

Gardner, R., & Lambert, W. (1972). *Attitudes and Motivation in Second Language Learning.* Cambridge, MA: Newbury House.

Gay, G. (1993). Ethnic minorities and educational equality. In J. A. Banks & C. A. McGee Banks (Eds.), *Multicultural education: Issues and perspectives,* pp. 171–194. Boston: Allyn and Bacon.

Gickling, E., & Havertape, J. (1981). *Curriculum-based assessment (CBA).* Minneapolis: National School Psychology Inservice Training Network.

Giles, H. C. (Jan.–Feb., 1990). Counseling Haitian students and their families: Issues and interventions. *Journal of Counseling and Development, 68,* 317–20.

Glutting, J. & McDermott, P. (1990). Principles and problems in learning potential. In C. R. Reynolds and R. W. Kamphaus (Eds.), *Handbook of psychological and educational assessment of children's intelligence and achievement* (pp. 296–347). New York: Guilford.

Golding, J. M., & Burnham, A. (1990). Immigration, stress and depressive symptoms in a Mexican-American community. *The Journal of Nervous and Mental Disease, 78*(3), 161–71.

Goldman, M. (1980). Effect of eye contact and distance on the verbal reinforcement of attitude. *The Journal of Social Psychology, 111,* 73–78.

Goldman, S., & McDermott, R. (1987). The culture of competition in American schools. In G. Spindler (Ed.), *Education and Cultural Process,* 2d. Ed. (pp. 282–99). Prospect Heights, IL: Waveland Press.

Goodenough, W. (1957). Cultural Anthropology and Linguistics. *University Monograph Series on Language and Linguistics, No. 9,* 167.

Gopaul-McNicol, S. (1993). *Working with West Indian families*. New York: Guilford.

Gopaul-McNicol, S. (1997). *Multicultural/multimodal/multisystems approach in working with culturally different families*. Connecticut: Praeger, Greenwood Publishing Group.

Gopaul-McNicol, S. (1997). The role of religion in psychotherapy: Cross-cultural issues and importance of psycho-spiritual training for professionals. *Journal of Contemporary Psychotherapy*.

Gopaul-McNicol, S., Black, K. & Clark-Castro, S. (1997). Introduction: Intelligence testing with minority children. *Cultural Diversity and Mental Health, Vol. 3, No. 2*, 1–4.

Gopaul-McNicol, S. & Armour-Thomas, E. (1997a). A case study on the bio-ecological approach to intellectual assessment. *Cultural Diversity and Mental Health, Vol. 3, No. 2*, 40–47.

Gopaul-McNicol, S. & Armour-Thomas, E. (1997b). The role of a bio-ecological assessment system in writing a culturally sensitive report: The importance of assessing other intelligences. *Journal of Social Distress and the Homeless, Vol. 6, No. 2*, 127–139.

Gopaul-McNicol, S., Thomas, T., & Irish, G. (1991). *A handbook for immigrants: Some basic educational and social issues in the United States of America*. New York: Caribbean Research Center.

Grant, C. A., & Sleeter, C. E. (1989). *Turning on Learning: Five Approaches for Multicultural Teaching Plans for Race, Class, Gender, and Disability*. New York: MacMillan.

Grimes, S. K. (1995). Targeting academic programs to student diversity utilizing learning styles and learning-study strategies. *Journal of College Student Development, 36(5)*, 422–30.

Grosjean, F. (1982). *Life with two languages*. Cambridge, MA: Harvard University Press.

Guadalupe Organization, Inc. v. Tempe Elementary School District (1972). No. CIV. 11-435, Phoenix, Arizona. January 24, 1972.

Guthrie, R. (1976). *Even the rat was white*. New York: Harper & Row.

Hacker, A. (1992). *Two nations*. New York: MacMillan.

Hale-Benson, J. (1982). *Black children: Their roots, culture and learning styles*. Provo, UT: Brigham Young Press.

Hamayan, E. V., & Damico, J. S. (1991). Developing and using a second language. In E. V. Hamayan & J. S. Damico (Eds.), *Limiting bias in the assessment of bilingual students* (pp. 39–75). Austin, TX: Pro-Ed.

Hanna, J. L. (1988). *Disruptive school behavior: Class, race and culture*. New York: Hanes and Meier.

Hanson, M. J. (1992). Families with Anglo-European roots. In E. W. Lynch & M. J. Hanson, *Developing cross-cultural competence* (pp. 181–257). Baltimore, MD: Paul Brookes Publishing Co.

Hargis, C. H. (1987). *Curriculum-based assessment: A primer*. Springfield, IL: Charles C. Thomas.

Hartman, A. (1978). Diagrammatic assessment of family relationships. *Social Casework, 59*, 465–476.

Hartman, A., & Laird, J. (1983). *Family centered social work practice*. New York: The Free Press.

Harwood, A. (1981). *Ethnicity and medical care*. Cambridge, MA: Harvard University Press.

Hayes, K. (1992). Attitudes toward education: Voluntary and involuntary immigrants from the same families. *Anthropology and Education Quarterly, 23*, 250–267.

Haynes, N., & Comer, J. (1993) The Yale School Development program: Process, outcomes and policy implications. *Urban Education, 28*(2), 166–169.

Haynes, N., & Gebneyesus, S. (1992). Cooperative Learning: A case for African-American students. *School Psychology Review, 21*(4), 577–85.

Heath, S. B. (1983). *Ways with words: Language, life and work in communities and classrooms.* New York: Cambridge University.

Helms, J. (1985). Cultural identity in the treatment process. In P. Pedersen, *Handbook of cross-cultural counseling and therapy.* Westport, CT: Greenwood Press.

Helms, J. E. (1992). Why is there no study of cultural equivalence in standardized cognitive ability testing? *American Psychologist, 47*(9), 1,083–1,101.

Helton, G. B., Workman, E. A., & Matuszek, P. A. (1982). *Psychoeducational assessment: Integrating concepts and techniques.* New York: Grune & Stratton.

Hendriques, F. (1953). *Family and color in Jamaica.* London: Eyre and Spottiswoode.

Hickson, J., Land, A., & Aikman, G. (1994). Learning style differences in middle school pupils from four ethnic backgrounds. *School Psychology International, 15*, 349–59.

High achieving Asian Americans are fastest growing minority. (October, 1985). *Population Today,* pp. 2, 8.

Hill, R. (1972). *The strengths of Black families.* New York: Emerson Hale.

Hilliard, A. G. (1979). Standardization and cultural bias as impediments to the scientific study and validation of "intelligence." *Journal of Research and Development in Education, 12*(2), 47–58.

Ho, C. K. (1990). An analysis of domestic violence in Asian American communities: A cultural approach to counseling. *Women and Therapy, 9*, 129–50.

Holman, A. (1983). *Family assessment: Tools for understanding and intervention.* Beverley Hills, CA: Sage.

Homel, P., Palif, M., & Aaronson, D. (Eds.). (1987). *Childhood bilingualism: Aspects of linguistic, cognitive and social development.* Hillsdale, NJ: Lawrence Erlbaum.

Hoppe, S. K., & Heller, P. L. (1975). Alienation, familism and utilization of health services by Mexican-Americans. *Journal of Health and Social Behavior, 16*, 304–14.

Howard, Gary R. (Sept., 1993). Whites in multicultural education. *Phi Delta Kappan,* 36–41.

Hughes, S. R., & Dodder, R. A. (1984). Alcohol consumption patterns among American Indian and White college students. *Journal of Studies on Alcohol, 45*, 433–39.

Hutt, M. I. (1977). *The Hutt adaptation of the Bender Gestalt test, 3rd Ed.* New York: Grune and Stratton.

Hvitfeldt, C. (1986). Traditional culture, perceptual style, and learning: The classroom behavior of Hmong adults. *Adult Education Quarterly, 36*, 65–77.

Irvine, J. (1988). *Teacher race as a factor in Black student achievement.* Paper presented at an annual meeting of the American Education Research Association, New Orleans.

Jacobson, E. (1938). *Progressive relaxation.* Chicago: University of Chicago Press.

Jensen, A. R. (1979). Outmoded theory or unconquered frontier? *Creative Science and Technology, 2*, 16–29.

Jensen, A. R., & Whang, P. A. (1994). Speed of accessing arithmetic facts in long-term memory: A comparison of Chinese-American and Anglo-American Children. *Contemporary Educational Psychology, 19*, 1–12.

Joe, J. R. & Malach, R. S. (1992). Families with native American roots. In E. W. Lynch & M. J. Hanson, *Developing Cross-Cultural Competence* (pp. 89–119). Baltimore, MD: Paul Brookes Publishing Co.

Johnson, S. D. (1990). Towards clarifying culture, race and ethnicity in the context of multicultural counseling. *Journal of Multicultural Counseling and Development, 18,* 4.

Jones, E. E., & Thorne, A. (1987). Rediscovery of the subject: Intercultural approaches to clinical assessment. *Journal of Consulting and Clinical Psychology, 55,* 488–95.

Jones, L. V. (1985). Interpreting Spearman's general factor. *The Behavioral and Brain Sciences, 8*(2), 233.

Jones, N. S. (1990). Black/White issues in psychotherapy. A framework for clinical practice. *Journal of Social Behavior and Personality, 5,* 305–22.

Joseph, C. B. (1984). The child, the family and the school in English-Haitian education. In C. R. Foster & A. Valman (Eds.), *Haiti—Today and tomorrow: An interdisciplinary study* (pp. 351–58). Lanham, MD: University Press.

Juarez, M. (1983). Assessment and treatment of minority language handicapped children: The role of the monolingual speech-language pathologist. *Topics in Language Disorder, 3,* 57–66.

Kagan, S. (1986). Cooperative learning and sociocultural factors in schools. In Bilingual Education Office (Ed.), *Beyond language: Social and cultural factors in schooling language minority students* (pp. 231–98). CA: Evaluation, Dissemination, and Assessment Center, California State University.

Kallen, H. M. (1924). *Culture and democracy in the United States: Studies in group psychology in the American people.* Boni and Lineright Publishers: New York.

Kashani, J. H., Beck, N. C., Heoper, E. W., Fallhi, C., Corcoran, C. M., McAllister, J. A., Rosenberg, T. K., & Reid, J. C. (1987). Psychiatric disorders in a community sample of adolescents. *American Journal of Psychiatry, 144,* 584–589.

Katz, D. (1974). Factors affecting social change: A social-psychological interpretation. *Journal of Social Issues 30*(3), 159–180.

Kessel, J., & Robbins, S. P. (1984). The Indian child welfare act: Dilemmas and needs. *Child Welfare, 63,* 225–32.

Kleinman, A. (1980). *Patients and healers in the context of culture.* Berkeley: University of California Press.

Kleinman, A. (1982). Neuracthenia and depression: A study of somatyallion and culture in China. *Culture, Medicine and Psychiatry, 6,* 117–90.

Kleinman, A., & Good, B. (Eds.). (1985). *Culture and depression.* Berkeley: University of California Press.

Kochman, T. (1981). *Black and White: Styles in conflict.* Chicago: University of Chicago Press.

Kochnomer, J., Richardson, E., & Di Benedetto, B. (1983). A comparison of the phonic decoding ability of normal and learning disabled children. *Journal of Learning Disability, 16,* 348–51.

Korman, M. (1974). National conference on levels and patterns of professional training in psychology: Major themes. *American Psychologist, 29,* 301–313.

Kozol, J. (1991). *Savage inequalities: Children in America's schools.* New York, NY: Crown Publishers, Inc.

Kozulin, A., & Falik, L. (1995). Dynamic cognitive assessement of the child. *Current Directions in Psychological Science, 4*(6), 192–196.

Krashen, S. (1982). *Principles and practice in second language acquisition.* Hayward, CA: Alemany Press.

Krashen, S. (1982). *Principles and practice in second language acquisition.* New York: Pergamon.

Kretschmer, R. E. (1991). Exceptionality and the limited English proficient students: Historical and practical contexts. In E. V. Hamayan & J. S. Davico (Eds.), *Limiting bias in the assessment of bilingual students* (pp. 2–38). Austin, TX: Pro-Ed.

Krueber, A. L., & Kluckhahn, C. (1952). *Culture: A critical review of concepts and definitions, 47,* pp. 85, 181. Cambridge, MA: Peabody Museum.

Kurtz, B. (1989). Individual differences in cognitive and metacognitive processing. In W. Schneider & F. Weinert (Eds.), *Interactions among Aptitudes, Strategies and Knowledge in Cognitive Performance.* New York: Springer-Verlag, 17–29.

LaFromboise, T. D. (1988). American Indian mental health palsey. *American Psychologist, 43,* 388–97.

Lambert, M. C., Weisz, J. R., Knight, F., Desrosiers, M., Overly, K., & Thesiger, C. (1992). Jamaica and American adult perspectives on child psychopathology: Further exploration of the threshold model. *Brief Reports, 60*(1), 146–49.

Langdon, H. W. (October 1988). Working with an interpreter/translator in the school and clinical setting. A presentation at the Council for Exceptional Children Symposia on Ethnic and Multicultural Concerns, Denver.

Lau v. Nichols, 414 U.S. 563; 39. L. Ed 2d 1, 94 S. Ct. 787 (1974).

Lazarus, A. A. (1976). *Multimodal behavior therapy.* New York: Springer.

Lee, E. (1982). A social systems approach to assessment & treatment for Chinese American families. In M. McGoldard, J. Peone, & J. Geonlaw (Eds.), *Ethnicity and Family Therapy,* (pp. 527–51). New York: Guilford.

Lee, E. (1989). Assessment and treatment of Chinese American immigrant families. *Journal of Psychotherapy and the Family, 6,* 99–122.

Lee Katz, L. (1991). Cultural scripts: the home-school connection. *Early Child Development and Care, Vol. 73,* pp. 95–102.

Lefley, H. P. (1979). Prevalence of potential falling-out cases among Black, Latin and non-White populations of the city of Miami. *Social Science and Medicine, 13B,* 113–128.

Leigh, J. W., & Green, J. W. (1982). The structure of the black community: The knowledge base for social services. In J. W. Green (Ed.), *Cultural awareness in the human services,* (pp. 94–121). Englewood Cliffs, NJ: Prentice-Hall.

Lequerica, M. (1993). Stress in immigrant families with handicapped children: A child advocacy approach. *American Ontopsychiatric Association, 63*(4), 545–52.

Levine, D. U. (1994). Instructional approaches and interventions that can improve the academic performance of African American students. *Journal of Negro Education, 63*(1), 46–63.

LeVine, E., & Padilla, A. (1980). *Crossing cultures in therapy: Pluralistic counseling for the Hispanic.* Belmont, CA: Wadsworth.

Lidz, C. S. (Ed.), (1987). *Dynamic assessment.* New York: Guilford.

Lidz, C. S. (1991). *Practitioner's guide to dynamic assessment.* New York: Guilford.

Lipsky, D. R., & Gartner, A. (1996). Inclusion, school restructuring, and the remaking of American society. *Harvard Educational Review. Vol. 66, No. 4,* (pp. 762–796).

London, C. (1990). Educating young, new immigrants: How can the United States cope? *International Journal of Adolescence and Youth, 2,* 81–100.

Longstreet, W. S. (1978). *Aspects of ethnicity: Understanding differences in pluralistic class-rooms*. New York: Teacher's College Press.

Lopez-Bushnell, F. K., Tyne, P., & Futness, M. (1992). Alcoholism and the Hispanic older adult. *Clinical Gerontologist, 11*, 123–30.

Lopez, E., & Gopaul-McNicol, S. (1997). English as a second language. In G. Beor, K. Minke, & A. Thomas (Eds.), *Children's needs II*. Washington, DC: National Association of School Psychologists (in press).

Lopez, S., & Nunez, J. A. (1987). Cultural factors considered in selected diagnostic criteria and interview schedule. *Journal of Abnormal Psychology, 96*(3), 270–72.

Lora et al. v. the Board of Education of the City of New York. 587 F. Supp. 1572 (EDNY 1984).

Lorion, R. P., & Filner, R. D. (1986). Research on mental health interventions with the disadvantaged. In S. L. Senfield, & A. E. Bergin (Eds.), *Handbook of psychotherapy and behavior change, 3rd Ed.*, (pp. 739–75). New York: Wiley.

Lynch, E. W. (1992). From culture shock to cultural learning. In E. W. Lynch & M. J. Hanson (Eds.), *Developing cross-cultural competence*, (pp. 19–34). Baltimore, MD: Paul H. Brookes Publishing Co.

Majors, R., & Billson, J. M. (1992). *Cool Pose: The Dilemmas of Black Manhood in America*. New York: The Free Press.

Maker, C. J. (1992). Intelligence and creativity in multiple intelligences: Identification and Development. *Educating Able Learners, Fall*, 12–19.

Malgady, R. G., Rogler, H. L., & Constantino, G. (1987). Ethnocultural and linguistic bias in mental health evaluation of Hispanics. *American Psychologist, 42*(3), 228–34.

Maloney, M. P., & Ward, M. P. (1976). *Psychological assessment: A conceptual approach*. New York: Oxford University Press.

Marcos, L. R. (1976). Bilinguals in psychotherapy: Language as an emotional barrier. *American Journal of Psychotherapy, 30*, 552–59.

Marcos, L. (1979). Effects of interpreters on the evaluation of psychopathology in non-English-speaking patients. *American Journal of Psychiatry, 136*, 171–74.

Marlin, O. (1994). Special issues in the analytic treatment of immigrants and refugees. *American Journal of Psychoanalysis, 16*(1), 7–17.

Marsella, A. J., Kinzie, D., & Gordon, P. (1973). Ethnic variation in the expression of depression. *Journal of Cross-Cultural Psychology, 4*, 435–458.

Marsella, A. J., & White, G. (Eds.). (1982). *Cultural conceptions of mental health therapy*. Dor Duecht, The Netherlands: D. Reidal.

Martinez, C., Jr. (1993). Psychiatric care of Mexican Americans. In A. C. Gou (Ed.), *Culture, Ethnicity, and Mental Illness* (pp. 431–66). Washington, DC: American Psychiatric Press.

Massey, D. S., & Denton, N. A. (1993). *American apartheid: Segregation and the making of the underclass*. Cambridge, MA: Harvard University Press.

McClure, E. (1981). Formal and functional aspects of the code-switched discourse of bilingual children. In R. Duran (Ed.), *Latino Language and Communicative Behavior*, 69–94. Norwood, NJ: ABLEX.

McGoldrick, M., Pearce, J. K., & Giordano, J. (1982). *Ethnicity and family therapy*. New York: Guilford.

McGrew, K. S. (1994). *Clinical interpretation of the Woodcock Johnson Tests of Cognitive Ability-Revised*. Boston: Allyn and Bacon.

McGrew, K. S. (1995). Analysis of the major intelligence batteries according to a proposed comprehensive Gf-Gc framework of human cognitive and knowledge abilities. In D. P. Flanagan, J. L. Genshaft, & P. L. Harrison (Eds.), *Beyond traditional intellectual assessment: Contemporary and emerging theories, tests and issues.* New York, NY: Guilford. Manuscript submitted for publication.

McLaughlin, B. (1977). Second language learning in children. *Psychological Bulletin, 84,* 438–59.

McMillan, D., & Meyers, C. (1980). Larry P.: An educational interpretation. *School Psychology Review, 9,* 136–48.

McMillan, D. L., Hendricks, I. G., & Watkins, A. V. (1988). Impact of Diana v. BOE, Larry, P., & P. L. 94–142 on minority students. *Exceptional Children, 54,* 426–32.

McNamara, J. (1967). The bilingual's linguistic performance—a psychological overview. *Journal of Social Issues, 23,* 58–77.

McNicol, M. (1991). *Helping children adjust to a new culture: A child's perspective.* New York: Multicultural Educational & Psychological Services.

McReynolds, P. (1975). Historical antecedents of personality assessment. In P. McReynolds (Ed.), *Advances in Psychological Assessment, 111,* 477–532. San Francisco: Jossey-Bass.

Meinchenbaum, D. H. (1977). *Cognitive-behavior modification.* New York: Plenum.

Mendoza, R. H., & Martinez, J. L. (1981). The measurement of acculturation. In A. Baron, Jr. (Ed.), *Explorations in Chicano psychology,* (pp. 71–82). New York: Praeger.

Menyuk, P., & Looney, P. (1972). A problem of language disorder: Length versus structure. *Journal of Speech and Hearing Research, 15,* 264–79.

Mercer, C. D. (1987). *Students with learning disabilities, 3rd Ed.* Columbus, OH: Merrill.

Mercer, J. R. (1979). In defense of racially and culturally non-discriminatory assessment. *School Psychology Digest, 8(1),* 89–115.

Mercer, J. R. (1983). Issues in the diagnosis of language disorders in students where primary language is not English. *Topics in Language Disorder, 3(3),* 46–56.

Meredith, W., & Cramer, S. (1982). Hmong refugees in Nebraska. In B. Droning & D. Olney (Eds.), *The Hmong in the West: Observations and Reports* (pp. 353–62). Minneapolis, MN: Southeast Asian Refugee Studies Project, Center for Urban and Regional Affairs, University of Minnesota.

Mickler, M. L. & Zippert, C. P. (1987). Teaching strategies based on learning styles of adult students. *Community/Junior College Quarterly, 11,* 33–37.

Minuchin, S. (1974). *Families and family therapy.* Cambridge, MA: Harvard University Press.

Minuchin, S., Montalvo, B., Guerney, B. G., Jr., Rosman, B. L., & Schumer, F. (1967). *Families of the slums.* New York: Basic Books.

Missiuna, C., & Samuels, M. (1988). Dynamic assessment: Review and critique. *Special Services in the Schools, Vol. 5(1-2),* 1–22.

Mollica, R. F., & Lavelle, J. (1988). Southeast Asia refugees. In L. Comas-Diaz and E. E. H. Griffith (Eds.), *Clinical Guidelines in Cross-cultural Mental Health* (pp. 262–93). New York: Wiley.

Mollica, R. F., & Wyshak, G., & Lowelle, J. (1987). The psychosocial impact of war trauma and torture on Southeast Asian refugees. *American Journal of Psychiatry, 144(12),* 1,567–72.

Montejano, D. (1987). *Anglos and Mexicans in the making of Texas, 1936–1986*. Austin: University of Texas Press.

Morgan, H. (1980). How schools fail Black children. *Social Policy*, 11, 49–54.

Morrow, R. (1987). Cultural differences: Be aware. *Academic Therapy*, 23(2), 143–149.

Mosley, J. C., & Lex, A. (1990). Identification of potentially stressful life events experienced by a population of urban minority youth. *Journal of Multicultural Counseling and Development*, 18, 118–25.

Mowder, B. (1980). A strategy for the assessment of bilingual handicapped children. *Psychology in the Schools*, 17(1), 7–11.

Moyerman, D. R. & Forman, B. D. (1992). Acculturation and adjustment: A meta-analytic study. *Hispanic Journal of Behavioral Science*, 14(2), 163–200.

Murrone, J., & Gynther, M. (1991). Teachers' implicit "theories" of children's intelligence. *Psychological Reports*, 69, 1,195–1,201.

Myers, L. J. (1991). Expanding the psychology of knowledge optimally: The importance of worldview revisited. In R. L. Jones (ed.), *Black psychology, 3rd Ed.* (pp. 15–28). Berkeley, CA: Cobb & Henry.

Myers, P. I., & Hammill, D. D. (1990). *Learning Disabilities: Basic Concepts, Assessment Practices and Instructural Strategies, 4th Ed.* Austin, TX: Pro-Ed.

National Assessment of Educational Program. (1985). *The Reading Report Card*. Princeton, NJ: Educational Testing Service.

Neisser, V., Boodoo, G., Bouchard, T. J. Jr., Boykin, A. W., Brody, N., Ceci, S. J., Halpern, D. F., Loehlin, J. C., Perloff, R., Sternberg, R. J., & Urbina, S. (1996). Intelligence: Knowns and unknowns. *American Psychologist*, 51(2), 77–101.

Nelson, K. (1985). *Making service: The acquisition of shared meaning*. New York: Academic Press.

New York City Department of Planning—Office of Immigrant Affairs and Population Analysis Division (1985, May 11). *Caribbean immigrants in New York City: A demographic summary*. Unpublished manuscript presented to the Caribbean Research Center.

Nicassio, P. M. (1985). The psychosocial adjustment of the Southeast Asian refugee. *Journal of Cross-cultural Psychology*, 16, 153–73.

Noble, C. E. (1969). Race, reality and experimental psychology. *Perspectives in Biology and Medicine*, 13, 10–30.

Northcutt, L., & Watson, D. (1986). *Implementing Sheltered English Effectively*. Caulbert, CA. BINET.

Oakes, J. (1990). *Multiplying inequalities*: The effects of race, social class, and tracking on opportunities to learn mathematics and science. Santa Monica: The Rand Corporation.

Oakland, T., & Phillips, B. N. (1973). *Assessing minority group children*. New York: Behavioral Publications.

Oakland, T. (1977). *Psychological and educational assessment of minority children*. New York: Brunner/Mazel.

Oberg, K. (1960). Cultural shock: Adjustment to new cultural environments. *Practical Anthropology*, 7, 177–82.

Office of Bilingual Education (1995). *Facts and Figures—1994–1995*. New York City Board of Education.

Ogbu, J. U. (1981). Origins of human competitive: A culture-ecological perspective. *Child Development, 52*, 413–29.

O'Hare, W. P., & Felt, J. C. (1991). *Asian Americans: America's fastest growing minority group.* Washington, DC: Population Reference Bureau.

O'Hare, W. P. (1992). America's minorities—the demographics of diversity. *Population Bulletin, 47*(4), 1–47.

O'Hare, W. P. (1989). Black demographic trends in the 1980s. In D. P. Willis (Ed.), *Health policies and Black Americans*, 37–55. New Brunswick, NJ: Transaction.

O'Hare, W. P., Pollard, K. M., Mann, T. L., & Kent, K. M. (1991). African Americans in the 1990s. *Population Bulletin, 46*, 1–40.

Okagaki, L., & Sternberg, R. J. (1993). Parental belief and children's school performance. *Child Development, 64*, 36–56.

Oldham, J., & Riba, M. (Eds.). (1995). *Review of psychiatry, Vol. 14.* Washington, DC: American Psychiatric Press, Inc.

Oller, J. W., Baca, L. L., & Vigil, A. (1978). Attitudes and attained proficiency in ESL: A sociolinguistic study of Mexican-Americans in the Southwest. *TESOL Quarterly, 11*, 173–83.

Oller, J. W., Hudson, A., & Liu, P. F. (1977). Attitudes and attained proficiency in ESL: A sociolinguistic study of native speakers of Chinese in the United States. *Language Learning, 27*, 1–27.

Omaggio, A. (1986). *Teaching Language in Context.* Boston: Heinle and Heinle.

Ortiz, A. A. (1984). Choosing the language of instruction for bilingual children. *Teaching Exceptional Children, 16*, 208–12.

Ortiz, A. A., Garcia, S. B., Holtzman, W. H., Jr., Poyzoi, E., Snell, W. E. Jr., Wilkinson, C. Y., & Willig, A. C. (1985). *Characteristics of limited English proficient students served in programs for the speech and language handicapped: Implication for policy, practice, and research.* Austin, TX: The University of Texas, Handicapped Minority Research Institute in Language Proficiency.

Ovando, C., & Collier, V. (1985). *Bilingual and ESL Classrooms.* New York: McGraw-Hill.

Padilla, A. M. (1979). Critical factors in the testing of Hispanic Americans: A review and some suggestions for the future. In R. W. Tyler & S. H. White (Eds.), *Testing, teaching and learning: Report of a conference on testing.* Washington, DC: U.S. Government Printing Office.

Payne, M. (1989). Use and abuse of corporal punishment: A Caribbean View. *Child Abuse and Neglect, 13*, 389–401.

Peck, S. (1993). Further along the road less traveled. New York: Simon & Schuster.

Pedersen P. (1985). *Handbook of cross-cultural counseling and therapy.* Westport, CT: Greenwood Press.

Pedersen, P. (1995). Culture-centered ethical guidelines for counselors. In J. G. Ponterotto, J. M. Casas, L. A. Suzuki, & C. M. Alexander (Eds.), *Handbook of multicultural counseling* (pp. 34–49). Newbury Park, CA: Sage.

Philippe, J., & Romain, J. B. (1979). Indisposition in Haiti. *Social Science and Medicine, 13B*, 129–133.

Podemski, R. S., Marsh II, G. E., Smith, T. E. C., & Price, B. J. (1995). *Comprehensive administration of special education (2nd ed.).* Englewood Cliffs, NJ: Prentice-Hall.

Ponterotto, J. G., & Casas, J. M. (1991). *Handbook of racial/ethnic minority counseling research.* Springfield, IL: Charles C. Thomas.

Prasse, D. P. (1986). Litigation and special education: An introduction. *Exceptional children, 52,* 311–312.

Prasse, D. P., & Reschly, D. J. (1986). Larry P.: A case of segregation, testing, or program efficacy? *Exceptional Children, 52*(4), 333–346.

Randall-David, E. (1989). *Strategies for working with culturally diverse communities and clients.* Washington, DC: Association for the Care of Children's Health.

Reder, S., Cohn, M., Arter, J., & Nelson, S. (1984). *A study of English language training for refugees.* (Public Regent, U.S. Department of Health and Human Services, Offices of Refugee Resettlement). Portland, OR: Northwest Regional Educational Laboratory.

Reid, J. (1986, February). Immigration and the future of U.S. Black population. *Population Today, 14,* 6–8.

Richards, J. (1972). Social factors, interlanguage and language learning. *Language Learning, 22,* 159–88.

Richardson, T. Q. (1993). Black cultural learning styles: Is it really a myth? *School Psychology Review, 22*(3), 562–67.

Rick, K., & Forward, J. (1992). Acculturation and perceived intergenerational differences among Hmong Youth. *Journal of Cross-Cultural Psychology, 23*(1), 85–94.

Ridley, C. R. (1985). Imperatives for ethnic and cultural relevance in psychology training programs. *Professional Psychology: Research and Practice, 16*(5), 611–622.

Rodriguez, R., Prieto, A., & Rueda, R. (1984). Issues in bilingual multicultural special education. *NABE Journal, 8,* 55–66.

Rodriguez-Fernandez, C. M. (1981). Testing and the Puerto Rican Child: A practical guidebook for psychologists and teachers (Doctoral dissertation, University of Massachusetts).

Roger, L. H., Cortes, D. E., & Malgudy, R. G. (1991). Acculturation and mental health status among Hispanics. *American Psychologist, 46*(6), 585–97.

Ronstrom, A. (1989). Children in Central America: victims of war. *Child Welfare League of America, 58*(2), 145–153.

Rosenthal, J. H. (1970). A preliminary psycholinguistic study of children with learning disabilities. *Journal of Learning Disabilities, 3,* 391–95.

Rothenberg, J. J., Lehman, L. B., & Hackman, J. D. (1979). An individualized learning disabilities program in the regular classroom. *Journal of Learning Disabilities, 12*(7), 72–75.

Rueda, R., & Matinez, I. (1992). Fiesta educativa: One community's approach to parent training in developmental disabilities for Latino families. *Journal of the Association of Severe Handicaps, 17*(2), 95–103.

Salomone, R. C. (1986). *Equal education under law: Legal rights and federal policy in the post-Brown era.* New York: St. Martin Press.

Samuda, R. (1975). From ethnocentrism to a multicultural perspective in educational testing. *Journal of Afro-American Issues, 3*(1), 4–17.

Samuda, R. (1976). Problems and issues in assessment of minority group children. In R. L. Jones (Ed.), *Mainstreaming and the minority child* (pp. 65–76). Reston, VA: Council for Exceptional Children.

Sattler, J. M. (1988). *Assessment of children.* San Diego, CA: Jerome M. Sattler Publisher.

Sattler, J. M., & Gwynne, J. (1982). Ethnicity and Bender Visual Motor Test performance. *Journal of School Psychology, 20*(1), 69–71.

Shade, B. J., & New, C. A. (1993). Cultural influences on learning: Teaching implications. In J. A. Banks and C. A. McGee Banks (Eds.), (pp. 317–331). *Multicultural Education: Issues and Perspectives, 2nd Ed.* Needham heights, MA: Allyn and Bacon.

Shapiro, E. S. (1987). *Behavioral assessment in school psychology.* Hillsdale, NJ: Lawrence Erlbaum.

Shinn, M. R. (Ed.). (1989). *Curriculum-based measurements: Assessing special children.* New York: Guilford.

Skinner, B. F. (1974). *About behaviorism.* New York: Knopf.

Slavin, R. E. (1987). *A review of research on elementary ability grouping.* Baltimore, MD: Johns Hopkins University Press.

Slavin, R. E. (1988). Cooperative learning and student achievement. *Educational Leadership, 45*(2), 31–33.

Slavin, R. E. (1990). Research in cooperative learning: Concerns and controversy. *Educational Leadership, 42,* 52–54.

Smith, K. J. (1992). Using multimedia with Navajo children: An effort to alleviate problems of cultural learning style background of experience and maturation. *Teaching and Writing Quarterly: Overcoming Learning Difficulties, 8,* 287–94.

Soldier, L. L. (February, 1989). Language learning of Native American students. *Educational Leadership, 42,* 74–5.

Sowell, T. (1981). *Ethnic America.* New York: Basic Books.

Sternberg, R. J. (1984). What should intelligence tests test? Implications of a triarchic theory of intelligence for intelligence testing. *Educational Researcher* (January) 5–15.

Sternberg, R. J. (1985). *Beyond IQ.* New York: Cambridge University Press.

Sternberg, R. J. (1986). *Intelligences applied.* New York: Harcourt Brace Jovanovich.

Sternberg, R. J., & Powell, J. S., & Kaye, D. B. (1982). The nature of verbal comprehending. *Poetics, 11,* 155–187.

Sternberg, R. J., & Powell, J. S., (1983). Comprehending verbal comprehension. *American Psychologist, 38,* 878–893.

Strom, R., Johnson, A., Strom, S., & Strom, P. (1992). Designing curriculum for parents of gifted children. *Journal for the Education of the Gifted, 15(2)* 182–200.

Strom, R., Johnson, A., Strom, S., & Strom, P. (1992). Educating gifted Hispanic children and their parents. *Hispanic Journal of Behavioral Sciences, 14(3),* 383–393.

Sue, S. (1981). *Counseling the culturally different.* New York: Wiley.

Sue, D. W. & Sue, D. (1990). *Counseling the culturally different: Theory and Practice, 2nd Ed.,* New York: Wiley.

Sue, D., Arredondo, P., & McDavis, R. (1992). Multicultural counseling competencies and standards: A call to the profession. *Journal of Multicultural Counseling and Development, 20,* 64–88.

Sue, S. & Zane, N. (1987, January). The role of culture and cultural techniques in psychotherapy. *American Psychologist, 42,* 37–45.

Super, C. M. (1980). Cognitive development: Looking across at growing up. In C. Super & M. Harkness (Eds.), *New directions for child development: Anthropological perspectives on child development, 8,* 59–69.

Surber, J. (1995). Best practices in a problem-solving approach to psychological report writing. In A. Thomas & J. Grimes (Eds.), *Best practices in school psychology III.* Washington, DC: The National Association of School Psychologists.

Swisher, K., & Deyhle, D. (1989). The styles of learning are different, but the teaching is just the same: Suggestions for teachers of American Indian youth. *Journal of American Indian Education*, 1–14.

Tallent, N. (1993). *Psychological report writing (4th ed)*. Englewood Cliffs, NJ: Prentice-Hall.

Tanaka-Matsumi, J., & Marsella, A. J. (1976). Cross-cultural variations in the phenomenological experience of depression. 1. World Association Studies. *Journal of Cross-Cultural Psychology, 7*, 379–96.

Tapp, J. L., Kelman, H., Triandis, H., Wrightsman, L., & Coelho, G. (1974). Advisory principles for ethical considerations in the conduct of cross-cultural research: Fall 1973 revision. *International Journal of Psychology, 9*, 231–349.

Taylor, O. (1973). Attitude toward black and non-standard English as measured by the language attitude scale. In R. Shuy & R. Fasald (Eds.), *Language attitudes: Current trends and prospects*, 174–201. Washington, DC: Georgetown University Press.

Teske, R. H. C., Jr., & Nelson, B. H. (1974). Acculturation and assimilation: A clarification. *American Ethnologist, 1*, 351–67.

Tharp, R. G. (1989). Psychocultural variables and constants. *American Psychologist, 44*, 349–359.

Tharp, R., & Gallimore, R. (1988). *Rousing Minds to Life: Teaching, Learning and Schooling in Social Context*. New York: Cambridge University Press.

Thomas, D. M. (1981). Limits of pluralism. *Phi Delta Kappan, 62(8)*, 589–92.

Thomas-Presswood, T. N. (1997). Cultural issues in the intellectual assessment of children from diverse cultural backgrounds. *Journal of Social Distress and the Homeless, 6(2)*, 113–127.

Thomas, T. (1991). *Post traumatic stress disorder in children*. Paper presented in August at the annual meeting of the American Psychological Association, Boston, MA.

Thomas, T. N. (1995). Acculturative stress in the adjustment of immigrant families. *Journal of Social Distress and the Homeless, 4(2)*, 131–42.

Thomas, T. N. (1992). Psychoeducational adjustment of English-speaking Caribbean and Central American immigrant children in the United States. *School Psychology Review. 21(4)*, 566–76.

Thomas, T. N. and Damino, J. (1985). *Specificity of encoding in Bilingual Memory*. Unpublished manuscript, Master's Thesis for Hofstra University.

Thomas, T. N., and Schare M. (in press). A cross-cultural analysis of alcoholism and social alienation in Panama and the United States. *International Journal of Psychology Research*.

Thomas, W. B. (1986). Mental testing and tracking for the social adjustment of an urban underclass, 1920–1930. *Journal of Education, 168(2)*, 9–30.

Thomas, T., & Gopaul-McNicol, S. (1991). *An immigrant handbook on special education in United States of America*. New York: Multicultural Educational & Psychological Services.

Thompson, R. W., & Hixson, P. (1984). Teaching parents to encourage independent problem solving in preschool-age children. *Language, Speech and Hearing Services in the Schools, 15*, 175–181.

Thorton, M. C. (1992). The quiet immigration: Foreign spouses of U.S. citizens, 1945–1985. In M. P. P. Root (Ed.), *Racially mixed people in America*, 64–76. Newbury Park, CA: Sage.

Thurstone, L. L. (1924). *The nature of intelligence*. New York: Harcourt Brace.

Toliver-Weddington, G., & Meyerson, M. D. (1983). Training paraprofessionals for identification and intervention with communicationally disordered bilinguals. In D. R. Omarx & J. G. Erickson (Eds.), *The bilingual exceptional child*, 379–95. Austin, TX: Pro-Ed.

Tollman, S. G., & Msengana, N. B. (1990). Neuropsychological assessment: Problems in evaluating the higher mental functioning of Zulu-speaking people using traditional Western techniques. *South-Africa Tydskr. Sielk. 20*(1), 20–24. *South African Journal of Psychology*.

Trennent, R. A., Jr. (1988). *The Phoenix Indian School: Forced Assimilation in Arizona, 1891-1935*. Norman: University of Oklahoma Press.

Triandis, H. (1987). Some major dimensions of cultural variation in client populations. In P. Pedersen (Ed.), *Handbook of cross-cultural counseling and therapy* (pp. 21–28). New York: Praeger.

Trimble, J. E. (1987). Self-perception and perceived alienation among American Indians. *Journal of Community Psychology, 15*, 316–33.

Tseng, W. S., & McDermott, Jr., J. F. (1981). *Culture, Mind, and Therapy*. New York: Brunner/Mazel.

Tseng, W., Xu, D., Ebata, K., Hsu, J., & Cul, Y. (1986). Diagnostic pattern for neuroses among China, Japan and America. *American Journal of Psychiatry, 143*, 1,010–1,014.

Tucker, G. R., Hamayan, E., & Genesee, F. (1976). Affective, cognitive and social factors in second language acquisition. *Canadian Modern Language Review, 23*, 214–26.

Tucker, J. A. (1980). *Nineteen steps for assuring non-biased placement of students in special education*. Reston, VA: ERIC Clearinghouse on Handicapped and Gifted Children.

Tyler, E. B. (1871). *Primitive Culture* (2 volumes). New York: Harper Torchbook. London: Murray, p. 1958.

U.S. Bureau of Census (1990). 1990 Census of population and housing—summary tape file 3. *Summary of Social, Economic, and Housing Characteristics*. Washington, DC: U.S. Government Printing Office.

U.S. Bureau of Census (1991). Race and Hispanic origin. *1990 Census Profile, No. 2*, 1–8.

U.S. Bureau of Census (1996). *1990 Census of Population. 1990 CP—1-4, General Population Characteristics*. Washington, DC: U.S. Government Printing Office.

U.S. Department of Commerce News. (1989, October 12). (Census Bureau Press Release). Hispanic population surpasses 20 million mark; grows by 39 percent, Census Bureau reports. (CB 89-58).

U.S. Department of Education (1994). *Summary of the Bilingual State Educational Agency Program Survey of States' Limited English Proficient Persons and Available Educational Services (1992–1993): Final Report*. Arlington, VA: Development Associates.

U.S. Department of Education (1995). *Individuals with Disabilities Education Act Amendments of 1995*.

U.S. Department of Justice, Immigration and Naturalization Service (1982–1987). *Statistical Yearbook*.

U.S. Office of Education (1977). Assistance to states for education of handicapped children: Procedures for evaluating specified learning disabilities. *Federal Register, 42*, 65082–65085.

United States v. Texas, 5th Cir. 1972, 342 F. Supp. 24 (E.D. Tex. 1971); aff'd, 466 F.2d 518.

Utley, C. (1983). A cross-cultural investigation of field-independence/field-dependence as a psychological variable in Menominee Native American and Euro-American grade school children. Madison: Wisconsin Center for Education and Research.

Valdivieso, R., & Davis, C. (1988). *U.S. Hispanics: Challenging issues for the 1990's.* Washington, DC: Population Reference Bureau.

Van Deusen, J. M. (1982). Health/mental health studies of Indochinese refugees: A critical review. *Journal of Medical Anthropology, 6,* 231–52.

Van De Vijuer, F. J. R., & Poortiga, Y. H. (1982). Cross-cultural generalization and universality. *Journal of Cross-Cultural Psychology, 13,* 387–408.

Vasquez-Nuttall, E. (1987). Survey of current practices in the psychological assessment of limited English proficiency handicapped children. *Journal of School Psychology, 25,* 53–61.

Vasquez-Nuttall, E., Goldman, P., & Landurand, P. (1983). *A study of mainstreamed limited English proficient handicapped students in bilingual education.* Newton, MA: Vasquez-Nuttall Associates.

Viadero, D. (April 10, 1996). Culture clash. *Education Week,* 39–42.

Vontress, C. E. (1995). The breakdown of authority: Implications for counseling young African American males. In J. G. Ponterotto, J. M. Casas, L. A. Suzuki, & C. M. Alexander (Eds.) *Handbook of multicultural counseling,* (pp. 457–73). Thousand Oaks, CA: Sage.

Vygotsky, L. S. (1978). *Mind in society: The development of higher psychological processes.* Cambridge, MA: Harvard University Press.

Walker, C. L. (1985). Learning English: The Southeast Asian refugee experience. *Topics in Language Disorders, 5(4),* 53–65.

Wallace, G., Larsen, S. C., & Elksnin, L. K. (1982). *Educational assessment of learning problems: Testing for teaching* (2nd Ed.). Boston: Allyn and Bacon.

Washburn, W. (1975). *The Indian in America.* New York: Harper and Row.

Watson, D. L., Northcutt, L., & Rydell, L. (February 1989). Teaching bilingual students successfully. *Educational Leadership, 42,* 59–61.

Weinstein, G. (1984). Literacy and second language acquisition: Issues and perspectives. *TESOL Quarterly, 18,* 471–84.

Weisner, T. S., Weibel-Orlando, J. C., & Long, J. (1984). "Serious drinking," "White man's drinking," and "tee totaling": Drinking levels and styles in an urban American Indian population. *Journal of Studies in Alcohol, 45,* 237–250.

Westermeyer, J. J. (1993). Cross-cultural psychiatric assessment. In A. C. Sow (Ed.), *Culture, ethnicity, and mental illness* (pp. 125–44). Washington, DC: American Psychiatric Press.

Westermeyer, J. (1989). *Mental Health for Refugees and Other Migrants.* Springfield, IL: Charles C. Thomas.

Whitehurst, G., Fischel, J., Lonigan, C., Valdez-Menchaca, M., Arnold, D., & Smith, M. (1991). Treatment of early expressive language delay: If, when, and how. *Topics in Language Disorders, 11(4),* 55–68.

Wiig, E. H. & Semel, E. M. (1976). *Language Disabilities in Children and Adolescents.* Columbus, OH: Charles E. Merrill.

Wiig, E., & Semel, E. (1984). *Language assessment and intervention for the learning disabled, 2d Ed.* Columbus, OH: Charles E. Merrill.

Wiggins, G. *Portfolio-based assessment: Considerations and examples.* Paper presented at a meeting of Southern Maine Partnership Network of Renewing Schools, Gorham, ME, 1990.

Wilcox, K. A. & Dasby, S. M. (1988). The performance of monolingual and bilingual Mexican children on the TACL. *Language, Speech, and Hearing Services in Schools, 19,* 34–40.

Williams, C. L. (1986). Mental health assessment of refugees. In C. L. Williams and J. Westermeyer (Eds.), *Refugee mental health in resettlement countries* (pp. 175–88). New York: Hemisphere.

Willis, W. (1992). Families with African-American roots. In E. W. Lynch & M. J. Hanson, *Developing cross-cultural competence,* 121–50. Baltimore, MD: Paul H. Brookes Publishing Co.

Wilson, M. N. (1989). Child development in the context of Black extended family. *American Psychologist, 44*(2), 380–85.

Wittkower, E. D. (1964). Spirit possession in Haitian voodoo ceremonies. *Acta Psychother, 12,* 72–80.

Wolpe, J. *The practice of behavior therapy.* Oxford: Pergamon, 1969.

Wong Fillmore, L. (1982). Language minority students and school participation: What kind of English is needed. *Journal of Education, 164,* 143–56.

Woodcock, R. W. (1990). Theoretical foundations of the WJ-R measures of cognitive ability. *Journal of Psychoeducational Assessment, 8,* 231–258.

Worlfalk, A. E. (1995). *Educational Psychology, 6th Ed.* Boston: Allyn and Bacon.

Wrenn, C. G. (1985). Afterward: The culturally encapsulated counselor revisited. In P. Pedersen (Ed.), *Handbook of cross-cultural counseling and therapy* (pp. 323–329). Westport, CT: Greenwood Press.

Yamamoto, J., James, Q. C., & Palley, N. (1968). Cultural problems in psychiatric therapy. *Archives of General Psychiatry, 19,* 45–49.

Yates, J., & Ortiz, A. (1995). Linguistic and culturally diverse students. In R. S. Podemiski, G. E. Marsh, T. E. C. Smith, & B. J. Price (Eds.), *Comprehensive administration of special education,* (2d ed.) (pp. 129–55). Englewood Cliffs, NJ: Prentice-Hall.

Yinger, J. M. (1981). Toward a theory of assimilation and dissimulation. *Ethnic and Social Studies, 4,* 249–64.

Zanger, V. V. (1991). Social and cultural dimensions of the education of language minority students. In A. N. Ambert (Ed.), *Bilingual education and English as a second language* (pp. 3–54). New York: Ganard Publishing.

Zeichner, K. (1993). *Educating teachers for cultural diversity.* University of Michigan, National Center for Research in Teaching Learning.

Zuniga, M. E (1992). Families with Latino roots. In E. W. Lynch & M. J. Hanson, (Eds.), *Developing cross-cultural competence* (pp. 151–77). Baltimore, MD: Paul H. Brookes Publishing Co.

Index

AACTE. *See* American Association of Colleges for Teacher Education
Academic achievement
  learning disabled children, 76
  second-language learning and, 72, 75
Acculturation, 6–11
  child discipline, 136, 141, 178
  children's obligation to parents, 137–138
  communication styles and, 138
  family-role changes, 110–111, 134–135
  phases, 7–8
  psychological impact of, 140–142
  second-language learning and, 70
  as stressor, 7–9, 14, 55–56, 140–142
  in treatment and counseling, 55–56
ADA. *See* American with Disabilities Act of 1990
ADD. *See* Attention deficit disorder
Additive bilingualism, 65, 66
Adolescents, psychotherapy with, 132–133
Advanced fluency, second-language learning, 61
African Americans, 23–27, 72–74
  classroom behavior, 119–120, 125, 182
  classroom placement, litigation, 166
  communication style, 121

dropout rate, 117
education, 27, 37, 117, 123–124
employment, 26
intelligence tests, litigation, 167
as involuntary immigrants, 17
learning style, 123–124
mortality, 26
poverty, 26
psychotherapy, 52, 146
racial identity, 23
racism, 23–25
religion, 27, 56
role flexibility, 27
strengths, 26
"verve," 119, 125
Afterschool programs, 156–157
Age
  at immigration, 9
  second-language acquisition, 16
Alcoholism, cross-cultural study, 53
American Association of Colleges for Teacher Education (AACTE), 92
American with Disabilities Act of 1990 (ADA), 165
Americanized families, 20
American Psychological Association, guidelines for psychologists, 163, 170–172
Anglo-European families and children, 31–35
Anxiety, racism-induced, 111
Asian Americans
  communication styles, 121
  community support system, 19
  disabilities, beliefs about, 53
  education, 37

immigration to US, 6
mental illness, beliefs about, 52
poverty rate, 13
psychotherapy, beliefs about, 52
racism against, 23
socioeconomic status, 13
Aspira of New York Inc. v. New York Board of Education (1972), 47, 167
Assessment of minority populations. *See also* Educational assessment of minority children; Intellectual assessment of minority children; Psychological assessment of minority populations
  APA guidelines, 171–172
  due process, 170
  lack of comprehensive models, 190–191
  legislative actions needed, 190–191
  limited English proficient (LEP) children, 58–59
  litigations, 164–170
  parental involvement, 170
Assimilated Native Americans, 30–31
Assimilation, 8, 34–35
Ataque nervioso, 53–54
ATLAS, 181
Attention
  LEP students, 78–79
  medical conditions affecting, 177
Attention deficit disorder (ADD), 78
Attitudinal racism, 22

221